Late imperial Russia

MANCHESTER
1824

Manchester University Press

Late imperial Russia

Problems and prospects
Essays in honour of R. B. McKean

edited by
Ian D. Thatcher

Manchester University Press
Manchester and New York
distributed exclusively in the USA by Palgrave

Published by Manchester University Press
Oxford Road, Manchester M13 9NR, UK
and Room 400, 175 Fifth Avenue, New York, NY 10010, USA
www.manchesteruniversitypress.co.uk

Distributed exclusively in the USA by
Palgrave, 175 Fifth Avenue, New York,
NY 10010, USA

Distributed exclusively in Canada by
UBC Press, University of British Columbia, 2029 West Mall,
Vancouver, BC, Canada V6T 1Z2

British Library Cataloguing-in-Publication Data
A catalogue record for this book is available from the British Library

Library of Congress Cataloging-in-Publication Data applied for

ISBN 0 7190 6786 3 *hardback*
EAN   978 0 7190 6786 0
ISBN 0 7190 6787 1 *paperback*
EAN   978 0 7190 6787 7

First published 2005

14 13 12 11 10 09 08 07 06 05   10 9 8 7 6 5 4 3 2 1

Typeset in Minion
by Northern Phototypesetting Co. Ltd, Bolton
Printed in Great Britain
by Bell & Bain Ltd, Glasgow

Contents

Contributors

Sarah Badcock, Lecturer, School of History, University of Nottingham

Vincent Barnett, Research Fellow, Centre of Russian and East European Studies, University of Birmingham

Paul Dukes, Professor Emeritus, Department of History, University of Aberdeen

Murray Frame, Lecturer, Department of History, University of Dundee

Iain Lauchlan, Lecturer, Department of History, University of Stirling

David Moon, Reader, Department of History, University of Strathclyde

Geoffrey Swain, Professor, School of History, University of the West of England

Ian D. Thatcher, Reader in Modern European History, Brunel University

Peter Waldron, Professor, Department of History, University of Sunderland

James D. White, Professor, Department of Central and East European Studies, University of Glasgow

1

Introduction

Ian D. Thatcher

Historians of late imperial Russia are often described as 'optimists' or 'pessimists'.[1] The optimists believe that tsarism could have evolved peacefully into a prosperous, capitalist democracy. After all, the economy was experiencing impressive growth, the shoots of democracy were flowering in the parliament, the Duma, that sat from 1906 to 1917, and society was becoming more independent of the state, evident in a burgeoning professional and entrepreneurial elite. For the optimists the revolutions of February and October 1917 were the outcome of an unfortunate combination of specific and unfortuitous circumstances, related largely to the course of the First World War. In 1917 Russia was diverted from an otherwise bright future into decades of turmoil. The pessimists argue that even before 1914 tsarism was in the throes of a looming revolutionary crisis. One only has to consider the gulf that separated regime and society. The tsar was held in general contempt and rightly so. A repressive government, clear in day-to-day policy as well as headline events such as Bloody Sunday 1905 when unarmed petitioners were shot, had effectively alienated support from the professional bodies to the workers. Tensions between the tsar and the people were compounded by economic and social change, for which the regime had no adequate response. Russia's urban centres were a breeding ground of discontent and the likely spark for an all-out assault on the autocracy. For the pessimists, it is not so much a question of whether Nicholas II was facing a revolution, but what type of revolution he would be replaced by: a palace coup, a parliamentary revolt, or a socialist revolution on the streets.

The question 'Whither imperial Russia?' has intrigued R. B. McKean for the duration of a rich academic career. McKean's scholarship defies classification as 'optimist' or 'pessimist'. There is potential comfort and discomfort for both outlooks.

McKean's engagement with late imperial Russia's 'problems and prospects' began with a PhD thesis at the University of East Anglia, 'Russia on the Eve of the Great War? Revolution or Evolution?' (1971). This contains a balanced assessment of the extent to which the late imperial regime was threatened by revolution in July 1914. Was Nicholas II driven to war as a tactical manoeuvre designed to escape from extreme domestic social and political upheaval? McKean accepts that Russia's ruling elite had many problems at home. The government lacked a firm direction; ministers and ministries pursued contradictory policies and objectives. There is evidence of a broader political crisis, most notably in the fraught relationship between the elected Duma that sought a greater involvement in policy-making and a Council of Ministers that resisted concessions to the popular will. Amongst society broadly defined, the Duma's lack of progress produced a general feeling of alienation from the regime and scepticism for the prospects of peaceful, evolutionary change. A particularly distressing aspect of Russia's maturing crisis was the dire situation of the empire's urban workers, most notably in the capital that housed the largest concentration of a modern proletariat. The government and factory owners alike had proven unable to construct a considered and consistent response to the many ills afflicting the urban workers, including poor health and bad working and living conditions. The development of a legal workers' movement that may have negotiated appropriate reforms was hindered by official suspicion and repression. The workers' frustrations were clear in a boisterous strike movement that periodically raised its head, most notably from 1912 onwards. It was in the pre-war period that most ominously the Bolsheviks began to win majorities in the workers' organisations that did exist.

Although he outlined a scenario in which the late imperial regime may indeed have been heading for a revolutionary clash with its opponents, McKean nevertheless felt that 'despite the political, economic and social divisions of tsarist Russia, revolution was not imminent on the eve of the Great War'. Indeed, 'Russia was further from revolution in 1914 than she had been even in 1904'.[2] The reasons for this were mainly of a negative character: the Duma opposition was split; the radical workers and the Bolsheviks were largely isolated in the capital and from the rest of the country; the peasantry was quiet; the army was loyal. Thus tsarism did not go to war as a release from domestic discontent. Rather the fateful decision to enter into hostilities flowed from the broad appeal of Russian chauvinism. State and society coalesced around an anti-German foreign policy. The war met with general approval.[3]

McKean's PhD thesis ended as war began. It did not address the issue of why tsarism eventually fell. The implication was that if Russia was not facing revolution on the war's eve, it was indeed the circumstances of the war that sealed Nicholas II's fate. The PhD's implication was made explicit by a monograph study that guaranteed McKean's standing as a leading scholar of late imperial Russia. *St Petersburg Between the Revolutions* (1990) was the culmination of many years of study.[4] It drew upon a broad range of sources, including materials from the not always accessible archives housed in the then USSR. It was the most thorough investigation to date of the capital's working class between 1907 and 1917. The nature and development of St Petersburg's workers were placed within the broader context of the city's, and Russia's, economic, social and political history. There was a particular emphasis upon the relationship between the workers and working-class organisations, from cultural and leisure associations to trade unions and professional revolutionaries.

McKean's monograph was even more assertive than the PhD that an upheaval of revolutionary proportions had not matured within Russia by 1914. It stressed, for example, the factors that had hindered the emergence of a working class, united by a hostility to tsarism and by a commitment to socialism. In actual fact, St Petersburg's workers were divided by numerous factors. Most workers laboured not in medium or large-scale factories targeted by socialist agitators, but in the domestic or service sectors. They were largely ignored by professional revolutionaries and were too fragmented to be easily unionised or mobilised. The distribution of the workers across St Petersburg's distinct and isolated districts also complicated any attempt at united action by the working class. Most workers, McKean makes clear, did not possess a socialist outlook prior to the February revolution of 1917. Pre-war strikes sought in the main to improve terms and conditions of labour, but they were not anti-capitalist as such. The politicisation of the workers, especially if one is thinking of socialism, occurred in the months following Nicholas II's abdication.

The reasons for the extremely limited penetration of socialist ideas amongst the capital's workers were many. Only a relatively small number of predominantly skilled, male metal workers were active in radical activity before 1917. They stood out from fellow workers, most of whom preferred the scandal stories of cheap novels and the penny press to socialist doctrine. Members of the skilled, male radical elite were also different from other workers in that they had put down roots in the city and had formed a hereditary working class. Most workers came to the capital for brief spells, counting the village as their true home. The security organs were very effective at breaking up socialist organisations. There was little or no continuity of personnel; members of cells and other bodies were soon arrested. Neither faction of the Russian Social Democratic Labour Party (RSDLP) managed to establish functioning city-wide structures. Committees were local and short-lived. The professional revolutionaries were likewise unsuccessful in controlling trade unions or other examples of a 'legal' labour movement. These bodies tended to be closed down as quickly as they appeared. Likewise the publication and distribution of socialist newspapers was attempted, but failed to make an impact in the face of regular seizures of copies or closure of titles. Lenin and other leaders in exile exerted minimal or no influence over the politics of the capital's workers. Local activists were mainly the skilled, young, male workers referred to above.

They were independently minded, desired the unity of all factions of the RSDLP, but isolated and easily dealt with. The regime was right to worry about industrial unrest pre-1914, but it was not in danger of being toppled by it.

The absolutist monarchy was eventually felled, McKean argued, by a particularly intense economic and social crisis that hit the capital from the autumn of 1916 onwards. Rampant inflation, shortages (particularly of basic necessities), the temporary closure of plants because of inadequate supplies, and the prevalence of rumours of possible treachery within the tsar's own family, were all factors that helped unite a broad coalition of opposition to Nicholas II. Duma liberals, for example, were drawing up the composition of a government-in-waiting as workers were thinking of a general strike to press their demands. The strength and depth of sentiment hostile to the tsar, from district to district and from class to class, distinguished the discontent of autumn 1916 onwards from pre-war turmoil such as the 'General Strike' of July 1914. The final nail in the monarchy's coffin, for McKean, was the response of the city's garrison. The soldiers, mainly new recruits, were unwilling to arrest or fire upon the demonstrators that were now filling the capital's central squares. Having lost effective control of the capital and finding no voices of support for him to stay on, Nicholas II stood down. He did so, not because there was a consensus of what should replace tsarism; socialism, certainly, was a distant and unlikely prospect.

St Petersburg Between the Revolutions was a healthy corrective to certain myths, generated largely by the Soviet regime, about St Petersburg's pre-revolutionary working class. The workers were not as radicalised, housed in large modern factories, and under Bolshevik party control, as suggested by certain Soviet historians. There were also suggested revisions to the work of several Western historians. Most notably, L. Haimson's influential notion first advanced in the mid-1960s that there was the likelihood of a 'revolutionary explosion' in the pre-war months was not supported by McKean's research.[5]

One should not conclude from the studies mentioned so far that McKean can be placed in the camp of the optimists. If suggestions that the late imperial monarchy was in the throes of a terminal crisis outside the winter of 1916–17 are rejected, so is the optimistic scenario that late imperial absolutism could have evolved peacefully into a constitutional monarchy. In several studies McKean illustrates that a 'constitutional path' for late imperial Russia was a very unlikely prospect.[6]

McKean is willing to concede that, following the publication of the Fundamental State Law of April 1906, Russia was a 'proper constitutional monarchy'.[7] Henceforth it had the possibility of evolving into a democratic state governed by the rule of law along Western lines. There were, however, many factors that constrained and hindered an evolutionary path of development.

First of all, the political elite, headed by Nicholas II, was at best ambivalent about important freedoms of expression and association enshrined in the

Fundamental Laws. The emergence of autonomous centres of power independent of the state, of a healthy civil society essential to a functioning democracy, was held back by a regime that constantly interfered with and restricted civic activity. This is evident, for example, in the refusal to register or the closure of political parties, trade unions and professional associations. Russian civil society, both in the major urban centres but also most crucially in the provinces, was simply denied the opportunity to develop firm social and political structures. At the same time, the extent to which a civil society was formed in pre-revolutionary Russia also undermined the chances of a constitutional monarchy taking root. Society was in a process of transformation from the old estate to a new class structure, but it was characterised above all by social fragmentation. No social force or grouping was sufficiently united and strong to provide a firm foundation for a constitutional order. Social fragmentation was reflected in a political fragmentation that helped to paralyse the country's parliament, the Duma. Prime Ministers were unable to engineer a majority of any political shading, with detrimental consequences for a coherent programme of reform. Russia's political institutions were noted for their deadlock, rather than any coherent programmes or strategies.

If the constitutional monarchy could not discover vital support in a rejuvenated civil society or healthy parliamentarianism, McKean also makes clear the shortcomings of traditional bodies. The Russian Orthodox Church, for example, still played a major role in the lives of most Russians. Yet it did not mobilise the population behind the constitutional monarchy. Serious internal divisions, as well as the odd scandal, lessened Orthodoxy's popular appeal. If anything, a weak, fragmented and politically reactionary Orthodox Church made matters worse by increasing hostility to it and the monarchy.

In the fragile and precarious situation into which the monarchy was thrust, it was vital that major international tensions be avoided. The military and diplomatic disasters of the Russo-Japanese War of 1904–5 had illustrated only too vividly the parlous state of the armed forces and the link between war and revolution. From 1906 onwards the constitutional monarchy did enjoy some success in reforming and rearming the military and in pursuing a peaceful foreign policy. Such gains could not last. The maintenance of great power status was seen to be vital to the constitutional monarchy's survival. By 1914 it was even considered that continued disengagement from an aggressive foreign policy could produce a domestic revolt rather than impede it. There was broad consensus that Russia could no longer stand idle as Germany continued to extend its power and prestige. Feeling that it could no longer resist the temptation to put Germany in its place, the constitutional monarchy made a fatal decision to become involved in the European war that it was essential for it to avoid if constitutionalism were to grow from its shaky foundations.

As a historian of late imperial Russia McKean thus defies easy classification. He is both variously optimist and pessimist, at each instance aware of the complexities and contingencies of history. It is precisely an open mind and a commitment to honest scholarship that renders his work so valuable and inspiring. He cautions against hasty suggestions not fully verifiable by evidence. In a field for which reliable statistics are not always available, McKean's conclusions are fair and balanced. The essays presented here in McKean's honour cover a range of optimistic and pessimistic outlooks.

Sarah Badcock argues that Nicholas II, for all the power concentrated in his person, was unable to perceive, let alone remedy, the basic demands of the Russian state and society. The former cried out for far-reaching reform to manage modernisation. The latter required freedom, participation and responsibility if it was to contribute to progress and the formation of an alliance of regime and society in a constitutional monarchy. Nicholas II did not rise to the demands of wise leadership and coherent policies. He oversaw the decline and disintegration of an antiquated system of rule. Peter Waldron shares Badcock's assessment of the shallow foundations of the constitutional order put in place during the 1905 revolution. The imperial regime was willing to concede only the façade of a parliament, as an analysis of the Duma between 1905 and 1917 makes clear. The unwillingness to engage seriously in parliamentary norms and to share power with an elected assembly helped only to discredit democratic politics in a Russian context. It is perhaps not surprising that the 'hollow constitutionalism' of 1905 onwards was so easily repressed post-1917.

Iain Lauchlan reveals that sections of the tsarist administration could be highly efficient. Despite having the characteristics of an undergoverned regime – limited resources and insufficient personnel – the secret police organisation (Okhrana) employed the latest techniques in an organised manner to good effect. It collected an impressive body of information on revolutionaries, successfully infiltrating and subverting a range of anti-regime organisations, as Geoffrey Swain's chapter on late imperial revolutionaries also illustrates. However, even the Okhrana was aware that alone its operations could not save the autocracy. The Okhrana not only reinforced tsarism's sinister reputation, it also heped to galvanise an ever-broadening opposition movement that it could not hope to contain. As Lauchlan concludes, the Okhrana fought hard and won many battles, but it lost the war to protect its master.

Two examinations of late imperial intellectuals perceive some rays of hope for the late imperial regime. Murray Frame puts forward an alternative reading of late imperial civil society. Rather than taking social fragmentation as another nail in the coffin of a constitutional monarchy as Peter Waldron suggests, Frame argues that the extent of cultural pluralism revealed by the activities of several patrons of the arts point to a vibrant civil society, one that could have formed the 'firm foundations' of a constitutional monarchy. Frame downplays the likely political motivations of the theatrical impresarios, viewing them as simply interested in culture. However, tsarism's failure to encouarge and seek agreement with an emerging and vibrant civil society lost it potential support. The regime instead seemed intent to feel threatened by its weakening capacity to influence cultural life. It may have felt that its fate was linked more to the state of the economy. According to Vincent Barnett, one leading student of the late imperial economy thought that it was undergoing an impressive expansion under tsarism. For Tugan-Baronovsky the late imperial economy, despite some peculiarities, was progressing as a healthy capitalist system. Barnett regrets that market economics was rejected along with tsarism in 1917.

Tugan-Baronovsky was not blind to the problems of capitalist development, not least the dire working conditions evident in many a Russian factory. Ian D. Thatcher examines the economic, political and social aspects of the late imperial urban workers. He agrees with McKean that the regime had no adequate response to the concerns and difficulties of the urban workers. He disagrees with McKean's view that the politicisation of the workers began only after the February revolution of 1917. The workers were fragmented by a variety of economic, social, political and cultural factors. Nevertheless, there is sufficient evidence of a shared hostility to the factory order and a commitment to workers' economic, social and political rights to claim that the workers were largely anti-autocracy well before the monarchy was toppled. As Geoffrey Swain shows in his examination of a fragmented late imperial revolutionary movement, local activists embraced a revolutionary, not reformist, outlook.

Although it was events in the capital that secured Nicholas II's downfall, the fate of the late imperial regime was perhaps more affected by its relations with the peasantry: the vast majority of the country's population. Yet, as David Moon illustrates, the government did not attempt systematically to turn peasants into loyal citizens. Late imperial peasants were remarkably impervious to outside influences, whether of the cities, schooling, or military service. The limited political reforms of 1905 onwards did not seek to engage the peasants in a national forum. When peasant voters did make an impact, it was to produce radical voices for land distribution. The government's response, in the electoral law of 3 June 1907, was to reduce peasant participation in national politics even further. Nicholas II effectively excluded peasants from the 'constitutional order'; it is not suprising that peasant subjects did not rally to his cause.

There could have been good reason why Nicholas II ignored the peasants. James D. White outlines the views of a radical historian of late imperial Russia's likely development, M. N. Pokrovskii. For Pokrovskii, the predominant influence on the policies of the Russian state was not peasants, but merchant capital. From this, Pokrovskii argued that the Russian executive, as in Western societies, merely reflected the concerns of the most powerful economic groups. Late imperial politics was likely therefore to progress along a Western pattern; the imperial monarchy would be replaced by a constitutional order along English lines. Paul Dukes accepts Pokrovskii's view that late imperial Russia has to be understood as part of a broader international system. Dukes argues that great power concerns undermined tsarism's chances of survival. Nicholas II was trapped in imperial battles for prestige and influence that eventually resulted in a fateful world war.

This volume's contributors are thus as optimistic and pessimistic as McKean, although we share his basic pessimism when we consider the likelihood that late imperial Russia could have evolved into a stable constitutional monarchy. It is to McKean's credit, however, that he was able to introduce genuine doubt into a scholarly community all too keen to write off Nicholas II, largely accepting Haimson's thesis that there was a crisis of revolutionary proportions affecting late imperial Russia pre-1914. It is a pity that Haimson has not openly responded to McKean's challenging and more nuanced interpretation of late imperial Russia.[8] Further research, particularly into civil society in the provinces, may well yet alter further our perceptions of late imperial Russia's problems and prospects.

Notes

1   For a recent summary of the historiography of the late imperial period see, for example, C. Read, 'In Search of Liberal Tsarism: The Historiography of Autocratic Decline', *Historical Journal*, 45(1), 2000, pp. 195–210.
2   R. B. McKean, 'Russia on the Eve of the Great War: Revolution or Evolution?', PhD Thesis, University of East Anglia, 1971, pp. 333–4.
3   Ibid., pp. 290, 307–8, 313.
4   R. B. McKean, *St Petersburg Between the Revolutions: Workers and Revolutionaries, June 1907 – February 1917* (London, 1990).
5   L. H. Haimson, 'The Problem of Social Stability in Urban Russia, 1905–7', *Slavic Review*, 23(4), 1964, pp. 619–42 and 24(1), 1965, pp. 1–22.
6   The summary of the 'pessimistic' McKean is taken from R. B. McKean, 'Constitutional Russia', *Revolutionary Russia*, 9(1), 1996, pp. 33–42; R. B. McKean, *Between the Revolutions: Russia 1905 to 1917* (London, 1998); R. B. McKean, 'The Constitutional Monarchy in Russia, 1906–17' in I. D. Thatcher (ed.), *Regime and Society in Twentieth-Century Russia* (Basingstoke, 1999), pp. 27–43.
7   R. B. McKean, 'The Russian Constitutional Monarchy in Comparative Perspective' in C. Brennan and M. Frame (eds), *Russia and the Wider World in Historical Perspective* (Basingstoke, 2000), p. 125.
8   It is quite an oversight that when Haimson revisited his thesis of the mid-1960s he simply ignored McKean's refutation. See L. H. Haimson, '"The Problem of Political and Social Stability in Urban Russia On the Eve of War and Revolution" Revisited', *Slavic Review*, 59(4), 2000, pp. 848–75.

2

Autocracy in crisis: Nicholas the last

Sarah Badcock

The collapse of the Soviet Union left Russia seeking both precedents and alternatives for its political future. The role and image of Nicholas II has been subject to particular revision and scrutiny. Though reviled by Soviet historians as 'Nicholas the bloody', post-Soviet society has harboured popular nostalgia for the Nicholaevan era. The last tsar's public rehabilitation was symbolically concluded by the ceremony held on Friday 17 July 1998, when Nicholas II's remains were interred in the Peter Paul Cathedral in St Petersburg with full state pomp and ceremony. Russia's then premier Boris Yeltsin described the tsar and his family, who had been murdered by the Bolsheviks on 17 July 1918, as the 'innocent victims' of the revolution.[1] This description epitomises the casting of Nicholas II as a hapless bystander to Russia's tumultuous revolution. Such an approach neglects the fundamental collision in Nicholaevan Russia between the demands of a rapidly modernising state structure and Russia's increasingly anachronistic style of government. Nicholas II remained true to his autocratic heritage and attempted to maintain personal autocratic power, which was unrealisable. The challenges laid down by very rapid industrial and economic change, alongside the weakness and vacillation of Nicholas II's policies, left Nicholaevan Russia in a state of crisis. This chapter asserts that while Nicholas II failed to respond to the challenges of governing Russia, his failure can be explained by the context in which he operated as much as by his personal failings.

Russia was undergoing profound social and economic change at the turn of the twentieth century. Nicholas II's reign coincided with an intensification of the collision between political traditions that Russia's rulers faced. Economic development and cultural influence increasingly pushed Russia towards Western-style political development, while Russia's increasingly anachronistic and inadequate system of government, and Nicholas II's own personal perceptions, clung to strictly autocratic rule. Many contemporaries and historians argued that Russia was 'in crisis' by the turn of the twentieth century. This crisis can be framed as the collision between Western-style civil society and economic development, which pointed towards the development of a more representative system of government, and an autocratic system which proved unable to respond effectively to the evolutionary challenges posed by modernisation. Modernisation required the state to take on a plethora of new roles in relation to society, and it needed to mobilise that society, and allow civil society to develop, if it was to fulfil its roles effectively. The state's rejection of society's attempts to become involved in Russia's governance doomed it to failure.

The private letters and diaries left by Nicholas provide only the most limited assistance in analysing his political motivations.[2] Students and some biographers have seized upon his diary entries as evidence of his naivety, stupidity and even cruelty. The tsar routinely commented on his day's exercise, hunting triumphs and the weather at far greater length than his terse comments on issues of a political or national character. Expressions of emotion or of political opinion were very rare. Diaries were not, however, a window into Nicholas's soul. Their reserved and routine character may well be a reflection more of his methodical approach to diary-keeping than his emotional state and political thought. Nicholas was an intensely private and reserved individual, whose phenomenal self-control left little evidence for historians as to his mental state. More recent historiographical trends have anyhow moved away from interest in Nicholas II as an individual. The ground-breaking work of Boris Kolonitskii and Orlando Figes has focused on the ways in which the tsar's image and popular standing were eroded in the public eye, and the enormous significance this was to have in Russia's revolutions.[3]

Up until 1906, Russia was an autocracy in principle and in fact. Preserving the inviolability of the autocratic principle was Nicholas II's first priority.[4] Rapid industrialisation and urbanisation exposed the inadequacies of the system and its supporting bureaucracy, however, and left autocracy looking increasingly unviable. The late imperial regime was overburdened with routine work, isolated from its subjects, and had neither time nor energy to conceive of 'bigger' policy ideas.[5] These administrative shortcomings were a key feature of the collapse of tsarism. Lack of co-ordination of policies, corruption, inefficiency and arbitrariness were to become watchwords of Russian administration. The overarching problem for the Russian system of government was the expansion of tasks that it was expected to fulfil. The state's original role, to defend the realm, maintain order and extract taxes, had been extended to providing the population with basic services. The acceleration of industrialisation and urbanisation forced the state into an ever more interventionist role, in managing the economy and directing industry, and in providing more social services for the population. Education, healthcare, water supply and legal means all came into state remit. Provision of such services was a truly mighty task, which required effective local self-government, as well as a more advanced system of central government, if it was to be administered effectively.

The Nicholaevan regime was thoroughly ambivalent about releasing its grip on the process of ruling so that local government could operate effectively. The expansion of government's administrative duties and local self-government both fuelled and required the development of a new societal strata of educated professionals: doctors, lawyers, educators, administrators, statisticians, survey-ors and so on. This new strata formed a nucleus for the development of civil society in Russia, which could conceivably have provided a bulwark for some degree of conservatism, but which would inevitably challenge the prerogatives of autocracy.[6] Nicholaevan government was unable to reconcile itself with the civil society that developed alongside a larger, more interventionist state. The fundamental problem for Nicholas II was the collision between his political convictions, which revolved around a nostalgic desire for maintenance of tra-ditional social structures and values, and the inexorably building pressure from Russian society and circumstances for extensive reform of the Russian state. Nicholas II's personality and attitudes did not fit comfortably into an auto-cratic mould. Though to the last he remained an unswerving defender of the sanctity of autocratic rule, he had taken the reins of autocratic power reluc-tantly, and always made it clear that he defended the principle of autocracy and not his own personal power. Nicholas's response to his abdication gives some indication of this. His diary entries report that he slept extremely well after the abdication,[7] and Gurko remarked that 'the ease with which he abdicated in 1917 and his subsequent life and actions conclusively prove that he had no appreciation of the unlimited authority he possessed.'[8]

He has been characterised by many historians and biographers as more interested in sport and family life than in the affairs of state, and sometimes as lacking intelligence. More recent biographers have accepted his preoccupa-tion with simple pleasures, but have noted his above-average intelligence and education.[9] Biographers cannot claim any deep insight into Nicholas's person-ality. Factors in his upbringing, however, give the biographer a sense of the basis for his perceptions of power. Dominic Lieven's sympathetic and nuanced portrait of Nicholas concluded that 'his ethics were those of an honourable if naïve guard's officer. His conception of patriotism and duty was a high one. The intrigue, ambition, jealousy and frequent pettiness of the political world revolted him.'[10]

One can see military influence in a range of aspects of Nicholas II's life. He was preoccupied with orderliness and self-discipline, with physical fitness and activity, and was saturated with convictions of moral duty and national service. He expressed almost childlike delight at military parades and ceremonies.[11] He did not, however, have any experience of senior command or of war first-hand, and this may offer some explanation for the abiding romanticism with which he imbued military conflict. His deeply held religious faith also played a signif-icant part in his outlook, both in terms of his certainty of his own God-given right to rule, and in his fatalistic attitude when faced with adversity, which was regarded by many as a political weakness.[12]

Nicholas adopted the popular myths of tsarism wholeheartedly in his attitudes towards autocratic power and his relationship with his subjects. He regarded himself as the 'little father' of his people, and believed that the problems he faced in governing Russia stemmed from the intrusion of bureaucrats, and the intrigues of various anti-state groups, namely Jews and revolutionaries.[13] His speech to the worker delegation presented to him on 19 January 1905, in the aftermath of Bloody Sunday, reveals just how deeply entrenched these beliefs were. He scolded the workers for 'having let traitors and enemies of the motherland lead you into error and delusion'.[14] In Nicholas's highly personalised perception of autocratic rule, the bureaucracy and any proposed representative government would only interfere in the communication between the tsar and his people. Nicholas II did not recognise the importance of effective local government and efficient central bureaucracy in managing the state. The existing systems of Russian governance did not provide the necessary framework of a self-maintaining and capable bureaucracy.

Nicholas was enormously frustrated by ministerial staff, and genuinely believed that the bureaucracy was the only thing that stood between the will of the tsar and his subjects. This lack of respect seems to have been mutual. While Nicholas mistrusted his ministers, his own vacillations were the subject of extensive censure on their part. Vladimir Lambsdorf, the Minister for Foreign Affairs between 1900 and 1906, commented that Nicholas 'changes his mind with terrifying speed'.[15] For ministers, this meant that they could not be assured that a policy of theirs that had won the tsar's approval would continue to be approved. This lack of stability and system in government was not a feature exclusive to Nicholas II; however, it was a feature of autocratic rule in a large and complex state. Both Alexander II and Alexander III manipulated their ministers and distrusted their officials. This system protected the power of the autocrat, and ensured the tsar was in absolute control of his court, but castrated ministers, leaving them reluctant to initiate reform. The crucial difference between Nicholas II and his predecessors was that he lacked their commanding personality and political acumen, while being faced with challenges of far greater magnitude.

Nicholas's failure to come to terms with the realities of modern government is well reflected in his own day-to-day schedule. Despite his position as the 'Emperor of all the Russians', trivialities and rituals absorbed his time, and he lacked an effective mechanism through which to impose his will on Russia's ever-growing bureaucracy. Nicholas had no personal secretariat, which was a serious weakness in his autocratic power. Without a private secretariat, he had limited control over appointments and promotions in the civil service, and no effective buffer to ensure that he dealt with only the most important issues.

While he was diligent in reading and commenting on official documents, he had no personal staff to ensure that his directions were implemented. A final irony is that the Russian Empire's supreme autocrat took great pride in doing his own filing and letter writing, and personally sealed all his own envelopes.[16] Such eccentricities left Nicholas with less time to wield some level of control over the mighty administrative machine, and to direct and implement concerted policy.

The mythical 'father tsar' had retained a number of his most archaic duties. Until 1913, for example, the emperor's personal permission was required for a wife to live apart from her husband, and the emperor's personal consent was required for names to be changed. Though the Petitions chancellery dealt with such petitions in the first instance, Nicholas himself spent ninety minutes each day discussing problematic cases. This was an extraordinary use of time for the ruler of a vast and modernising empire. At no time was this strange state of affairs more apparent than in the build-up to the outbreak of the First World War. Nicholas's diary entries reveal that despite the ever-increasing likelihood of a massive European war, his time continued to be filled with his usual activities – ceremonial duties, family meals, reading papers. Though Nicholas was profoundly distressed by unfolding events, his personal schedule was not significantly affected.[17] The creaking autocratic machine was unable to manoeuvre with sufficient speed and dexterity in times of crisis.

The highly personalised power favoured by Nicholas II relied heavily on the tsar's own image and personal prestige, and offered those close to him massive opportunities for political power. This scope was heightened further by the state's lack of a tightly accountable and functioning bureaucracy. The roles of the tsar's wife Alexandra and the colourful figure of Grigorii Rasputin are often highlighted as examples of the irresponsible way in which power was wielded. Ironically, when one puts aside the hype, the significance of Alexandra and Rasputin was predominantly in the ways that they undermined the emperor's public profile, and much less on tangible policy decisions. Cultural history helps us distinguish between Rasputin's actual political role, which was minor, and his role in undermining popular perceptions of autocracy, which may have been huge. While the influence of Rasputin at court was widely held to have decided ministerial positions and to have directed the autocrat's decision-making, his influence on political decisions was not in fact as significant as has been suggested.[18] As for the Empress Alexandra, she was never comfortable in Russian high society, and her shyness and reserve did not endear her to the Russian population. Her association with the debauched and erratic Rasputin led to accusations of adultery and depravity from the popular press, which were widely believed, despite the fact that there was no substantiation for the scurrilous rumours in circulation. Alexandra was believed to be 'wearing the trousers' in her relationship with Nicholas II, to the extent that she was heavily involved in government policy.[19] These rumours were perceived to have a considerable impact on the desacralisation of the monarchy among the lower classes, and were apparently received among educated circles as well.[20] They irreparably weakened Nicholas II's position. He was portrayed as a weak cuckold, the antithesis of the authoritative father tsar that Nicholas II's own propaganda propounded.[21] Alexandra was also, by virtue of her unpopularity and her German family connections, widely accused of treason in the First World War period, aided and abetted, it was believed, by Rasputin. Lack of substantiation for these rumours was an irrelevance. As Figes and Kolonitskii astutely note, 'the point of all these rumours was not their truth or their untruth, but their ability to unify and mobilise an angry public against the monarchy'.[22]

Failings in the governance of Russia can be found from every angle. While many of them were systemic in origin, they were exacerbated by the inadequacies of Nicholas II as an autocrat. Among the most conspicuous weaknesses was the fierce competition between the ministries, particularly between the two most important ministries, the Ministry of Finance and the Ministry of Internal Affairs. This competition had its origins in the reorganisation of central government in the 1860s when political power was parcelled out to separate ministries, but no measures were taken to ensure co-ordination between the ministries.[23] Nicholas II did nothing to rein in rivalries, which impeded ministerial power and could therefore be seen to bolster his own position. Competition between ministries is inevitable in any system of government. In an autocracy, however, where ministers were all competing for the ear of the tsar, competition led to erratic policy-making without collaboration between the various departments involved, and the impression of arbitrary government. The final decision of all questions of policy lay, in theory, with the tsar himself, but there was no clearly defined decision-making process leading towards the tsar. As departments became bigger and more specialised, it became more difficult for a non-specialist to understand their workings, much less direct policy. Realistically, the tsar could not make informed and harmonious decisions on all areas of policy without coherent and highly informed advice, which he needed to be willing to accept.

An important explanation for Nicholas II's inability to direct policy effectively and to keep his ministries working efficiently was his lack of both a clearly defined political agenda and close political associates. Close links with senior statesmen were crucial if an autocrat was to effectively stamp his line on the state. Nicholas was not, however, a natural political operator. On his accession to the throne, his political profile and opinions were not publicly known, and indeed can only be understood in the broadest of terms, encapsulating little more than notions of the sanctity of his rule and fond nostalgia for an imagined Russian past. There was a great deal of continuity between the reign of Alexander III and Nicholas II, both in policy and in ministerial staff. This was not least because it took until the turn of the century for Nicholas to make any discernible impact on policy or on ministers. Nicholas lacked experience and a close cohort of advisors. Though he was considered polite and charming to his political advisors, he was aloof and apparently unwilling to establish close links with his ministers. Nicholas's reserved personality was a central explanation for his distaste for ministers and political wrangling,[24] and proved to be a serious impediment in developing a political coterie. Of his political upper strata, he had almost no personal friends on accession to the throne; only General Orlov was his friend and contemporary, and Orlov died in 1908.[25] This lack of friends or close acquaintances in the power structures caused Nicholas many difficulties. In the early years of his reign, he relied on the 'old guard' of ministers, like Sergei Witte, who had served under his father.

Nicholas was pleasant and unconfrontational in his dealings with ministers, but his mild manner did not offer ministers any surety of his support. His apparently diplomatic handling of his senior advisors, whereby he gave all an audience and seemed to take their views into account, obscured what was in fact the tsar's inherent dislike of argument and discord; he was essentially unwilling to countenance an opinion which ran counter to his own.[26] His inability to engage effectively with reasoned argument left ministers feeling insecure and even powerless. This insecurity in the ministerial mind did not make for effective government. It was entirely conceivable for a minister to have in his department an individual who held the ear of Nicholas more closely than he did himself. All this contributed to government's biggest failing before 1905, that it lacked co-ordination, cohesion, consistency and a grand plan. Nicholas did attempt to tackle this problem by calling a weekly meeting of ministers, but in the absence of an effective and energetic chair, these meetings came to nothing. Pobedonostsev, chief procurator of the Holy Synod, laid this lack of co-ordination firmly at the tsar's feet.[27]

It is ironic that one of the potential benefits of autocratic rule was clear and well-directed policy (as it emanated from one man), and yet this was flagrantly lacking in Nicholas's government. Marked vacillations in policy occurred with little clear direction from the top, and little apparent awareness of their potential for inflaming public opinion. A pertinent example of feckless policy direction was the replacement of the assassinated and hugely unpopular Viacheslav Von Plehve, Minister of the Interior, in 1904. The post of Minister of the Interior was of particular political importance, as its holder had significant influence on domestic policy. The post was filled by Prince Sviatopolk-Mirksy. Plehve and his predecessor had been old school conservatives, who believed that concessions to liberal society would only heighten Russia's domestic instablity, and who sought to establish order through firmness and repression. Sviatopolk-Mirsky, on the other hand, was of known liberal sentiments, and openly expressed concern to Nicholas that his own policies would in no way be comparable to those of Plehve. He proposed significant concessions to the development of what was essentially civil society. But Sviatopolk-Mirsky, like other ministers, proved able to win the emperor's ear without actually winning his whole-hearted support, and his moment in the sun lasted less than five months. His appointment raised great expectations about the possibility of political change among educated society, but his ambitious ten-point reform programme was in the main part rejected by the emperor, leaving Sviatopolk-Mirsky isolated and society frustrated. His appointment raised public expectations of a general softening of the regime's position, when in fact it presaged nothing of the sort. Societal tensions and opposition to the autocracy were heightened rather than relaxed by such erratic policy.

The department of agriculture offers an excellent example of the inadequacies of Russian government, and the truly enormous challenges it faced. Formed in 1894, it was a relatively new department, but was vast in size, and was faced with a mounting sense of crisis over the state of the peasantry. Russia's backbone was her peasant population, both socially and economically. The state of the peasantry at the turn of the twentieth century was a contemporary as well as an oft-debated historical conundrum. Though historians have differed over the extent to which there was an economic crisis in rural Russia,[28] the famine of 1891–92 gave Russian government and society an impression of rural impoverishment and crisis. Concerned observers saw the wave of unprecedented peasant unrest and violence that emerged in the 1905–7 revolutionary period as the culmination of peasant woes.

Nicholas showed particular interest in agrarian issues, and was kept well informed about the peasantry debate and its connection with Russia's impending financial crisis. There were fundamental divisions among his advisors over the extent and causes of peasant unrest. Nicholas's own perspective embraced the sentimentally inclined notions of the peasantry as naïve, but profoundly loyal, God-fearing and innocent subjects.[29] Peasant unrest and disorder was interpreted from such a position as the product of misunderstandings, or of the malign intervention of non-peasant, anti-state forces. If there was a challenge to peasant life, it was the forces of modernisation, which brought the corrupting influences of the towns closer to the unsullied villages. This naïve and traditionalist view of the peasantry was at odds with the rather better informed views held by two of the most significant figures in Nicholas's reign, Sergei Witte and Petr Stolypin. They held that the very structures of traditional peasant life, in particular the commune, themselves retarded Russia's economic development, and promoted the Russian peasantry's disregard for the importance of private property. Stolypin sought to modernise Russian peasant life, and to erode the traditional village structures held dear by traditionalists. This was an important distinction between the tsar's perspective and that of his senior advisors. While the traditionalist view held the forces of modernity, industrialisation and urbanisation, to be at fault in provoking peasant unrest,

Stolypin recognised the inevitability of social and economic change and development, and sought to reform peasant society to allow it easier access to these forces of modernisation.

Despite the efforts of a number of his advisors, including the senior statesman Alexander Polovtsov, even the long-feared mass peasant disorders of 1905–7 failed to impress upon Nicholas II the dangers of semi-socialistic landholding and its capacity to unite peasants against landowners. Nicholas's response to impending crisis was very cautious: he appointed a commission to investigate agricultural conditions in January 1902, headed by Witte, but encouraged the Ministry of Internal Affairs to run rival committees, and ultimately it was the arch-conservative Goremykin who was appointed to head a rural reform programme. Witte regarded Nicholas's position on this issue as 'the epitome of indecisiveness and bad faith'.[30] Setting one ministry against another was an unsurprising tactic from a tsar who had little faith in any of his senior bureaucracy, and lacked strong personal conviction to drive through his own policy proposals.

Government relations with Russia's nascent working class provide a further example of governmental incompetence, and in particular the tsar's inability to grasp the fundamentals of the challenges he faced. Nicholaevan labour policy demonstrated the lack of convergence between the Ministry of Internal Affairs and the Ministry of Finance, and the absence of effective leadership from Nicholas II. Russia's developing labour movement was a significant contributor to the sense of crisis that pervaded Russia at the turn of the century. Urbanisation had proceeded at a dramatic pace since the economic reforms of the 1890s, and brought with it a whole tranche of further problems. The industrial workforce more than doubled between 1890 and 1912, from 1.4 million to 2.9 million. The impact of this growth was acutely felt particularly because of high geographical concentration; more than 60 per cent of Russia's workers in 1900 were situated in Petrograd, Moscow, Poland and Ukraine. This put enormous pressure on urban infrastructure, and housing and sanitation suffered. The creaking Russian governmental machine was ill equipped to cope with such challenges. In addition to the practical issues surrounding rapid growth of urban areas, there was the new problem of labour relations and state intervention and regulation.

While Witte recognised that the growth of a large industrial workforce would inevitably create labour conflict, and that protective pre-emptive legislation was the best way to manage this, the Ministry of Internal Affairs instinctively sought to repress self-organising groups. This conflict was writ large in Nicholaevan policies regarding labour. The department of factory inspectors, which operated under the wing of the Ministry of Finance, sought to protect workers to some extent and to encourage better labour relations, while the Ministry of Internal Affairs maintained a hostile position on any labour protection.

The brief experiment of legal workers' organisations was an example of the short-sightedness of the regime in this respect. S. V. Zubatov, chief of Moscow's secret police, initiated a pioneering scheme for limited state-sponsored workers' unions.[31] These 'Zubatov unions', established in 1902, aimed to operate as a safety valve for worker discontent, providing legal workers' organisations under the firm guidance of the state. By the summer of 1903, Zubatov's experiment was abruptly terminated, as the unions became increasingly unmanageable and radical. The elemental forces of workers' organisation were not to be easily funnelled into safe channels. The only conceivable way of staunching the rising tide of labour radicalism would have been to initiate labour protection at a level that Nicholas II's regime was incapable of contemplating. Such innovative policies required boldness and concerted policy direction, neither of which qualities Nicholas II possessed.

The regime's inability to tackle the growing labour movement is most poignantly illustrated by its disastrous mishandling of the peaceful workers' demonstration on 9 January 1905, which came to be known as Bloody Sunday. The first failing of the regime's handling was in the failure to repress Father Gapon's movement, which had been overlooked by the usually zealous police authorities as part of the sanctioned actions of the Zubatov unions. The second failing was polar to the first, that of excessive force and repression. Having allowed the movement to develop, the demonstration was policed with a heavy-handedness that the regime was to rue in the months of civil unrest that followed. More than a hundred unarmed demonstrators were killed by infantry troops in various locations around the city, with the focal point of unrest outside the tsar's city residence on Palace Square. The shooting of unarmed, peaceful petitioners before the tsar's very windows carried immeasurable symbolic significance. The aims and actions of the demonstrators in many respects accorded with the model of faithful subjects addressing their little father tsar; the unarmed supplicants sought to present their petition into the tsar's hands personally, carried his picture and religious icons, and symbolically at least can be seen to have approached the palace with heads bowed and bared. The shooting of these supplicants literally outside Nicholas's front door tarred him indelibly with bloodshed and oppression. Nicholas II's personal response to the events of Bloody Sunday reveals his total incomprehension of the forces of change his regime faced. For Nicholas II, worker unrest was a symptom of a narrow malaise, the activities of a handful of revolutionaries. The notion that social unrest reflected a broader need for change went unheeded.

Possibly the most dangerous field of policy for an ill-advised and under-supported autocrat to operate in was that of foreign affairs. As Figes acerbically notes, 'unfortunately foreign policy was the one area of government where Nicholas felt competent to lead from the front'.[32] This danger was exacerbated by the patronage-ridden inadequacy of the Foreign Ministry.[33] The example which stands out in discussing Nicholas's foreign policy follies is Russia's involvement in the Russo-Japanese War, a conflict that was predicated on Nicholas's enthusiastic pursuit of expansionist aims and his inability to recognise the need for an economically weak Russia to avoid war at all costs. The naivety of a Russian patriot officer was allowed to run amok, and to draw Russia into a war against an enemy it underestimated and was ill prepared to fight. Nicholas was confident of victory and apparently unconcerned about the financial implications of the war.[34] The Russo-Japanese War came about as a result of intrinsic territorial and influence conflict between Russia and Japan, but more than that as a result of ministerial bungling on the part of Nicholas and his myriad advisors, in particular the speculator Alexander Bezobrazov. The tsar's grand visions for Russia in the Far East had not been weighed against Russia's other interests.

Perhaps the final great misjudgement from Nicholas was his takeover of absolute control of the Russian army in summer 1915, replacing his cousin the Grand Duke Nicholas Nicholaevich. The tsar's ministers were not even consulted, and were appalled by the decision. There was no semblance of understanding or effective communication between tsar and ministers, which, were it not so grave, would be comedic in a modern state at war. Anna Viroubova, a close confidante of the tsar and his wife, reported Nicholas's words on returning from his meeting with ministers to inform them of his decision to assume command:

> The Emperor, entirely exhausted, returned from the conference. Throwing himself into an armchair, he stretched himself out like a man spent after extreme exertion, and I could see that his brow and hands were wet with perspiration. 'They did not move me,' he said in a low, tense voice. 'I listened to their long dull speeches, and when all had finished I said "Gentlemen, in two days from now I leave for Stavka."'[35]

There was some sense in his decision, which was taken primarily to raise the army's morale, by having God's anointed leader at the head of the troops. There were other more pragmatic reasons that favoured the decision. Having Grand Duke Nicholas Nicholaevich in such a powerful post strengthened the position of the grand dukes, whose relations with Nicholas II were troubled.[36] More importantly, by taking control himself, Nicholas could offer better co-ordination between civil and military authorities. Nicholas did not decide military and strategic operations, which were left to his chief of staff General Alekseev.[37] The decision to take over as commander-in-chief is, however, often credited as the beginning of the end for the tsar, as the post allowed him to be associated personally with the Russian army's disasters at the front. Also, it fed negative perceptions of the monarchy by leaving Alexandra and by proxy Rasputin in charge in the capital during his enforced prolonged absences.

The theme of impending crisis dogged Nicholas's reign, despite the fact that he was the first Romanov to have taken the throne in apparent calm rather than political crisis in the nineteenth century.[38] It is impossible to quantify this sense of crisis that was remarked upon by almost all contemporaries in turn-of-the-century Russia. By 1902–3, revolution was in the air, and even the establishment's most conservative figures were countenancing constitutional change. As early as 1901, the well-known Slavophile publicist General Kireev noted that 'in the eyes of the great majority a constitutional order is the [monarchy's] only salvation'.[39] The tsar himself was reluctant to accept that Russia was in a state of crisis, and that the very monarchy was at risk. Nicholas and Alexandra shared the belief that the tsar was 'truly loved' by ordinary Russians, the *narod*. Alexandra, reflecting on the apparent success of the Romanov Jubilee celebrations in 1913, said: 'They [the state ministers] are constantly frightening the Emperor with threats of revolution and here – you can see it for yourself – we need merely to show ourselves and at once their hearts are ours'.[40]

The revolutions of 1905 and 1917 confirmed that the sense of crisis was not a chimera, but reflected a very real turning-point in Russia's political development. In such times of tumultuous change, a clear sighted and assertive tsar was required to provide some ballast to the unsteady empire. Nicholas's response to the rising sense of governmental disquiet was to become ever more interventionist in government policy, a response which did not result in the desired for strong leadership, but instead only further muddled and weakened government policy. One can argue that the sense of crisis was a direct result of the tsar's refusal to countenance any sort of political change without the immediate threat of revolution hanging over him. Where the forces of change were given no legitimate arenas in which to operate, unstinting opposition to the regime became the only alternative. Nicholas stated unambiguously at the outset of his reign that he was absolutely committed to preserving the principles of autocracy, and he declared that the hopes of *zemstvo* representatives (elected district councillors) for more involvement in government affairs were 'senseless dreams'.[41] The general fear that the *zemstva* were in some way encroaching on the autocratic prerogative persisted through Nicholas's reign, and became most marked in the context of Russia in crisis during the First World War. This is a good example of the problems raised by the protection of autocracy in the context of a modern state. By rejecting the role of some degree of local self-government, Nicholas set himself up both on a collision course with society, and on a sure-fire tactic for incompetent government. *Zemstva* were absolutely crucial in the administration of rural Russia. This was recognised by the legislators of emancipation, yet Nicholas refused to acknowledge the changes wrought by modernisation, and instead preferred to cling to the myth of Russia one and indivisible, and of the naïve, trusting, steadfast Russian people.

The period between war and revolutions in Russia between 1905 and 1914 was perhaps the most critical for Nicholas II's rule. The concessions made by the tsar in the October Manifesto of 1905 were given only with the greatest of reluctance. His diary entry on 17 October, the day he signed the manifesto, included a rare emotional outburst: 'Lord, help us, save and pacify Russia!'[42] The October Manifesto promised civil liberties and a meaningful legislature and offered Russia an opportunity to develop a constitutional monarchy, along the lines of the models of France and Germany.[43] The Russian Fundamental State Laws which were drawn up in 1906 to clarify Russia's constitutional position did not, however, give as much to reformists as the October Manifesto had seemed to offer. The tsar refused to relinquish any fundamental aspects of his autocratic power, and would not allow the word 'constitution' to be used.[44] Further, while aspects of the Fundamental Laws seemed to enshrine rule of law and civil rights, the intransigence of the tsar himself limited the impact of these apparently far-reaching statements. The lack of clear legal challenges to autocratic rule meant that any reforms relied on the goodwill of the autocrat to succeed. Nicholas II's personal hostility to these reforms assured their impotence.[45]

The October Manifesto presented a challenge to Nicholas's personal power, which was his central objection to it. Even in areas where reform was aimed towards efficiency rather than at directly challenging the tsar, he was obdurate. The October Manifesto and Fundamental Laws established a Council of Ministers headed by a President, and was directed towards the co-ordination of policies and ministerial actions. Such co-ordination was vital in making government more effective and less arbitrary. The emperor, however, was unwilling to allow it to operate effectively, and despite article 17 of the October Manifesto, which placed the President of the Council of Ministers as an intermediate between tsar and ministers, ministers continued to be individually responsible to the emperor, and to report directly to the tsar. There was a bewildering level of ministerial shuffling in the period 1905–17, reflecting Nicholas's increasingly interventionist attitude to government. The problems of uncoordinated government continued, and tensions between Ministries, most notably between the ministries of Finance and of the Interior, were unresolved.

The role of the Prime Minister was particularly vexed. Petr Stolypin is a useful personification of Russia's move towards twentieth-century rule, and the tsar's continued resistance to the forces of modernisation. From taking the premiership in July 1906 up until his assassination on 14 September 1911, Stolypin was the dominant individual in government, and seemed to have won the respect and support of the tsar for the first two years of his period in office. He was generally regarded as a character who could bring order to Russia, despite his concessions to parliamentarism. In the years 1909–10, however, his opponents gathered as he alienated a range of important interest groups, including the Orthodox Church and landowners. The tsar, rather than offering absolute support to this exceptional minister, came to feel challenged by Stolypin, particularly after Stolypin forced the tsar's hand in pushing through his western *zemstvo* bill in March 1911. Though Stolypin was assassinated before his political denouement could occur, no one doubted it was on the cards. The tsar's failure to support Stolypin wholeheartedly can be regarded as a significant political misjudgement, but was entirely to be expected. Stolypin was energetic, charismatic and far-sighted. His vision of his ministerial role presented a challenge to Nicholas's personalised conception of his own power. Stolypin had been a glimmer of hope for Russian government, a strong premier with the necessary good relations with the tsar to enable some sort of cohesion to be drawn between the disparate elements of tsar, ministers and parliament. Without Stolypin, governance slipped back to the old patterns of uncoordinated autonomous action.

The alienation of those political groups that could have provided a bulwark for the regime epitomises the damage the tsarist regime did to itself by its uncompromising defence of absolute autocracy. The Constitutional Democratic Party (referred to as the Kadets), which was formed in 1905, provided a political voice for Russian liberalism. Despite the reformist beliefs of its members, and an unswerving hostility to revolution, the Kadet party presented a far more intransigent attitude to the autocratic regime than it would naturally have occupied. This is perhaps most apparent in the history of the short-lived first State Duma (27 April – 8 August 1906). This Duma was Russia's first flirtation with representative government, and the Kadets, for the only time in their existence, formed its majority grouping. Headed by Miliukov and Maklakov, the Kadets made far-reaching demands for representative government and broad civil liberties in their response to Nicholas's address from the throne. Their demands were categorically refused, and when they demanded the resignation of the tsar's cabinet, the Duma was dissolved. Unbowed, more than 200 leading Kadets signed the so-called 'Vyborg Manifesto', which endorsed civil disobedience as a method of protest.[46] Despite being committed supporters of the monarchy, Kadets were forced into radicalism by the regime's unswerving resistance to any political change or encroachments on the autocratic prerogative.[47]

The outbreak of war in 1914 'deeply stirred the patriotic sentiments of the educated classes'.[48] The tsar himself, though not eager to enter into war, did believe that the war would strengthen national feeling.[49] The challenge to the nation constituted by war offered a brief window for national endorsement of the tsar's personal rule. The initial mobilisation of soldiers in July and August went surprisingly well,[50] and scholars have remarked on a wave of patriotic fervour in the first months of the war.[51] The occasion of war offered the tsar a unique opportunity to capitalise on this patriotic surge. The Fourth Duma, unsurprisingly given its heavy bias towards the right, expressed openly patriotic and supportive sentiments. Its President, Mikhail Rodzianko, even went so far as to suggest that the Duma did not sit in wartime so as not to disrupt the war effort, though this provoked the rancour of the moderate Duma deputies. The 'Union sacree', an agreement on the part of Duma deputies to suspend all internal conflict for the duration of the war, and to offer the government its full support, lasted until July 1915. Though its formation was predicated partly out of healthy self-interest on the part of the Octobrists and Kadets who were threatened by internal dissent in 1914, its existence presented a brief period of apparent concord between tsar and Duma. In 1915, some of the most hated reactionary ministers, including the Minister of War Sukhomlinov and Minister of the Interior Nikolai Maklakov, were removed and replaced with more moderate figures.[52]

The breakdown of cordial relations between government and Duma, and the formation of the Progressive bloc in August 1915, demonstrated the regime's inability to co-operate with society even in favourable conditions, and was testament to its increasingly incompetent handling of the war effort. The Progressive bloc's first quarrel was not with the government itself, but with the corruption and incompetence it fostered. The tsar's isolation in government was demonstrated by the support of many of his ministers for the Progressive bloc, whose main demand was the establishment of a 'responsible ministry'. The tsar contemptuously prorogued the Duma on 3 September 1915, only to be faced by a rebellion from his own ministers, who largely recognised the need for a more responsible ministry. Having courted more liberal ideas over the summer, the tsar swung back to an unconciliatory position, and dismissed those ministers who were opposed to his choice of chairman, the old conservative stalwart Goremykin.

The tsar became increasingly distanced from the domestic politics he so despised in the course of 1916, even basing himself in Stavka, the military headquarters, from April onwards. By October 1916, the secret police (Okhrana) repeatedly warned of the alarming popular mood, driven predominantly by food crisis fears, and the rising tide of opposition. Distanced geographically and emotionally from these reports, Nicholas failed to respond. His reliance on the incompetent Sturmer, and then the enormously unpopular Protopopov, forced even the reluctant Duma moderates into an oppositional position. Nicholas insistently held on to his personal prerogatives and hindered the formation of competent government. When he concentrated on his military role, the 1916 'paralysis of authority' in domestic affairs was the result. Miliukov's infamous speech of 2 November 1916, in which he asked rhetorically of Sturmer's incompetence, 'Is this stupidity, or is it treason?',[53] was in retrospect regarded as a clarion call to revolution, but Miliukov's intentions were very different. He was forced into an attack on government by the malcontents in his party and the Progressive bloc, and was frightened by society's resonant response to his illegally circulated speech.[54]

It is not only the tsar's relations with Russia's elected representatives that were highlighted by the First World War. Society more generally was mobilised by the outbreak of war, and this mobilisation was perceived as challenging Nicholas's autocratic power. The disastrous shortage of ammunition and weapons, and the massive logistical problems thrown up by incompetent and ill-prepared war leadership, forced Nicholas's government to look to society for assistance. Educated society jumped at the chance afforded by the war to become more closely involved in public life, to display patriotic zeal, and to serve the country. The *zemstva* were critical to the war effort, organising food campaigns, hospitals, care of refugees, appeals to the population, and keeping statistical information on the war.[55] The Union of Towns and the *Zemstvo* Union, both of which first cut their teeth in the Russo-Japanese War, reformed at the outset of the First World War.[56] The War Industries Committee, created by the Ninth Congress of Trade and Industry in May 1915, was set up by industrialists in an attempt to improve technical and administrative efficiency in industry, and to synchronise its efforts with the war. The war was a catalyst for the more effective organisation of Russia's industrialists, especially those based in Moscow, into a national pressure group. It was inevitable that this group became involved in politics, as it sought to influence policy-making and decisions at the highest level.[57]

The government's relations with these organisations were highly ambivalent. On the one hand, the contribution of voluntary organisations to the war effort was absolutely necessary, and had to be courted by government. On the other hand, heavy police surveillance and curtailing of voluntary organisations' activities demonstrated that Nicholas's government was engaged in the feeblest sort of ceasefire with societal forces, rather than any real rapprochement. As early as November 1914, the Minister of the Interior Nikolai Maklakov voiced suspicion about the intentions of the Unions of *Zemstva* and Towns, and warned that their activities be restricted to medical and sanitary assistance. In the September 1915 political crisis, Nicholas displayed his disdain for the public organisations by refusing to meet with their representatives. While the war impressed as nothing else had the necessity of societal support if the state was to be administered effectively, Nicholas was unable to recognise the need to solder firmer relations with society.

This survey of the last of the Romanovs allows us to draw some tentative conclusions. The institution of autocracy was itself anachronistic in the context of a modern and developing state. The personal control of one man over an empire whose governance required that the state take an ever-larger role was simply not possible. If the semblance of autocracy was to be retained, it required a large and highly effective bureaucracy to support it, and to implement its rulings. Despite Nicholas II's theoretically untrammelled autocratic power, he actually had very limited control over policy direction and political decisions, exactly because he lacked the sort of highly developed and proficient bureaucratic machine he needed. The absence of a sufficiently advanced and effective bureaucracy had its origins partly in Nicholas's own anachronistic view of his own power. He was unable to recognise that his will would not be magically visited upon his people, and maintained a hostile attitude towards the governmental apparatus that should have allowed him to rule. Finally, Nicholaevan government never really came to terms with Russia's developing civil society. Educated society could potentially have become a bulwark for some form of constitutional monarchy, much-needed ballast for the empire in times of profound social and economic change. Nicholas refused to sacrifice his autocratic prerogatives on the altar of constitutional monarchy. This refusal closed the doors to the development of a more meritocratic society, more efficient government, and a future for the Romanov dynasty.

Notes

1   So described by Boris Yeltsin, then Russian premier, during his opening speech for the interment ceremony. (Speech quoted in full in *The New York Times*, 18 July 1998, p. 4.)

2   E. J. Bing, *The Secret Letters of the Last Tsar: Being the Confidential Correspondence Between Nicholas II and his Mother, Dowager Empress Maria Feodorovna* (London, 1937); J. T. Fuhrmann, *The Complete Wartime Correspondence of Tsar Nicholas II and the Empress Alexandra, April 1914 – March 1917* (Westport, CT, 1998); V. P. Kozlov, T. F. Pavlova and Z. E. Pereudova, *Dnevnik Imperatora Nikolaia II* (Moscow, 1991).

3   O. Figes, and B. I. Kolonitskii, *Interpreting the Russian Revolution: The Language and Symbols of 1917* (New Haven, CT, 1999).

4   B. V. Ananich and R. S. Ganelin, 'Nicholas II', in D. J. Raleigh and A. A. Iskenderov (eds), *The Emperors and Empresses of Russia* (London, 1996), pp. 334–68, 374.

5   T. S. Pearson, *Russian Officialdom in Crisis: Autocracy and Local Self Government 1861–1900* (Cambridge, 1989), p. 258.

6   E. W. Clowes, S. D. Kassow and J. L. West, *Between Tsar and People: Educated Society and the Quest for Public Identity in Late Imperial Russia* (Princeton, NJ, 1991), ch. 1 provides an insightful commentary on the difficulties of the Russian 'middle', and its relationship with the state.

7   Kozlov et al., *Dnevnik Imperatora Nikolaia II*, p. 625.

8   V. I. Gurko, *Features and Figures of the Past: Government and Opinion in the Reign of Nicholas II* (Stanford, CA, 1939), p. 493.

9   M. D. Steinberg and V. M. Khrustalev (eds), *The Fall of the Romanovs* (New Haven, CT, 1995), p. 4; Ananich and Ganelin, 'Nicholas II', p. 371 outlines Nicholas's twelve-year educational programme.

10   D. Lieven, *Nicholas II: Emperor of all Russians* (Cambridge, 1994), p. 107.

11   E. L. Hynes, *Letters of the Tsar to the Tsarina* (London, 1929) provides numerous examples of the tsar's naïve joy at inspecting troops and 'playing' with his fleet (see, for example, pp. 50–1, 94, 109).

12   Steinberg and Khrustalev, *The Fall of the Romanovs*, p. 14.
13   On his virulent anti-Semitism, see R. D. Warth, *Nicholas II: The LIfe and Reign of Russia's Last Monarch* (Westport, CT, 1997), p. 132.
14   Ibid., p. 92.
15   Lieven, *Nicholas II*, p. 102.
16   A. A. Mossolov, *At the Court of the Last Tsar* (London, 1935), pp. 12–13.
17   Kozlovet et al., *Dnevnik Imperatora Nikolaia II*, pp. 474–8.
18   Lieven, *Nicholas II*, pp. 164–5. Warth states that Nicholas II regarded Rasputin as a 'good, religious, simple-minded Russian', hardly an indication that he was a primary political influence (Warth, *Nicholas II*, p. 165).
19   P. von Reenen, 'Alexandra Fedorovna's Intervention in Russian Domestic Policies during the First World War', *Slovo*, 10(1–2), 1998, pp. 71–82 argues that her political interventions were 'extraordinarily damaging'.
20   Figes and Kolonitskii, *Interpreting the Russian Revolution*, p. 16.
21   See O. Figes, *A People's Tragedy: The Russian Revolution 1891–1924* (London, 1996), pp. 1–24.
22   Figes and Kolonitskii, *Interpreting the Russian Revolution*, p. 19.
23   Pearson, *Russian Officialdom in Crisis*, p. 14.
24   Lieven, *Nicholas II*, p. 107.
25   Ibid., p. 69.
26   Mossolov, *At the Court of the Last Tsar*, pp. 8–11 provides a good explanation of this. Mossolov was the head of the Court Chancellery between 1900 and 1916.
27   As cited in Lieven, *Nicholas II*, p. 106.
28   The best-known discussion on the state of the peasantry is to be found in the articles of James Simms, and in John Bushnell's review of Teodor Shanin's seminal work. J. Bushnell, 'Peasant Economy and Peasant Revolution at the Turn of the Century: Neither Immiseration nor Autonomy', *Russian Review*, 47(1), 1988, pp. 75–88; T. M. Shanin, *Russia as a 'Developing Society'. Volume 1: The Roots of Otherness: Russia's Turn of the Century* (London, 1985); J. Y. Simms, 'The Crisis in Russian Agriculture at the End of the Nineteenth Century: A Different View', *Slavic Review*, 36, 1977, pp. 377–98; J. Y. Simms, 'The Economic Impact of the Russian Famine of 1891–1892', *Slavonic and East European Review*, 60(1), 1982, pp. 63–74. J. Y. Simms, 'A Closer Look at the Indirect Tax Receipts and the Condition of the Russian Peasantry, 1881–1889', *Slavic Review*, 43(4), 1984, pp. 667–71; J. Y. Simms, 'More Grist for the Mill: A Further Look at the Crisis in Russian Agriculture at the End of the Ninetenth Century', *Slavic Review*, 50(4), 1991, pp. 999–1009.
29   For a discussion of these notions of the Russian peasantry, see C. A. Frierson, *Peasant Icons: Representations of Rural People in Late Nineteenth Century Russia* (Oxford, 1993), pp. 32–53.
30   Lieven, *Nicholas II*, p. 85.
31   See J. Schneiderman, *Sergei Zubatov and Revolutionary Marxism: The Struggle for the Working Class in Tsarist Russia* (Ithaca, NY, 1976), on the Zubatov unions experiment.
32   Figes, *A People's Tragedy*, p. 168.
33   Warth, *Nicholas II*, p. 47.
34   Ibid., p. 67.

35 A. Viroubova, *Memories of the Russian Court* (London, 1923), p. 125.
36 See Ananich and Ganelin, 'Nicholas II', p. 390.
37 Lieven, *Nicholas II*, pp. 212ff.
38 Nicholas I took charge in 1825 in the wake of the failed Decembrist uprising, Alexander II took over with Russia in the throes of the disastrous Crimean War in 1855, and Alexander III was crowned in the wake of Alexander II's assassination in 1881.
39 Cited in Lieven, *Nicholas II*, p. 89.
40 Cited in Figes, *A People's Tragedy*, p. 12.
41 Variants of the speech are presented in 'Slyshalis golosa liudei, uvlekavshikhsia bessmyslennymi mechtaniiami', *Istoricheskii Arkhiv*, 4, 1999, pp. 213–20.
42 Kozlov et al., *Dnevnik Imperatora Nikolaia II*, p. 285.
43 For an insightful comparison of Russia's constitutional monarchy with those of other European countries, see the essay of our dedicatee, R. B. McKean, 'The Russian Constitutional Monarchy in Comparative Perspective', in M. Frame and C. Brennan (eds), *Russia and the Wider World in Historical Perspective* (London, 2000), pp 109–25.
44 Ibid., p. 112. The text of the Fundamental Laws is reproduced in G. Vernadsky et al. (eds), *A Source Book for Russian History from Early Times to 1917. Volume 3: From Alexander II to the February Revolution* (New Haven, 1972), pp. 772–4.
45 McKean, 'The Russian Constitutional Monarchy', p. 118.
46 Incidentally, the Vyborg Manifesto's call went unheeded, leaving its authors exposed and embarassed. The failure of this tactic was to ghost the Kadets for the rest of their existence, as even on the brink of revolution in 1916 they fought shy of appeals to the general population.
47 See A. Kroner, 'The Role of the Kadets in Three Attempts to Form Coalition Cabinets in 1905–06', *Revolutionary Russia*, 5(1), 1992, pp. 22–45; S. Galai, 'The Kadet Quest for the Masses', in R. B. McKean (ed.), *New Perspectives in Modern Russian History* (London, 1992), pp. 80–98.
48 Gurko, *Features and Figures of the Past*, p. 538.
49 As reported by Viroubova, *Memories of the Russian Court*, p. 104.
50 J. A. Sanborn, *Drafting the Russian Nation: Military Conscription, Total War and Mass Politics, 1905–1925* (DeKalb, IL, 2003), pp. 29–30.
51 H. F. Jahn, *Patriotic Culture During World War 1* (New York, 1995), p. 171.
52 See R. Pearson, *The Russian Moderates and the Crisis of Tsardom* (London, 1977), p. 41.
53 Full text of speech available in F. Golder, *Documents of Russian History 1914–1917* (Massachusetts, 1964), pp. 154–66.
54 See Pearson, *The Russian Moderates*, p. 113.
55 W. Gleason, 'The All Russian Union of Zemstvos and World War One', in T. Emmons and W. S. Vucinich (eds), *The Zemstvo in Russia: An Experiment in Local Self Government* (Cambridge, 1982), pp. 365–82.; K. Matsuzato, 'The Role of the Zemstva in the Creation and Collapse of Tsarism's War Efforts during World War One', *Jahrbucher fur Geschichte Osteuropas*, 46, 1998, p. 322.
56 Figes, *A People's Tragedy*, p. 271.
57 Pearson, *The Russian Moderates*, p. 34.

3

Late imperial constitutionalism

Peter Waldron

The Provisional Government which was installed after the 1917 February revolution appeared to represent the culmination of the post-1905 constitutional system. The tsarist autocracy had disappeared and had been replaced by a government which drew its legitimacy from the Duma. The triumph of parliamentarianism and the future of representative government in Russia seemed assured. Yet, within eight months Russian constitutionalism had been snuffed out as the Bolsheviks seized power and for a further seventy-five years Russia lived under a regime which had scant regard for law or for representative institutions. The constitutional experiment of the post-1905 years proved to be just that: an experiment which failed. The roots of the constitutional structure turned out to be shallow and unable to sustain the Provisional Government, so that the Bolsheviks were easily able to dispense with the apparatus of constitutionalism after October 1917. There was no popular upsurge of support for the Provisional Government in the wake of the Bolshevik *coup*, and no great wave of public opinion protested against the forcible dissolution of the Constituent Assembly at the beginning of 1918. The Civil War of 1918–21 was fought to try to rid Russia of the Bolsheviks, rather than to restore constitutional government. Less than twelve months after the Provisional Government had come into being, the high hopes provoked by its formation had turned to dust. This chapter will suggest reasons for the failure of constitutional Russia to establish itself in the decade after 1905.

The October Manifesto of 1905 gave Russia an elected legislative representative assembly for the first time. A popularly elected parliament, the Duma, was to be established and in the spring of 1906 the system was made more complex by the transformation of the existing consultative State Council into a second legislative chamber, with half its members appointed by the tsar and half elected by interest and corporate groups such as the nobility, universities and business.[1] Lastly, the emperor was given the final say in the legislative process; all three elements of the system – Duma, State Council and emperor

– had to agree before a bill became law. Nascent Russian political opinion was overjoyed at the concessions that the tsarist regime had made in giving up its unlimited autocratic power, and there was a firm belief among those who had pressed for a constitutional regime that the changes heralded by the October Manifesto marked the beginning of a new era of change in Russia.

However, it quickly became clear that the apparatus of the constitutional system was incapable of meeting the aspirations aroused by its creation. For those on the left and in the centre of Russian politics, the establishment of the Duma was to be merely the beginning of a process of reform. The centrist Octobrists and the liberal Kadets both wanted to use the parliamentary assembly to bring about major change to the Russian Empire, but the Duma proved to be an inadequate forum for these purposes. Political differences between government and the political parties meant that the relationship between government and Duma was never easy. From the beginning of its existence the majority of the Duma's members saw their task as being to keep a watch on the activities of the government and to prevent the administration from overstepping the limits which each party saw as correct. This attitude dated from the Duma's first convocation: the first speaker of the Duma, the Kadet S. A. Muromtsev, saw himself as being the most important political figure in Russia after the tsar. After an initial snub from Nicholas II, he would only use his right to report to the monarch if he was summoned by the emperor, and met Nicholas only twice during the First Duma's existence. Muromtsev also kept his distance from the government itself and took no steps to meet Goremykin, the Prime Minister, to help establish workable relations between executive and legislature. As contemporary observers noted, Muromtsev failed to take the opportunity to establish himself as the intermediary between the new parliament and the government.[2]

The fault did not lie wholly with the Duma, however. The Goremykin government was fundamentally antagonistic to the new parliament and believed that it should be kept at arm's length. After Nicholas II had addressed the opening session of the First Duma, Muromtsev asked if he could present the emperor with a copy of the Duma's response: his request was swiftly and sharply rebuffed. This was not entirely surprising, since the Duma's Answer to the Throne was a resolution that called for fundamental political reforms. The government's approach was reflected in the speech made by Goremykin, the 66-year-old Prime Minister, to the First Duma soon after its official opening. He addressed the Duma deputies much as a headmaster might deal with a potentially troublesome pupil, warning the Duma that certain policies, in particular the compulsory expropriation of noble-owned land, had already been rejected by the government and that there was therefore no point in the Duma entertaining false hopes as to its ability to influence matters. Goremykin wanted to make it plain that the government would not tolerate any overstepping of the limits it wanted the Duma to observe.[3] The majority of deputies in the First Duma had no intention of falling into line with the government's view of their role.[4] The radical-dominated Duma pressed for a wide range of significant reforms, especially in the areas of land reform and civil rights, and found itself at loggerheads with Goremykin's government on almost every issue. The Russian government was wholly unused to dealing with legitimate institutional opposition and its initial reaction was to deal with this problem as it would confront any other type of opposition. The First Duma was thus summarily dissolved after only two months. The government believed that the political composition of the First Duma had been an aberration, and that once the Russian people were given another chance to elect deputies a more moderate Duma would emerge. Ministers also felt that their display of firmness in dealing with the extreme ideas of the First Duma would demonstrate plainly that it was pointless for the voters to elect another radical Duma, since it would have as little chance of achieving positive results as its predecessor. However, fresh elections produced much the same result and the Second Duma was equally radical in its outlook.[5] The new parliamentary system offered no mechanism, other than dissolution, by which such an *impasse* between executive and legislature could be resolved.

Even when Stolypin came to power as a Prime Minister personally committed to radical reform, the structure and mechanics of the Duma meant that most of his reform proposals became bogged down in a legislative morass. The fundamental relationship that existed between the government and the legislative institutions made the workings of the Duma difficult, and this was exacerbated by the barely restrained, and often overt, antagonism that existed between these two parts of the Russian constitutional structure for a significant part of the period between 1905 and 1917. The Russian Duma was not controlled by a government party and this meant that the government was therefore unable to guarantee that its legislation would become law. Government ministers were not members of the Duma, but instead could only appear to make statements or to answer interpellations from Duma deputies. The government was thus detached from the legislature and was often the target of angry and highly critical interpellations, especially in relation to its policy of repression and the infringements of civil rights that this involved. The relationship between government and the first two Dumas was fundamentally one of mistrust. This did improve somewhat after the election of the Third Duma under a different electoral law that produced a more moderate legislature, but the atmosphere that had been created during the brief sessions of the first two Dumas continued to underlie relations between executive and legislature and to poison the relationship between the government and political parties on the left.

The dissolution of the First Duma had produced a furious response from the Kadet party, and many of its Duma deputies travelled the short distance to

Vyborg in autonomous Finland to issue a manifesto calling for a campaign of civil disobedience to protest against the government's decision. The government had responded to the Vyborg Manifesto with equal vigour, closing down Kadet clubs, dismissing Kadet party members from government service and prosecuting the signatories of the manifesto. This final move had severe consequences for the Kadet party, since the 230 accused were disqualified from standing for election to the Second Duma. When the case eventually came to court, 166 Kadets were found guilty and sentenced to imprisonment, and were permanently prohibited from taking part in political activities. The level of antagonism that was engendered between the Kadet party and the government was immense and ensured that this liberal political party would treat even a reforming regime with deep scepticism. The government was so frustrated with the behaviour of the First and Second Dumas that, when it dissolved the Second Duma, its only solution to the problem was to unilaterally change the electoral law. This action served to damage relations with parties on the left and liberal wings even further, since it was unconstitutional as legislation required the approval of the new parliamentary institutions.[6] The new electoral law of 3 June 1907 achieved the government's aim of ensuring a more pliant Duma, by reducing the representation given to the peasantry and enhancing the position of the provincial and essentially conservative nobility. When the Third Duma met in November 1907, the Kadets saw their representation halved and the radical Trudovik party's 104 members in the Second Duma were reduced to a rump of only ten. The largest single party in the Third Duma was the Octobrists: they comprised more than one-third of the Duma's membership and this appeared to offer the promise of a more stable parliamentary system. While this revised electoral law provided the government with a less awkward Duma after 1907, it did little to deal with the real sources of antagonism that separated government from the newly created parliament.

The constitutional system that was established during 1905 and 1906 was intended to maintain this formal distance between government and the political parties, but the architects of the 1905 settlement failed to recognise the problems this would pose in establishing a workable legislature. No party in the Duma was under any imperative to see a bill approved, for as there was no governing party, a party's position did not depend on its ability to see a piece of legislation successfully through parliament. This gave political parties no stake in the success of the new legislature and allowed them to adopt attitudes that were highly critical of the government, with little fear that this would have repercussions for them. The political parties had no power to lose by opposing or delaying government bills, and this was especially true of the liberal and radical groups that had seen the government take vigorous steps to curb their influence. The Octobrist party did try to demonstrate that it had special links with Stolypin's government, but this did nothing to persuade members of the party to present a united front in support of the government and splits developed within the party.[7] The genesis of the Octobrist party was its commitment to the October Manifesto and the party's acceptance of the constitutional arrangements that were set up as a result of the 1905 revolution; the Octobrists wanted to work through the new institutions to promote change. But the Octobrists proved to be as willing as any other party to criticise government policy: it was Octobrist amendments, for example, which substantially altered a key part of the Stolypin government's civil rights reforms, the bill to regularise the position of the Old Believers. Parties further to the left, however, maintained much more consistent opposition to the government. The Kadet party continued to voice fierce antagonism towards the government: during 1908 and 1909, other political parties came to believe that the Kadets were simply using the Duma as a tribune from which they could attack the government. Kadets certainly took a leading role in putting down interpellations to ministers which concentrated on laying bare the government's record on civil rights: in December 1908 they invited the Duma to condemn the widening use of the death penalty against participants in the revolutionary movement. When their proposal was rejected, the Kadets walked out of the session, along with Trudovik and Social Democrat deputies.[8] Kadet antipathy to the tsarist government continued right up until the end of the regime: the famous 'Is it stupidity or is it treason?' speech by Miliukov, one of the Kadet leaders, in the Duma in November 1916 had a powerful effect on public opinion and demonstrated that, for the Kadets, the only answer to the crisis that had beset Russia was the removal of the imperial regime.[9]

The attitude of parties on the right towards the new structures was also overwhelmingly negative. At this end of the political spectrum there was a deep mistrust of the fundamental principle of representative institutions, and the experience of the first two Dumas had only served to intensify this belief. The instinct of parties on the right was to support the authority of the tsar and to oppose anything that they believed would encroach on his prerogatives. Conservative parties were also deeply suspicious of reform, believing that the autocracy's traditional repressive policies were a more effective way of dealing with discontent. The emperor himself was sympathetic to this approach. Nicholas II's instincts during 1905 itself had been to try to deal with revolt by crushing opposition and he had only been persuaded to make concessions under great pressure. Parties on the right took their cue from the atmosphere around Nicholas II and wanted the Duma's role to be constrained, with it acting more as a consultative body than possessing any real power. The right was strongly opposed to the reforms that Stolypin tried to introduce after 1906, believing that they would undermine the traditional basis of the Russian state by weakening the authority of the nobility and the Orthodox Church.[10] The influence of interest groups such as the United Nobility and the Orthodox

Church at this end of the political spectrum was very considerable and they proved able, along with their allies in the Duma and State Council, to delay and defeat the majority of Stolypin's reform programme. It proved much easier for parties on both left and right to be critical of the government's work than it was for them to offer support. Stolypin himself had said that he expected the Third Duma to display moderate opposition to the government.[11] The government never expected to be able to work closely with the Duma, while no Duma party found itself able to offer whole-hearted support to Stolypin's government. This friction between executive and legislature was not conducive to the enactment of a major programme of reform. It was only after Stolypin's assassination in 1911, and his replacement as Prime Minister by the colourless Kokovtsov, that relations between government and legislature became easier. Kokovtsov had no desire to make reforms of any real substance and this helped to quieten the right, who saw the new Prime Minister as somebody who also wanted to curtail the activities of the legislature. While this did negate the most dangerous source of opposition to the government, it did not stifle the commotion from the left about the government's actions. But, while this was articulate and vocal, the government was able to ignore most of the criticism from this source. This period of relative calm proved, however, to be short-lived.

The outbreak of the First World War in the summer of 1914 and Russia's immediate and dramatic military reverses served to provoke further and increasingly severe criticism. The government sought to limit the extent of such criticism by denying its opponents a public forum. It restricted the length of the Duma's sessions: the Duma met for a single day in the summer of 1914 to give its support to Russia's entry into the war, and then for three days in January 1915. A six-week session in the summer of 1915 was followed by nearly six months during which the Duma was in recess. During 1916, the Duma was in session from February until June and again in November, but attendance was not high. This limitation on the part the Duma could play during a time of national crisis served to provoke Duma members even further. In the summer of 1915, the majority of the Duma's members formed the Progressive bloc, and issued a programme calling for the formation of a government which enjoyed 'the confidence of the country' and which could work with the legislature.[12] The bloc included members from all but parties at the two extremes of the Duma and could count on support from more than two-thirds of the Duma. Its programme emphasised that Russia could only be victorious in war if the government was able to make real changes and it called for the implementation of a wide range of reforms, essentially aimed at dismantling much of the repressive apparatus of the tsarist state. This move by Duma members infuriated Nicholas II and his closest advisers, and the emperor absolutely rejected the idea of allowing elected representatives to take any part in the government of Russia. Even though there was considerable disunity among government ministers, especially over the tsar's decision to take on the post of Commander-in-Chief himself, Nicholas held firm and continued to hold the Duma at arm's length. The relationship between Duma and government became one of absolute mistrust, as Nicholas II believed that the Duma's members were seeking to usurp his own authority. While the Duma's activities were circumscribed, the government itself was undergoing rapid changes. Between September 1915 and February 1917, a process of 'ministerial leapfrog' gave Russia four Prime Ministers, five Ministers of Internal Affairs, three Ministers of Foreign Affairs, three Ministers of War, three Ministers of Transport and four Ministers of Agriculture. The chronic instability of Russia's government demonstrated the growing isolation of Nicholas II and his closest advisers from both the Duma and increasingly from his own moderate ministers. The crisis of the First World War served to increase the difficulties inherent in the post-1905 Russian constitutional system.

The new Russian constitution proved to have structural problems that rendered it ineffective, but the detailed procedures for legislating also contributed to the new system's difficulties. The problems which Stolypin's government encountered in trying to steer contentious reform legislation through the Duma stemmed partly from the workload which the government placed upon the new parliament. During the Third Duma's first session, the government introduced 610 bills, of which only 332 were approved during that session, leaving the remainder to be dealt with later. Over the five years of the Third Duma's life, over 2,500 measures were submitted to it by the government and 90 per cent of them were eventually approved.[13] Most of these bills, however, were of the so-called 'vermicelli' variety, which legislated for very minor matters but did nevertheless take up valuable time. The government was unable to draw any distinction between matters which needed primary legislation and those which, in other parliamentary regimes, were dealt with by government regulation. By the beginning of 1909 the pressure of time on the Duma was so severe that the number of full sessions had to be increased from three to four per week, solely to deal with this minor business.[14] But in the autumn of 1909 there was a return to three sessions weekly, not because the amount of work had decreased, but because the increased number of full sessions meant that Duma deputies were unable to devote sufficient time to the examination of bills in committee.[15]

The burden of legislation was intensified by the lack of any fixed timetable for the progress of legislation through the Duma. The main stumbling block was the commissions which were established to examine each bill: those dealing with major bills had 66 members, while less significant measures were debated by commissions of 33. These unwieldy bodies were intended to allow the party structure of the Duma to be reproduced in miniature, but made proper discussion very difficult indeed.[16] There was no requirement that a commission finish its work within a specified period, and when dealing with a major piece of reform legislation it was not uncommon for a commission to take eighteen months over its deliberations.[17] The lack of fixed procedure for a commission's work was repeated when a bill came to be debated in the full session of the Duma. There was no provision for a timetable to be set out for a bill's passage through the Duma, and no mechanism that the government could use to speed up the bill's progress. There was no means of introducing a 'guillotine' motion which would allow the government to set a time limit for debates on a particular measure. In certain cases, the Duma itself voted to restrict the length of speeches, but this was only resorted to in exceptional circumstances.[18] The decision to limit debate rested with the Duma itself rather than with the government, and there was little incentive for the Duma to conclude its deliberations quickly.

Many of the Stolypin government's major reform bills were introduced into the Duma at the very beginning of the 1907–8 session and this paved the way for severe legislative congestion. Each bill's passage through the commissions took at least a year and it was impossible to predict when a commission would complete its work of examining a bill and it would be ready for consideration by the full session of the Duma. Although in the autumn of 1908 Stolypin tried to influence the chairman of the Duma to debate the local government reforms first,[19] it was decided by the leaders of the different parties in the Duma that the order of business should be determined according to the preferences of the Duma parties themselves.[20] An informal committee consisting of sixteen representatives from the political groupings in the Duma had been established by N. A. Khomiakov, the Duma's speaker, so that 'they could become acquainted with the opinions which existed in different groups concerning the various questions of Duma activity, and so achieve as much agreement as possible'.[21] It was this committee which was responsible for deciding the pattern of the Duma's work. But there was no agreement between the different parties on the order in which bills should be debated. The situation was further complicated by the inability of commissions to conclude their examination of bills to coincide with the Duma leaders' preferences. Discussion of the agrarian measures occupied the Duma for much of 1909, but there was no consensus on what should be dealt with afterwards. Suggestions by Guchkov, the Octobrist leader, that two bills could be debated in parallel were rejected because it was felt that the complexity of the measures he suggested – reform of the local court and the enshrining in law of personal inviolability – would make this impractical.[22] It was eventually decided to debate the local court bill first, but when Guchkov became the Duma speaker in the spring of 1910, he abandoned the meetings of this committee, believing that they served no useful purpose and that the views that were expressed could just as easily be put on the floor of the Duma.

This lack of effective organisation in arranging the Duma's timetable had a serious effect on the government's legislative programme, for it meant that the amount of time devoted to different bills could vary considerably. More than six months of the 1909 session were given over to the agrarian legislation, whereas the bill restricting Finnish autonomy was considered in a single week in 1910. Political parties could delay or speed up a bill as a political manoeuvre, and the government remained powerless in such a situation: relations between the government and the Duma had not reached the stage where informal contacts could ensure the smooth passage of legislation. It is clear that the leaders of the Duma parties themselves found their lack of control over the work of parliament to be frustrating, for it meant that it was difficult to plan any sort of reliable legislative timetable and the Duma parties could not be sure that their preferred reforms received priority. The government too was adversely affected by the delays in the legislative programme, for opposition to its proposals was given time to crystallise and organise itself, thus making the government's task much more difficult.

The mere existence of representative institutions in the Russian Empire was no guarantee that they were able to complete any useful work. Although the government wanted to see the Duma work effectively, and most of the parties inside the Duma intended that it should be seen to justify its existence by bringing benefit to Russia, the Duma was never able to find a satisfactory system for its prime purpose of legislating. The conscientious approach which many Duma members adopted to their job did not help in pushing through reform: deputies were, in the main, unwilling to approve legislation without having first examined and discussed it fully, and this process often involved much time being spent on research into the subject.[23] In the full sessions of the Duma, members were eager to speak, often at considerable length, and showed great reluctance to shorten speeches, either by the imposition of a time limit or by allowing only a given number of speakers on an issue. The problems which the Duma encountered were those produced by having a set of inexperienced legislators attempting to deal with an overfull programme of major reform bills without a clear set of procedural rules to guide them. This caused delays which neither the Duma nor the government had the power or will to avoid. If Stolypin had been able to legislate without the Duma, his proposals would undoubtably have had more success in becoming law, but the existence of the Duma – brought into being following widespread popular pressure – succeeded in slowing down the reform progress. It is ironic that an institution which was created to bring about reform actually acted to slow down reform, and ultimately to delay Stolypin's reform programme so much that organised opposition was able to defeat them.

The State Council provided different problems in the new constitutional structures. The newly reformed body was designed to be a conservative body that could act as a counterweight to a radical Duma. This did not mean that its members came exclusively from the right of the political spectrum: a small group of Kadet sympathisers were members of the Council, while a centre grouping appeared to have the support of a majority of the Council's members.[24] This political framework did give the government some expectation that the Council could act in concert with the Duma, especially after the 1907 elections had produced a less radical Third Duma. But these expectations too came to naught. The State Council centre group proved to be an amorphous collection of men, without clear leadership or a coherent set of principles and policies. Attempts at co-ordinating the work of the Duma centrist parties with like-minded members of the State Council proved unsuccessful, while the emperor's annual appointments to the Council served to strengthen the right. The lengthy process of legislating in the Duma meant that the State Council hardly had the opportunity to consider any of Stolypin's reform programme before the political atmosphere moved away from promoting reform and the efforts of the right became focused on defeating Stolypin and his proposals for reform. The State Council demonstrated its independence from the government by coming close to defeating Stolypin on the issue of the Naval General Staff in 1908,[25] and then by adopting a strongly nationalist outlook. Eventually, in 1911, the Council defeated the government's bill to introduce *zemstva* into the western provinces of the empire, showing how far relations between government and legislature had deteriorated.

The new Russian parliamentary system quickly became paralysed after 1905. The radical First Duma clashed with the conservative Goremykin government and this set the tone for relations between executive and legislature. When Stolypin came into office he had to cope with an atmosphere that was already soured and it proved very difficult to retrieve the situation and bridge the gulf between the two institutions. The government's actions made this process no easier: Stolypin took resolute action to counter unrest across Russia and he gained a reputation as a tough and uncompromising opponent of revolt. This served to antagonise political groups on the left of the Russian political spectrum, while the Prime Minister's espousal of reform aroused great misgivings on the right. No element in the new constitutional structure was willing to take the steps needed to compromise and work with people of opposing views. The constitutional structures that were put in place in 1905 and 1906 essentially institutionalised the divisions in the Russian political scene that had been evident before the October Manifesto.

The roots of the practical problems encountered in legislating lay in the political culture of imperial Russia. By the beginning of the twentieth century, the social structure of Russia was changing. The emancipation of the serfs in 1861 had helped to give the peasant population of the empire greater independence.

More peasants began to work in the growing industrial cities as the ties between urban and rural Russia developed. The process of industrialisation – particularly powerful during the 1890s – changed the urban landscape of the empire by bringing into existence a class of industrial workers, and by enabling the rapid growth of entrepreneurial and professional groups. The establishment of elected councils – *zemstva* – in much of rural European Russia in 1864, along with the introduction of elected urban councils six years later, had provided the opportunity for prominent provincial figures to gain practical experience of governing their local region. *Zemstvo* involvement in education, social services, public health matters and the provision of local infrastructure had laid the basis for the growth of employment opportunities right across European Russia for educated professional people. The twin trends of industrial growth and the development of local self-government helped to give a sharp stimulus to the growth of a Russian middle class. Professional bodies, industrial and commercial trade organisations and a wide variety of cultural societies were all coming into being by 1900. The greater freedom of association which was promised by the government during 1905 gave a further impetus to the establishment of groups which brought together the nascent Russian middle class. A more heterogeneous press, together with a better system of education, contributed to the widening influence of the sector of Russian society that stood between the nobility and the peasantry. During the first decade of the twentieth century, the Russian Empire was undergoing a process of social diversification. The vacuum left by the declining power of the nobility was very gradually being filled by a vigorous and varied middle class.[26]

This process of social change was not, however, reflected in the post-1905 political structures of the empire. The traditional social elite continued to retain power and influence, both in the formal legislative institutions of Duma and State Council and in the informal channels through which much of the work of the imperial government was still done. Nicholas II and his coterie proved to be insuperable obstacles to real reform and the tsar deeply regretted that he had ever been persuaded to concede the establishment of the Duma.[27] The Fundamental Laws which were issued in April 1906 created a legislative system which contained a permanent bias to the right; legislation had to be approved not just by the Duma, but also by the State Council and by the tsar. Nicholas II's conservatism was never in doubt, while his appointment of half the membership of the State Council ensured that the council would also have a large inbuilt right bloc. The elections to the First and Second Dumas had allowed a wider constituency to play a part in the political process, but the outcome had proved unpalatable to the government. The revised 1907 franchise, while producing an easier relationship between government and Duma, had done so by restricting the participation of – in the government's view – the Duma's most awkward elements and by shifting the balance of the Duma firmly towards the right. The sections of Russian society which believed that they had the most to gain from the new constitutional structures found themselves heavily outnumbered in the post-1907 legislative system by those groups which had most to lose.

In particular, the growing middle classes found that their views were poorly represented. Even though the Octobrist party drew much of its support from urban voters, and might have been expected to reflect the views of the industrial and commercial populations of the great cities of the empire, the landowners who dominated the leadership of the party had divided loyalties. It was also true that in the first decade of the twentieth century, the level of development of the middle classes had hardly reached the stage where they saw themselves as having coherent political objectives. While the long-established merchants and industrialists of Moscow, St Petersburg and Nizhnii-Novgorod demonstrated a cohesiveness that allowed them to pursue political objectives, the growing professional and entrepreneurial classes had not yet achieved that degree of common purpose. The concerns of these people were expressed through their disparate sectional organisations, and as the formal political arena was barely open to these groups, their congresses became a vital forum for the articulation of their aspirations. The more open political environment after 1905 quickly helped to promote the discussion of matters of social and political concern. As the Duma failed to provide an appropriate arena for this debate, the varied congresses came to provide what one contemporary described as a 'parliament of public opinion'.[28] Even though meetings such as congresses on fire insurance, on alcoholism or of librarians could by no stretch of the imagination be described as overtly political, they – and many other gatherings – passed resolutions which addressed questions of political importance. There was little connection, however, between these unofficial expressions of opinion and the formal political institutions of the empire. Indeed, conservative newspapers attacked the holding of such congresses and called for government action to prevent meetings at which political questions were debated. Russian political life failed to live up to the expectations aroused by the upheaval of 1905. The new political structures ossified rapidly and failed properly to represent the transformations that Russian society was undergoing. The façade of reformed political institutions concealed an established political class which was intent on resisting real change.

It is here that McKean's comments on the weakness of the social foundations of the constitutional regime are relevant.[29] The dynamic nature of Russia's social development was not reflected in the political institutions of constitutional Russia. This made it very difficult for reform to be implemented in the years immediately after 1905, but it had an even greater effect during the First World War. Even though the tsarist regime showed itself to be an incompetent manager of the war effort, the industrial and business community found it difficult to gain access to the decision-making machinery of the state. The crisis that engulfed the Russian state during the war made the rulers of the empire even more reluctant to allow proper social involvement in the work of government. The War Industries Committees which represented the industrial bourgeoisie were marginalised by the government and found themselves reduced to a state of 'patriotic despair'.[30] During the war the Duma was even more marginal to the war effort. The government resisted summoning the Duma, allowing it to meet only briefly during the summer of 1915 and again in February and November 1916. The Duma's members could only rant in impotent rage as Russia slid further and further into disarray.

The opportunity for wider social participation in the work of government had, however, existed during 1906. Discussions had taken place between Stolypin and leading 'public figures' including D. N. Shipov, A. I. Guchkov, Prince G. E. Lvov – later to head the Provisional Government[31] – and N. N. Lvov to discover if there was sufficient common ground to allow them to take up ministerial appointments. Neither side, however, was prepared to move far enough to compromise: the tsar expressed extreme scepticism about the principle of public participation in government, while the public figures themselves demanded far-reaching guarantees both about the nature of the posts which they would occupy and about the overall policy of the government. This failure to draw government and society together had significant results: it polarised government and Duma and it meant that the government's retreat from reform after 1909 could be accomplished without substantial opposition from its own ministers. This was particularly important since there was a sharp and rapid decline in the willingness of the Russian political elite to contemplate measures which would enhance the new constitutional structures. As the regime regained control of the empire during 1906, many on the right believed that there was no need to embark on further reform and that the constitutional changes which had been conceded during 1905 should be hemmed about to reduce the new parliament to impotence. After 1906 the empire's elites were congratulating themselves on having defeated revolution, rather than recognising that it had merely been held at bay. The constitutional changes of 1905 proved only skin-deep: the conservative establishment of Russia proved as able to reassert its authority as conservatives across much of Europe had been able to do after 1848.

The failure of constitutional Russia raises important issues about the nature of both state and society in late imperial Russia. During the eighteenth and nineteenth centuries the tsarist regime had proved resilient and capable of maintaining its authority at successive times of crisis. It had demonstrated its ability both to embark on imperial expansion and to fight wars while remaining financially solvent. Uniquely among the great powers of Europe, imperial

Russia had been able to resist reform until 1905, and even after the proclamation of the October Manifesto the government was able to hedge the concessions it had granted with measures which severely reduced the manifesto's impact. The tsarist state had, thus, sufficient confidence in its own durability to act to restrict the extent of constitutionalism in the Russian Empire. Peter Gatrell suggests that an examination of the reasons for the autocracy's failure to subvert the entire constitutional system after 1905 would be appropriate,[32] yet essentially fails to recognise that the resurgent coercive power of the state in the aftermath of 1905 rendered such a course of action unnecessary. Tsarism found it helpful to maintain the structures of a constitutional system, especially to enhance the image of the regime that was projected abroad, but was able to render the apparatus so ineffective that it came to pose no real threat to the imperial regime. The Russian state appeared re-invigorated after 1905: the existence of the Duma gave it the appearance of having undergone reform, while the crushing of rebellion after 1905 appeared to have enhanced the power of tsarism. The imperial regime believed that it had regained its authority, but this self-delusion was to have fatal consequences.

The weakness of the state was made manifest by the reaction of important groups in imperial society when crisis struck again after 1914. Many national groups were excluded from the system of constitutional politics or else found their representation limited. Non-Russian nationalities seized the opportunity presented by war and revolution to rebel against their Russian masters, and in some cases were able to gain their independence. The unity of the Russian Empire was superficial. The fracturing of the empire along national lines after 1914 demonstrated the failure of successive tsars' attempts to Russify their imperial domains; the post-1905 structures had taken no account of the national stresses which Russia faced. The peasant population of the empire proved equally unwilling to sustain tsarism. The Stolypin land reform had not been greeted with overwhelming enthusiasm by the peasant population and it had failed in its aim of providing a stable and reliable base of support for the imperial regime. Peasant interest in politics, as evidenced by the flood of petitions presented after the edict of 18 February 1905,[33] was not destroyed by the suppression of the First and Second Dumas and the reduction in peasant representation brought about by the June 1907 electoral law. More analysis is needed of peasant attitudes in the period after 1905 to gain greater insight into the mentality of the rural population, but it seems fair to assert that peasant expectations of change provoked by the constitutional changes of 1905 were dashed and that this played a vital part in making the divorce between monarch and people final. Social fragmentation was vital in bringing about the collapse of constitutionalism: when the people of the Russian Empire had the opportunity to spring to the defence of constitutional politics after February 1917, they signally failed to respond. The failure of constitutional politics

in Russia demonstrated that, even when the strength of the tsarist state had
been shown to be a myth, there was no adequate social base for a new political
culture.

Notes

1   See A. S. Korros, *A Reluctant Parliament: Stolypin, Nationalism, and the Politics of
    the Russian Imperial State Council, 1906–1911* (London, 2002), chs 1 and 2 for a
    discussion of the State Council's structure and composition.
2   A. Ascher, *The Revolution of 1905: Authority Restored* (Stanford, CA, 1992), p. 90.
3   *Gosudarstvennaia Duma. Stenograficheskie otchety*, I Duma, vol. 1 (St Petersburg,
    1906), cols 321–4.
4   The political composition of the First Duma is set out in M. McCauley and
    P. Waldron, *From Octobrists to Bolsheviks: Imperial Russia 1905–1917* (London,
    1984), p. 16.
5   See ibid., p. 16 for the political composition of the Second Duma.
6   The new electoral law was issued under Article 87 of the Fundamental Laws which
    allowed for legislation to be issued while the Duma was in recess, but specifically
    excluded the use of this article to make changes to the electoral law.
7   The weakening of Octobrist unity accelerated after the spring of 1909 when Ia.
    G. Gololobov, a party adherent acting as *rapporteur* for an interpellation on trade
    unions, mounted a vigorous attack on Octobrist policy. See A. S. Viziagin,
    Gololobovskii intsident: stranichka iz istorii politicheskikh partii v Rossii (Khar'kov,
    1909), pp. 9–71.
8   V. S. Diakin, *Samoderzhavie, burzhuaziia i dvorianstvo v 1907–1911gg* (Leningrad,
    1978), p. 124.
9   See R. Pearson, *The Russian Moderates and the Crisis of Tsarism 1914–1917*
    (London, 1977).
10 P. Waldron, *Between Two Revolutions: Stolypin and the Politics of Renewal in Russia*
    (London, 1998), pp. 143–6.
11 London, Public Record Office FO 418/38, p. 203.
12 *Krasnyy Arkhiv*, 50–1, 1932, pp. 133–6.
13 *Obzor deiatel'nosti Gosudarstvennoi Dumy tret'ego sozyva, 1907–1912* (St Peters-
    burg, 1912), vol. 1, p. 172.
14 St Petersburg, Rossiiskii Gosudarstvennyi Istoricheskii Arkhiv (RGIA), f. 1278, op.
    3, d. 171, l. 63.
15 Ibid., l. 73.
16 S. I. Shidlovskii, *Vospominaniia*, vol. 1 (Berlin, 1923), p. 113.
17 An exception was the agrarian bill, which after its introduction into the Third
    Duma took only three months to gain the approval of the commission examining
    it. This bill had previously been introduced into the Second Duma and it had been
    partially examined there, while it also commanded a measure of support amongst
    different political parties.
18 This was done during the debate on the agrarian bill, but deputies were able to
    avoid the restriction by making speeches under an article of the Duma's rules

which allowed them to speak 'to explain their voting'. Shidlovskii, *Vospominaniia*, vol. 1, p. 113.

19 P. A. Stolypin to N. A. Khomiakov, 17 October 1908. RGIA, f. 1278, op. 3, d. 171, l. 41.

20 RGIA, f. 1278, op. 3, d. 171, l. 73, 8 November 1908.

21 Ibid., l. 1

22 Ibid., l. 87.

23 The diligence with which the commission dealing with the Old Believer bill went about its work – interviewing interested parties and asking them for their comments on the government's proposals – is not untypical of the commissions.

24 Korros, *Reluctant Parliament*, p. 91.

25 See G. Hosking, *The Russian Constitutional Experiment: Government and Duma 1907–1914* (Cambridge, 1973), pp. 80–5.

26 See E. Clowes, S. D. Kassow and J. L. West (eds), *Between Tsar and People: Educated Society in the Quest for Public Identity in Late Imperial Russia* (Princeton, NJ, 1991); A. Rieber, *Merchants and Entrepreneurs in Imperial Russia* (Chapel Hill, NC, 1982); and J. A. Ruckman, *The Moscow Business Elite: A Social and Cultural Portrait of Two Generations, 1840–1905* (DeKalb, IL, 1984).

27 Waldron, *Between Two Revolutions*, p. 123.

28 Cited in J. Bradley, 'Russia's Parliament of Public Opinion: Association, Assembly, and the Autocracy, 1906–1914' in T. Taranovski (ed.) *Reform in Modern Russian History: Progress or Cycle?* (Cambridge, 1995), p. 235.

29 R. B. McKean, 'Constitutional Russia', *Revolutionary Russia*, 9, 1996, pp. 34–7.

30 See L. Siegelbaum, *The Politics of Industrial Mobilization in Russia, 1914–17: A Study of the War-Industries Committees* (London, 1983), esp. pp. 183–9.

31 See O. Figes, *A People's Tragedy: The Russian Revolution 1891–1924* (London, 1996), esp. pp. 49–51 and 354–8 for background on Lvov.

32 P. Gatrell, 'Constitutional Russia: A Response', *Revolutionary Russia*, 9, 1996, p. 91.

33 See R. Sh. Ganelin, 'Ukaz 18 fevralia 1905 g. o petitsiiakh i pravitel'stvennaia politika', *Vspomogatel'nye istoricheskie distsipliny*, 15, 1983, pp. 170–85.

4

The Okhrana:
security policing in late imperial Russia

Iain Lauchlan

The Okhrana is one of the great grey areas of late tsarist history. 'Okhrana' or more accurately 'okhranka' was the nickname for a loosely bound collection of police and intelligence agencies waging war against the forces of revolution and left-wing terror in the Russian Empire from 1881 to 1917.[1] Like many other espionage agencies, the secrecy surrounding the Okhrana meant that it has been the subject of rumour, exaggeration and myth. It has been depicted as a progenitor of the Cheka, yet its members were systematically arrested and executed by the early Soviet secret police. It was frequently referred to by the totalitarian school as a prototype of the all-seeing Big Brother police system, and yet the Okhrana was a relatively small organisation – with only a few thousand employees in a country of over 140 million people. It has been cited both as one of the principal causes of the revolution and as the pillar of Russian reaction, and yet it was reviled by revolutionaries and reactionaries alike. Many have presented the Okhrana as evidence of the anachronistic and backward nature of the late imperial regime, and yet it was a technological and methodological innovator in the arts of political control and surveillance.

To gain a more realistic picture of this paradoxical organisation we must first look at its origins. Most of the Okhrana's leading officers were recruited from – and members of – the Separate Corps of Gendarmes. This was a paramilitary force distinct from the ordinary police. Up until 1880 the Separate Corps enjoyed a great deal of independence – it was subordinated only to a special office of the tsar's court: the Third Section. Some have seen the Third Section as evidence of a uniquely Russian brand of police despotism, yet it was based on similar organisations in Metternich's Austria and Napoleonic France, and part of a pan-European process systematising modern police methods.[2] The Third Section was Nicholas I's response to the liberal Decembrist uprising of 1825, whereby the emperor borrowed and re-tailored his opponents' ideas to prove that autocracy was the best possible means of securing the greatest happiness for the greatest number. The true founder of the Third Section, Count A. Kh.

Benckendorff, frequently reminded the gendarmes of their noble mission: 'Every man will see in you an official who through my agency can bring the voice of suffering mankind to the throne of the tsars, who can instantly place the defenceless and voiceless citizen under the protection of the sovereign emperor'.[3]

However, the gendarmerie was soon distracted from this utopian dream, notably by threats to the status quo from Polish parts of the empire in the 1830s and 1860s and from a burgeoning radical intelligentsia in Russia proper. In response the Third Section took on the role of a more mundane security police agency – as defenders of the state rather than guardians of the people's happiness. Consequently, the benign posturing of the new higher police force came to be viewed by many as a purely cynical method of socio-political control, and not without some justice: 'Public opinion', the founder noted, 'has the same importance for the authorities as a topographical map has for an army commander'.[4] In other words gendarme surveillance of the 'mood of the populace' (*nastroenie naseleniia*) was merely a means of defence *against* – rather than a purer form of – democracy. The gendarmes' particular brand of meddlesome altruism won them few friends amongst the new intelligentsia, who referred to these snoops as 'unwanted guests'.

Benckendorff envisaged an organisation that would be 'feared and respected'. Events in the 1860s and 1870s seemed to indicate that the Third Section had failed on both counts. The old methods of open, demonstrative repression through arrest, exile and censorship were rendered partially obsolete by a number of new developments. Society had changed: the growing pace of urbanisation, a free peasantry and the granting of university autonomy in the 1860s gave birth to more radical, home-grown ideologies: particularly what Turgenev dubbed 'nihilism' – based on D. I. Pisarev's calls for society and state to be smashed and built anew on a scientific basis, rejecting the passive acceptance of all tradition and superstition, including old codes of morality and respect for authority. Technology had also changed: rail travel, the high-speed rotary printing press (1865) and the invention of dynamite (1866) gave the radicalised opposition groups mobility, the chance for wider dissemination of their ideas and a weapon to intimidate the flesh and blood representatives of autocratic power. And the tactics of oppositionists had changed. Police repression was substantially to blame for this: as radical groups moved away from esoteric intellectual debate, calling themselves Populists, they sought to engage and learn from the peasantry and 'ordinary' Russian folk. The gendarmerie responded with wide-scale arrests of the young radical agitators 'going to the people' (particularly in the summer of 1874). Consequently, one section of the opposition movement turned away from open non-violent action and devoted itself to conspiracy and terror. By 1879 the new elements had crystallised into the People's Will movement. The gendarmerie was ill-equipped to deal with the changed methods of subversion: decked in rather extravagant blue uniforms, with white gloves, frock-coat and sultan spike of white horse hair on the lamb skin parade helmet, they were hardly what you would call a *secret* police force. Their founding directives in 1826 explicitly rejected conspiratorial work as dishonourable. People's Will had good reason to believe that through secret cells – so-called *piaterki* ('groups of five') – they had identified tsardom's Achilles' heel.

Moreover, the training of gendarmes equipped them with only a shallow understanding of the difference between harmless freethinking and hostile radicalism. For example, the head of the gendarmerie in Kiev at the turn of the twentieth century, General V. D. Novitskii, was said to be so out of touch that he considered the poetry of Lermontov and Pushkin to be subversive and to have never heard of Marx, Plekhanov or Lenin.

Added to this was the fact that civil rights in imperial Russia were codified for the first time in 1864. This seemed to vindicate tsarist claims that the autocratic legal system was the mildest in Europe. The state's ability to crush political unrest through judicial methods was significantly curtailed at the very moment when violent attacks on the state began. Many judges and juries of a liberal persuasion tended to allow political considerations to influence verdicts: for example, at the Nechaev trial of 1871 60 of the 87 were cleared despite clear evidence against them and in 1878 Vera Zasulich was acquitted of the attempted murder of the Petersburg Governor-General despite the fact that she did not even try to conceal her guilt. It seemed that the selective assassination of leading government figures – what Populists called the 'propaganda of the deed' – would 'give history a push' and topple the out-dated regime. This campaign culminated in the assassination of Alexander II in 1881.

And yet the tsarist regime did not collapse. The revolution–reaction duet merely grew in complexity. Just as police repression prompted the birth of People's Will, so in turn the latter's wave of terror prompted a reconstruction of the security police system. Starting from the 1870s the state created loopholes in the liberal legal system, which allowed governors to declare states of emergency. The governors could then grant extra-legal powers of search and arrest to the gendarmerie and police, and to three agencies in particular: St Petersburg, Moscow and Warsaw 'security sections' (*okhrannye otdeleniia*). The government attempted to rationalise and harmonise the hotchpotch of laws and institutions by means of the Security Law (*Polozhenie ob okhrane*) of 14 August 1881 and the unification of all policing institutions under the Interior Ministry's Department of Police. This was intended in many ways as a reformist gesture: the hated Third Section was, after all, dissolved in 1880 in an attempt to rein in the arbitrary powers of the political police. Thus, the direct connection of the gendarmerie to the tsar was severed. Divorced from court milieu, political policing was to be a cog in the bureaucratic machine. These measures were intended as a preliminary to the creation of a consultative legislative assembly. 'Ironically, such suspensions [i.e. the security laws] were the hallmark of transitions from absolutist to constitutional rule, from early modern *Polizeistaat,* or rationalised absolutism, to the rule of law.'[5] Yet, inevitably given the timing of events, the new system was viewed as a step backwards, a knee-jerk reaction to terrorism. The bureaucratic reforms, combined with the devastating wave of political arrests in the early 1880s, created the impression that Alexander III had created a new vast 'security' (*okhrana*) organisation: 'all-powerful, all-knowing, and all-capable'.[6] There was no official government agency called 'the Okhrana' (*okhranka*). Yet the term surfaced at this point in time as a convenient soubriquet, coined by the opposition to denote the confusing mass of secret police agencies. This invention allowed them to put a name to the intangible, invisible, central pillar of Russian reaction.

On the face of things the radical opposition had good reason to fear the new organisation: as a section of the Interior Ministry it was now part of the largest government institution outside the army. By 1900 the Department of Police had 50,000 employees. With the assistance of the commune watchmen, there were roughly 100,000 policemen in the Russian Empire. The Interior Minister also had control of the entire 15,000-strong Corps of Gendarmes. The Interior Minister was directly answerable to the tsar alone. A series of gifted, forceful and courageous Interior Ministers, such as V. K. Plehve, P. N. Durnovo and P. A. Stolypin, took an active interest in the war against subversives and came to embody the tsarist regime's 'terrible mystique of power'.[7] Many Okhrana officers relished this fearsome reputation:

> scattered throughout the country, with its departments, investigation points, and gendarme directorates, patiently listening to the reports of countless spies and scouts, constantly arresting, hanging and deporting, strong in its fund of bottomless human baseness, strong in the amount of blood and tears shed, strong in the annual ten million ruble fund, the Okhrana affected directly and indirectly all the measures of the government . . . The Okhrana set the tone.[8]

Nevertheless, the fight was far from over. George Kennan remarked on Russia in the 1890s:

> we have at present a strange spectacle. Before our eyes there has taken place something like a duel between the mightiest power on earth armed with all the attributes of authority on one side, and an insignificant gang of discharged telegraph operators, half-educated seminarists, high-school boys, and university students, miserable little Jews and loose women on the other, and in this unequal contest success was far from being on the side of strength.[9]

But was this really an 'unequal contest'? Russian nihilistic Populism did not fade away, it fused with Marxism, refined its methods and gave birth to the Socialist Revolutionary party and a ferocious campaign of terror that would claim the lives of over 10,000 government officials from 1901 to 1914. Contrary to popular perceptions, Russia was relatively *under*governed: the tsarist empire at the turn of the century had only 4 administrators per thousand inhabitants compared to 7.3 in England and Wales, 12.6 in Imperial Germany and 17.6 in France. To be sure, the Corps of Gendarmes was on the face of things an imposing political police force, with a staff of 15,000. However, only 2,500 were even vaguely connected to the political security policing (and most these were not involved in actual investigative work). As a force for social control the Okhrana was even weaker. In the villages it was dependent on the local police for all information. Even in the cities the co-operation of the ordinary police was essential in performing arrests and mundane surveillance work.[10] Russian per capita spending on the police was half that of Austria-Hungary, Italy and France and a sixth that of Great Britain. As a result ordinary Russian police were extremely underequipped, poorly educated and paid less than most factory workers. In the countryside one constable with a few sergeants might have a beat of 1,800 square kilometres encompassing 50,000–100,000 inhabitants. So, instead of walking a beat, three-quarters of Russian police constables, even in the cities, were positioned at stationary posts and supposedly 'slept like hibernating bears'.[11]

The Okhrana was not, therefore, an administrative megalith. The centralised and specialised structure – not the size – was the source of its power. Overall supervision of all police affairs, including Okhrana operations, was carried out by the Department of Police at its headquarters on the Fontanka canal (no. 16) in St Petersburg. Staff steadily increased in number over the decades from 161 full-time employees in 1895 to 387 in 1914. The overwhelming majority of these officials, however, were not directly involved in security police affairs – they worked instead in nine secretariats dealing with non-political and non-secret operations. A separate office inside the Department of Police exclusively devoted to secret political security policing – the Special Section (Osobyi otdel) – was only created in 1898. This occupied the entire top floor of the Fontanka headquarters. As its name indicated, the Special Section was different from the other offices of the Department of Police – it was closed to outsiders with an office staff of about fifteen intelligence officers representing an elite, 'a breed apart'.[12]

Beneath the Special Section, and the principal source of information, were the 'Security Sections'. These were the active directors of the physical collation of intelligence and the executive arm of police repression. They carried out surveillance, infiltration, arrests and interrogations. Officers in these sections were usually gendarmes with a military education. Directors of the Department of Police, in contrast, were usually university educated, legally trained, career bureaucrats. The Special Section meanwhile involved a mixture of the two types of personnel and provided a link between operatives in the field and analysts at headquarters. Security Sections – outside St Petersburg, Moscow and Warsaw – were only created in the rest of the major cities of the empire in 1902.

Employees of Security Sections consisted of three types of personnel. At the top were the gendarmes and bureaucrats who acted as directors, case-officers, interrogators, recruiters, record-keepers, clerks and analysts. They came to be known as *okhranniki*. Secondly there were surveillance operatives (known as 'external agents') who secretly tailed 'political unreliables' and acted as bodyguards to government officials. Many of their training manuals survive and seem to have been imitated by the KGB.[13] These show that external agents received highly competent training in the art of surveillance. Nevertheless, they had their critics. Their appearance was a curious juxtaposition of the inconspicuous and the blindly obvious. Prime Minister Sergei Witte noted that they 'can usually be spotted by their umbrellas and bowler hats'.[14] They usually wore ex-army issue greatcoats, which were easily recognisable. This poor attempt at urban camouflage gave rise to another nickname: 'Green coats'. All the same, they were often the only source of information, and the very rumour of their existence tended to unnerve revolutionary conspirators. The third breed of spy was the infamous 'internal agent': informers who were in contact with – or even members of – the political opposition. The internal agency was the most valuable source: 'without the Internal Agency' wrote General Aleksandr Gerasimov (the Petersburg Okhrana chief, 1905–9), 'the director of the political police is blind. The internal life of a revolutionary organisation, acting underground, is a wholly separate world, completely inaccessible to those who do not become members of the organisations.'[15] Rather than sending loyal police officers out to infiltrate revolutionary cells, it was simpler for the Okhrana to scout for spies amongst ready-made members of the political underworld. These agents would usually be recruited after arrest. The technique of 'turning' a committed radical into a loyal servant of the Okhrana, developed at the tail end of the nineteenth century, involved subjecting an arrested radical to a carefully paced, individually tailored 'seduction': a mixture of solitary confinement, tea and sympathy, threats of dire punishment (prison, exile or execution), and the promise of serving a good cause once more, or of money, power, prestige etc.

Secrecy was the key to the entire plan of attack. Officially, the very existence of the Special Section was secret. The location of a city's Security Section was, on the other hand, usually well-known; nevertheless, these fortified offices maintained a multitude of points of entry and exit so that officers could sneak in and out unnoticed. Group photographs of Okhrana employees were banned after one picture fell into the hands of the revolutionary underground in 1911. Most Okhrana chiefs wore plain clothes rather than gendarme uniform, they frequently changed address and often lived under an assumed name.

There was even a furtive air to the tsarist regime's acts of political repression. Like the NKVD, the Okhrana preferred to perform its arrests at night. Security Section officers often avoided attending these arrests in person in order to preserve their anonymity. Bail was usually set at a large amount. If evidence was too flimsy for a trial the political prisoners were either released or banished from the locality in secret. Arrests, whenever possible, were performed simultaneously to prevent the opportunity for the arrestees to destroy any compromising materials. These operations were referred to by the suitably opaque bureaucratic term 'liquidation'. A liquidation would thus often lead to the sudden disappearance of a whole group of acquaintances over night. It is not difficult to see why the term began to take on the sinister connotations that reached fruition in the Stalin era.

One of the most secret aspects of the Okhrana's work was the establishment of so-called 'Black Cabinets'. These were concealed offices based at major postal depots, which supplied the political police with access to all correspondence by mail and telegraph throughout the empire. The Okhrana's legal right to intercept and copy mail, known as perlustration, was tenuous to say the least, and consecutive Ministers of the Interior were obliged to deny that the practice even took place. Nevertheless, most opponents of the tsarist regime knew full well that the authorities read their mail.

The high level of secrecy meant that revolutionaries could only guess at the size and nature of the Okhrana. Consequently, the opposition seem to have over-estimated the omniscience of the secret police. Most thought that there was a Black Cabinet in every city and even many towns of the empire. When one Soviet historian dredged the archives he only found evidence of seven such offices with a grand total of 49 employees before 1914; reports of others, he noted, 'were sheer hallucinations'.[16] Activists in the political underground imagined the cities to be infested with watchers and informers, and feared that their ranks were riddled with traitors. Early detractors of the Okhrana estimated that it employed up to 40,000 spies and referred to it as the most important prop to the tsarist regime. Yet when the police archives fell into the hands of the Provisional Government in 1917 they only managed to uncover 600 informers. Recent surveys of the archives have revealed that the Department of Police never employed more than 2,000 informers at any one time and most of these were not high-level spies.[17] The entire Okhrana budget usually accounted for less than 10 per cent of the total expenditure on police, reaching a peak of around five million rubles in 1914: generous, but hardly what one would expect for a 'police state'.

This level of expense on the Okhrana was shared between a reasonably modest number of agents. St Petersburg Security Section at its height had some 750 plus employees: 25 officials of officer rank, 250 detectives engaged in bodyguard duties, 220 shadowing 'political unreliables' and performing various other miscellaneous tasks, 70 case officers and intelligence analysts, and 200 informers. St Petersburg's security force was about twice the size of the Moscow branch. The Okhrana had a 'Foreign Agency' based in Paris, which became notorious in Western Europe. Yet this branch was also rather small – with 4 case officers, 40 detectives and 25 secret agents. The entire Okhrana outside these three centres probably amounted to little more than a thousand employees. Low staff numbers may well have been the key to their success: it meant that salaries were high and consequently they attracted more talented and ambitious officers than the ordinary police or military (though also, of course, a fair number who were greedy and unscrupulous). From 1905 to 1911 the Okhrana was used as a model for imitation by the other security services: the ordinary police, criminal investigations and military intelligence.

The *okhranniki* were imitated because they were pioneers in the science of modern espionage. Just as the 1860s brought technical innovations which strengthened subversive movements, the 1890s saw developments which greatly enhanced police counter-subversion across the globe. The tsarist secret police were among the first in Europe to utilise new 'tradecraft' and technology such as fingerprinting, Bertillon's anthropometric system,[18] photographic identification, photo-fits, code-breaking, bugs, phone taps, typewriters, telegraphy, bullet-proof vests, tear gas, 'tranquilising guns' etc.[19] They also made prophetic warnings about the possible use of aeroplanes and trains for terrorist acts.

Technological breakthroughs, ambitious personnel and the unscrupulous practice of conspiracy, espionage, disinformation and intimidation formed a potent combination. Most inside accounts depict the offices of the Okhrana as an incredibly dynamic milieu: 'like an enormous machine . . . the surveillance agents spied, the translators translated, the "region" wrote to the province, the "top secret" office tried to get copies of letters, the "clearing" office cleared, the office recorded and reported to higher authorities, and clerks dashed from office to office, they were always busy pounding typewriters, using hectographs, making inquiries, and writing endless memoranda'.[20] The whole impression is of an organisation that never rested and never slept (indeed a large part of its business was conducted at night).

When considered purely in terms of data collation the Okhrana's intelligence output was exceedingly impressive. By 1900 the Special Section had amassed a card index of 55,000 names, a library of 5,000 revolutionary publications and 20,000 photographs. By 1917 the card index was rumoured to contain up to three million names. Reports were regularly issued to the lower rungs of the Okhrana through twice-monthly circulars and in a twice-weekly synopsis that was sent to the Minister of the Interior and the tsar. To disseminate a digested form of this information the Department of Police produced an 'alphabetical list of persons under investigation', a sort of who's who of the revolutionary underground. The 1889 list had only 221 names and in 1899 still only 624 names, but the 1910 list contained some 13,000 names in a series of huge grey volumes. The Department of Police's card index was said to contain 'the names of all social activists, a card for almost any intelligent person who at one time in life had ever thought about politics'.[21]

The Okhrana handled this data with greater subtlety and cunning than is often recognised. It has been viewed as a heavy-handed reactionary forefather of the Soviet terror machine. It has also been cited as evidence of the Russian *Sonderweg* or 'exceptionalism'.[22] However, it must be borne in mind that the Okhrana was by no means unique in Europe and was an organisation that had originally based it methods on Western systems of political surveillance and control.[23] Rather than evolving into the Cheka, the Okhrana was the most notable case of discontinuity between tsarist and Soviet regimes. For example, while large sections of the lower-ranking tsarist bureaucracy went on to work for the Soviet state (for example, up to 90 per cent of the staff of the Soviet Justice Commissariat were inherited from the tsarist regime), there are only a handful of documented examples of Okhrana officers joining the Cheka.[24] In fact the revolutionary Cheka avoided any association with the counter-revolutionary Okhrana. By the mid-1920s the Soviet secret police spearheaded a witch-hunt for former Okhrana agents as a means of 'purging' society. In contrast to the Cheka, attitudes of the *okhranniki* to their deadly enemies were surprisingly moderate. True, both policemen and revolutionaries were hardened by the protracted conspiratorial struggle. Yet even Soviet historians admitted that, aside from isolated examples, the Okhrana did not systematically employ any kind of torture. Attitudes varied of course, but S. P. Beletskii, a vigorous and aggressive police chief, gave a fairly typical insight into Okhrana attitudes to the radical opposition when he said that: 'I understand the struggle with the revolution, with the enemies of the state order. It is an honest struggle, eyeball to eyeball. They blow us up and we prosecute them and penalise them.'[25] This counter-subversive war was less bitter than under the early Soviets because the tsarist secret police pursued enemies of the state not 'enemies of the people'; it aimed to contain, not annihilate, hostile elements; to control, not transform, society.

The Okhrana's attitudes to the liberal political parties have often been misunderstood. The small number of spies in the centre parties and the comments of police chiefs seem to indicate that the Okhrana, particularly between 1906 and 1914, was never as anti-liberal as its enemies claimed. Relations with the moderate reformist Kadets were soured not due to their 'liberalism', but by the simple fact that the Kadets refused to condemn left-wing terrorists and that their slightly naïve demands for wider civil liberties might make them a Trojan horse for the revolutionary movement.[26] The *okhranniki* felt that they had a fairly valid reason to cling to their authoritarian ways: they observed that revolutionary violence was worse after, rather than before, the liberal October Manifesto. They were driven by Stolypin's conservative belief that: 'The punishment of a few prevents a sea of blood'.[27] In assisting Prime Minister Stolypin in the 'coup' of 3 June 1907 – whereby parliament was dissolved and a more conservative electoral law introduced – the Okhrana could, paradoxically, even be said to have helped to save the Duma from complete abolition at the hands of the tsar. Events following the brief flowering of liberty in 1917 seemed to vindicate the policy of extreme caution.

The hostility of the liberal parties to the tsarist state has also perhaps been overstated. Russian moderates were shocked by the mass, spontaneous, revolutionary violence of 1905–7 and briefly felt that they should fear the masses, 'more than all the government's executions, and must bless this regime which alone, with its bayonets and prisons, still protects us from the people's wrath'.[28] Many moderates even recognised after 1917 that they were as much to blame as the tsarist regime for failing to find a workable compromise between security and reform in the long run.

Rather than viewing the opposition groups as a single amorphous mass, the Okhrana established separate desks to study different parties, with tactics individually tailored and changing over time to meet the varying threats of mainly Socialist Revolutionaries (SRs), Bolsheviks, Mensheviks, anarchist communists, other Russian Social Democrats (SDs), Jewish workers' parties, Polish socialists, Latvian SDs, Armenian nationalists (Droshak/Dashnaktsutiun), the Georgian Social Revolutionary federalist party (Sakartvelo), the Party of Active Resistance in Finland, Zionists, and the liberal Union of Liberation (1904–5). There is a tactile quality to the Okhrana studies of the revolutionary movement: SRs were registered on red cards, SDs on blue cards, anarchists on green cards, students on yellow cards and all others involved in politics on white cards. All houses in major cities were colour-coded in the police records if the buildings had any connection with the movement of revolutionaries (not only if a political suspect lived there, but also if one ever happened to visit). The analysis of the tangled mass of ideologies, parties, individuals and social groups was graphically represented in vast spidery synoptic charts.

The intelligence processed was not merely the fuel for repression: security police often sympathised with some of the grievances which gave rise to rebellion. For example, one gendarme reported in 1885 that: 'Having had the opportunity to examine closely the life of factory workers I can find very little difference between their position and that of the earlier serfs; the same want, the same need, the same rights; the same contempt for their spiritual needs . . . [As yet the workers do not seem to be interested in politics, but] that evil day is coming closer and closer.'[29] The pressure from such reports had led to progressive Bismarckian Factory Acts in 1882, 1885 and 1897 and the Factory Regulations of 1886 and Sickness and Accident Insurance Bill of 1912. The reasoning behind Okhrana conciliation was summed up by the head of the secret police in Moscow, Sergei Zubatov, thus: 'economics are for the working man infinitely more important than any political principles. Satisfy the people's requirements in this respect, and they will not only not go into politics but will turn over to you all the radicals; revolutionaries without the mass are generals without an army.'[30]

Zubatov's mentalité goes some way to explain why in general the more sophisticated security police officers were loath to 'liquidate' revolutionary groups unless it was felt to be strictly necessary: indiscriminate arrests and harassment only tended to widen opposition to the tsarist regime. Consequently, the Okhrana appears to have given oppositionists a fair amount of room to slip in and out of the police net (as the pre-1917 careers of Lenin, Stalin, Trotsky et al. testify). Yet, when the Okhrana did act, the impact on the revolutionary movement was profound. Plehve and Sudeikin decimated People's Will in St Petersburg thanks to their spy Sergei Degaev; and A. S. Skandrakov, a director of Moscow Okhrana, was able to annihilate the leading cells of Black Repartition in 1884 thanks to information of his spy, S. K. Belov. The Okhrana effectively took control of the SR terrorist campaign after 1905 when the agents Evno Azef in St Petersburg and Zinaida Zhuchenko in Moscow were promoted to the top rank of the SR Battle Organisation. The SR leadership fled abroad once more in the post-1905 years of 'Stolypin reaction', but the Okhrana was never far behind: in 1910–14 of the 140 registered members of the SR party in Paris fourteen were spies.[31]

Police Director S. P. Beletskii pursued a particularly devious strategy of divide and rule against the Marxist Social Democratic party, so as to prevent the evolution of a broad-based popular socialist party on German lines. The key agent in this campaign was the party activist Roman Malinovskii, who was persuaded to shift from the moderate wing of the SDs (the Mensheviks) to the more extremist Bolshevik faction to promote division among Marxists and weaken their influence over the trade unions. Malinovskii went on to become the leading Bolshevik representative in the State Duma. The Okhrana produced detailed analyses of divisive issues within the SD party. This entailed developing a holistic approach to intelligence-gathering. For example, the secret police monitored not just their targets' movements and beliefs, but their personal lives, and those of their families. The Bolshevik party was consequently riddled with Okhrana spies at the highest level – including the editor of *Pravda*, Miron Chernomazov. It was rumoured that at the Prague conference of January 1912 ten out of the thirteen Bolshevik delegates were Okhrana informers. Allegations persist that Stalin himself was an Okhrana spy.

The system backfires

And so the Okhrana achieved great success. But at what cost? Repression decimated the political opposition at the expense of the moral credibility of the tsarist regime. The Okhrana was viewed as 'the living symbol of all that is most repressive, cruel, mean and revolting in autocracy'.[32] Consequently – to put it in today's newspeak – the regime lost the battle to win hearts and minds in the war against terror. The Habsburg Ambassador in St Petersburg, Count Alois von Aehrenthal, observed in the wake of the assassination of the Okhrana's chief architect, V. K. von Plehve, in 1904 that:

> The most striking aspect of the present situation is the total indifference of society to an event that constituted a heavy blow to the principles of the Government . . . I have found only totally indifferent people or people so cynical that they say that no other outcome was to be expected. People are prepared to say that further catastrophes similar to Plehve's murder will be necessary in order to bring about a change of mind on the part of the highest authority.[33]

Secrecy enabled the Okhrana to sow suspicion and discord among the radical opposition, but it also aroused many of the same feelings inside the government itself. Well-to-do members of society, the court camarilla and senior officials (viz. the Okhrana's natural constituency of supporters) looked askance at an organisation that concealed its activities even from Russian officialdom.

Moral concerns over the actions of the Okhrana inside the government led to disputes over security police methods. Consequently a rival camp emerged inside the Separate Corps of Gendarmes. These opponents came mostly from those officers not directly involved in secret political work: those assigned to police provincial towns, canals, railways and border areas – the 'crumbs' of security work, as one bored gendarme put it. These gendarmes considered themselves to be of the old school and resented the fact that this new breed of secret policemen had pushed them into the second rank of political investigations. The *okhranniki* had little respect for the ordinary 'blues' who attempted to penetrate the exclusive world of espionage: 'In the environs of the Corps of Gendarmes some amateurs liked to play Sherlock Holmes. But in reality they usually proved to be bad detectives.'[34]

The SR Viktor Chernov mocked this as a 'battle of mice and frogs'. In 1910 he characterised the contrasting behaviour of the two competing police cliques with a theatrical analogy – the conservative style of the reactionary camp in court under Kurlov versus the 'reactionary *style moderne*' of *okhranniki* under Stolypin:

> One proceeding proscenium, face to face, the other backstage: one proceeding officially – carrying out searches, seizures, arrests, formal investigations; the other – the exact opposite, conducting everything with a monopoly of secrecy . . . He who does not risk, does not gain – that is their slogan. The old gendarmerie would have had a completely different slogan – their's would have been 'A bird in the hand' . . . And so the friction grows. The Okhrana looks on the gendarmes with contempt. The gendarmes look on the *okhranniki* with mistrust. They speak different languages, they are 'barbarians to one another'.[35]

These internal feuds meant that the supply of intelligence was sometimes tainted by the desire of police officials to cultivate powerful patrons. Patronage could elevate a talented security official to the helm of the Okhrana, but it also meant that amoral intriguers often rose to the top. Attempts to cultivate the support of courtiers were partly to blame for the rank flirtation of some maverick *okhranniki* with extreme right-wing parties between 1905 and 1914, the composition of dubious reports on the dire threat of Russian Freemasonry and their shenanigans involving shady characters in court such as Rasputin.[36]

The human factor

A second flaw in the machine-like system – based as it was on a frantic workload and claustrophobic levels of secrecy, deceit and danger – was that it took a heavy toll on the human cogs. For example, the security police officials became, not surprisingly, the principal targets for terrorist attacks. Three out of the six Ministers of the Interior were killed by terrorists between 1902 and 1911 (Sipiagin in 1902, Plehve in 1904 and Stolypin in 1911). Two attempts were made to kill another, P. N. Durnovo, in 1905 and 1906. During the more tumultuous months of 1905 police were often too afraid to leave their homes as Okhrana offices were subjected to bomb attacks, and assassins – prepared to take pot-shots at anyone in a uniform – could be hired in the western provinces for as little as three rubles.[37] A police report in 1909 lists 190 high government officials who were victims of political attacks from 13 May 1903 to 2 March 1909; of these 58 were senior police officials (29 killed, 18 wounded and 11 other attempts). From February 1905 to May 1906 over 700 police officials of various ranks were killed in terrorist attacks.

Even the Petersburg Okhrana officers who escaped assassination often ended their careers in disgrace as they were blamed for any security mishaps. The Director of the Department of Police, A. A. Lopukhin, was branded a murderer by his boss for failing to prevent the assassination of Grand Duke Sergei in 1905. The head of St Petersburg Security Section, L. N. Kremenetskii, lost his job after the Bloody Sunday massacre in 1905, even though the atrocity was carried out by soldiers, and not the security police. A. V. Gerasimov himself was undone by the Azef scandal and the virulent wave and bureaucratic backstabbing which followed it in 1909. And the Assistant Minister of the Interior, P. G. Kurlov, was dismissed for dereliction of duty after the assassination of his boss, the Prime Minister, Stolypin, by the Okhrana agent Dmitrii Bogrov in 1911. These cases were all the more poignant because all were the result of 'turned' spies betraying their Okhrana supervisors and rejoining the revolutionary cause. This danger had been apparent ever since the pioneer of the internal agent system, G. P. Sudeikin, was shot and beaten to death by a gang directed by one of his own secret agents, Sergei Degaev, in 1883. The tsarist regime was literally hoist with its own petard.

The psychological pressure of this sort of work was immense. The Moscow revolt of December 1905 caused the head of the local Security Section, A. G. Peterson, to have a nervous breakdown. A Department of Police circular records a 'lamentable episode' in 1909 in which the Okhrana warned a local Governor that terrorists were planning an attempt on his life. The anxiety prompted by this warning caused the unfortunate Governor to die of a heart attack.[38] Fear and stress undoubtedly contributed to the moral degeneration of a number of agents. Okhrana officers of the besieged Warsaw and Riga sections were accused of torturing prisoners.[39]

The root of this alleged ethical breakdown was the fact that the Okhrana occupied such an ambiguous position: as fanatical defenders of tsarism, working in confusingly close proximity to the revolutionary underground it was nigh on impossible for any security chief to pursue a lengthy career in this labyrinth of deceit without getting a little sullied in the working. The lines between right and wrong, ally and enemy, reactionary and revolutionary were wholly blurred. Some of the leading police chiefs – such as S. V. Zubatov,[40] P. I. Rachkovskii,[41] M. E. Bakai,[42] L. P. Menshchikov[43] and A. M. Harting.[44] – began their conspiratorial careers as revolutionaries. Zubatov's trade unions spiralled out of control and were one direct cause of the 1905 revolution.[45] Bakai and Menshchikov crossed back over to the revolutionary camp after 1905.

In fact the secret police had always been locked in a strange symbiotic relationship of mutual fear and imitation with the revolutionary movement. Like the revolutionary movement it was a polycentric, amorphous entity, constantly evolving, defying simplistic definition. Like the revolutionary movement, the secret police traced its roots to the Decembrist uprising of 1825. Each side largely existed because of the other. Both claimed to serve the interests of the people. Tsarist police repression was unleashed to combat violent radical opposition; and the radical opposition to the tsarist regime grew often because the regime unleashed police repression. People's Will developed conspiratorial cells and the Okhrana trumped them with 'an ultrasecret form of organising political investigations'.[46] Nechaev conceived the 'Revolutionary Catechism' and gendarmerie responded by attempting to cultivate a 'moral superiority over the enemy . . . [whereby] revolutionary fanaticism must be counterbalanced by fanatical loyalty to the service'.[47] *Okhranniki* claimed that the revolutionaries 'preyed on the psychologically disturbed'[48] in order to recruit new members. The same accusation could be levelled at the Okhrana's methods of enlisting secret agents: 'Some provocateurs', a police chief confessed, 'exhibit an element of sadism . . . [they seek] to derive pleasure from a double degradation of people . . . To dominate people, to send them to the gallows, to play with them as a cat plays with a mouse.'[49]

Both secret police and revolutionaries were prey to corrosive effects of pro-longed submersion in the conspiratorial milieu:

> The very way of life of the terrorist has a stupefying effect. It is the life of a hunted wolf ... Apart from five to ten like-minded persons, one must deceive from morning to night literally everyone; one must hide from everyone, suspect in everyone an enemy ... One needs extraordinary fortitude to think and work at all under such unnatural conditions. But even those who possess it, unless they extricate themselves quickly from the quagmire of their situation, quickly go under. For individuals of less calibre, these perpetual intrigues with spies, false passports, conspiratorial apartments, dynamites, ambushes, dreams of murders and escapes prove even more disastrous.[50]

The secret police and revolutionary underground were so interconnected that it was not always entirely clear who benefited most from the actions of Okhrana spies. Vladimir Burtsev, a leading *émigré* opponent of tsarism, launched a campaign of counter-Okhrana publicity, whereby he persuaded a number of police agents to defect to the revolutionary camp and expose this 'world of vileness and desolation'.[51] Yet the exposés seem to have depressed and embarrassed the revolutionary movement more than it damaged the Okhrana. On the other hand, Roman Malinovskii's election to the Duma had been made possible by the assistance of the Department of Police. In the Duma Malinovskii proved an inspiring orator, speaking on 22 occasions in the first session of the Fourth Duma and on 38 in the second session, and he signed 54 inter-pellations and made five legislative proposals. This could hardly have been defined as doing only the bare minimum in order to preserve his cover. Lenin may well have been aware of and tolerated Malinovskii's Okhrana connections because this police agent was so useful to the Bolshevik fraction. It is also odd that the most successful Okhrana spy, Evno Azef, was alleged to have master-minded a total of 28 terrorist attacks on government officials. Rumours circu-lated that the *okhranniki* were themselves 'secret revolutionaries' and that they plotted the assassination of rivals inside the government.

A war against society

A third and fatal flaw in the tsarist security police system was the fact that it was designed to isolate and remove individual troublemakers: to infiltrate and paralyse small, conspiratorial subversive groups. Yet the political struggle had widened exponentially by 1905 and came to involve, to varying degrees, all sec-tions of society. The cancer could no longer be dealt with by surgical extraction. Attempts to do so often only made matters worse and alienated moderates such as ex-police chief A. A. Lopukhin: 'The whole political outlook of the ranks of the Corps of Gendarmes boils down to the following propositions', he wrote, 'there is the people and there is the state ... As a result [of this bipolar view], the protection of the state ... turns into a war against all of society ... By widening the gulf between the state and the people, the police engender a revolution.'[52]

The sheer scale of the upheavals of 1905 was the turning-point in this regard. Peasant *jacqueries* ravaged central Russia from 1905 to 1907, destroying around 2,000 estates. From 1905 to 1910 alone over 9,000 persons were killed in 'terrorist' attacks, the overwhelming majority of whom were government officials. The Okhrana specialised in the infiltration and suppression of small conspiratorial cells. Yet these attacks were, on the whole, not perpetrated by organised groups. Affiliates of the main pro-terror party – the SRs – claimed direct credit for less than ten terrorist attacks during 1901–4, only 44 out of a total of 591 committed in 1905, 78 in 1906 and 62 in 1907.[53]

In the face of mass spontaneous violence the Okhrana's subtle tactics tended to fall by the wayside: 'either the revolutionaries will use us to adorn the Petersburg lamp-posts', the capital's Okhrana chief said, 'or we must send them to jail and the gibbet'.[54] St Petersburg Security Section directed the arrest of nearly 2,000 people from 25 December 1905 to 25 January 1906. In all, the Interior Ministry arrested 70,000 people between October 1905 and April 1906.

The pursuit of organised subversive groups inevitably spilled over into ordinary society as these groups sought to hide behind various non-partisan legal organisations – such as trade unions, professional associations and pressure groups which were permitted to exist after the 1905 October Manifesto. Police repression from 1907 to 1910 reduced the trade union movement in St Petersburg from 63,000 members (22 per cent of the labour force) to 12,000 members (5 per cent of the labour force). This created the unnerving impression, albeit erroneous, that the Okhrana was omniscient: 'There was not a single party, nor a single mill, factory, nor a single organisation, nor society, union, club committee, university, institute, there was not even a single newspaper editorial staff in which among its members and collaborators there would not have been several secret agents.'[55]

The Okhrana did not have the resources to combat mass opposition. Consequently, the military often had to be called in to lend a heavy-hand. The regime had to fall back on the services of the army on 1,500 occasions from 1883 to 1903 to curb large-scale public disturbances. This was a disastrously clumsy policy: soldiers do not usually make good policemen. It resulted in massacres in St Petersburg on 9 January 1905 and in the Lena Goldfields in April 1912. From 1896 to 1912 3,767 persons were sentenced to death after summary trial by District Military Courts.[56] Stolypin introduced even more extreme measures, under some pressure from the tsar, with the institution of the Field Courts Martial in August 1906. During the short duration of their existence these courts executed over 700 people a year. Over the course of three decades before 1914 the tsarist military-police counter-revolution claimed the lives of over 14,000 people. This level of violence may well have paled in comparison with subsequent upheavals; nevertheless, it was a bloody reign of brutality by the standards of the age.

Relying on the armed forces to do the work of policemen was particularly troublesome because the army itself was not the reliable pillar of old: there had been over 400 mutinies from 1905 to 1906. The Okhrana's answer to this was to recruit spies inside the military in an attempt to expunge revolutionary influence. This caused a great deal of resentment among the army's top brass. And they came to influence the security police when the gendarme 'old school' gained ascendancy inside the Okhrana in 1913 with the appointment of V. F. Dzhunkovskii as Assistant Minister of the Interior. Dzhunkovskii declared that the secret police should 'sniff rather than stink'. He launched what the press called a 'purge' of the Okhrana – sacking many leading security police officers. He slashed the police budget and ordered the dismissal of all spies in the army. This was a popular gesture but it critically weakened the state's ability to monitor the reliability of the armed forces on the eve of war.

In the end it was the war and not the revolutionary movement that was the undoing of the tsarist regime. The Okhrana recognised that society and state had little chance of surviving a protracted military conflict. The so-called Durnovo Memorandum to Nicholas II in February 1914, which seemed to predict the cause and course of all the later disasters, is perhaps the most striking evidence that the *okhranniki* fully understood the gravity of their situation. Imperial Russia was teetering on the edge of an abyss and security police measures would be insufficient should the regime fall over the brink. The Okhrana zealously continued to do its job all the same and paralysed the organised opposition from 1914 to 1917. The professional revolutionaries were, after all, conspicuously absent from the February revolution. 'The development of mass revolutionary consciousness in the form of a commitment to a specific socialist party or political philosophies was fundamentally a phenomenon of the months after the fall of Nicholas II, when the politicisation of the masses began in earnest.'[57] The Okhrana secured a futile victory: it had won the battle of wits against the revolutionary underground but lost the war.

Notes

1   The principal archives of the Okhrana are the Department of Police records held in Moscow, *Gosudarstvennyi arkhiv Rossiiskoi Federatsii* (hereafter GARF). See GARF, *Putevoditel'. Tom 1. Fondy GARF po istorii Rossii XIX- nachala XX vv.* (Moscow, 1994); and Stanford University, California, Hoover Institution (hereafter Hoover), Okhrana Collection.

2   On this subject see C. Emsley, *Gendarmes and State in Nineteenth Century Europe* (Oxford, 1999); S. Monas, *The Third Section: Police and Society in Russia under Nicholas I* (Oxford, 1961).

3   P. S. Squire, *The Third Department: The Establishment and Practices of the Political Police in the Russia of Nicholas I* (London, 1968), p. 78.

4   Ibid., p. 201.

5   J. W. Daly, 'On the Significance of Emergency Legislation in Late Imperial Russia', *Slavic Review*, 54(3), 1995, p. 603. See also P. Waldron, 'States of Emergency: Autocracy and Emergency Legislation, 1881–1917', *Revolutionary Russia*, 8, 1995, pp. 1–25.

6   V. Zhilinskii, 'Organizatsiia i zhizn' okhrannogo otdeleniia vo vremena tsarskoi vlasti', *Golos minuvshago*, 9/10, Sept./Oct. 1917, p. 306.

7   See J. Daly, *Autocracy Under Siege: Security Police and Opposition in Russia, 1866–1905* (DeKalb, IL, 1998), pp. 149–50.

8   V. N. Russiian, 'The Work of Okhrana Departments in Russia', MS in Hoover, Russian Collection, pp. 4–6.

9   G. Kennan cited in W. B. Walsh, *Russia and the Soviet Union* (London, 1958), p. 395.

10 See R. G. Robbins Jr., *The Tsar's Viceroys: Russian Provincial Governors in the Last Years of the Empire* (London, 1987).

11 N. Weissman, 'Regular Police in Tsarist Russia, 1900–1914', *Russian Review*, 20, 1985, p. 65.

12 For insiders accounts of the workings of the Okhrana see P. E. Shchegolev (ed.), *Padenie tsarskogo rezhima*, 7 vols (Leningrad, 1924–27); quotation from vol. 3, Komissarov, p. 145.

13 See C. Andrew and V. Mitrokhin, *The Mitrokhin Archive: The KGB in Europe and the West* (London, 1999), p. 31 with reference to Dmitrii Gavrilovich Evseev, *Basic Tenets of Intelligence* and *How to Conduct Intelligence* (training manuals for the Chekisty in the 1920s). Compare: *Essential Handbook for KGB Agents* (published in London by the Industrial Information Index, 1978), pp. 23–40; 'Instruction for External Surveillance' and instructions on the Okhrana's external surveillance: 'Instruktsiia no. 298', Hoover, Okhrana, box 41, folder VIf.

14 S. Witte, *The Memoirs of Count Witte*, ed. Sidney Harcave (New York, 1990), p. 433.

15 A. V. Gerasimov, *Na lezvii s terroristami* (Paris, 1985), p. 56.

16 R. Kantor, 'K istorii chernykh kabinetov', *Katorga i ssylka*, 37, 1927, p. 93.

17 Z. I. Peregudova, 'Istochnik izucheniia sotsial-demokraticheskogo dvizheniia v Rossii', *Voprosy istorii*, 9, 1988, p. 96.

18 The measuring and recording of physical dimensions of prisoners as a means of future identification – a system still employed by Interpol to this day.

19 For example, see A. T. Vassilyev, *The Ochrana: The Russian Secret Police* (London, 1930), pp. 93–5; D. Kahn, *The Codebreakers: The Story of Secret Writing* (New York, 1976).

20 Russiian, 'The Work', pp. 4–5.

21 Zhilinskii, 'Organizatsiia i zhizn' , p. 267.

22 See, for example, H. Arendt, *The Origins of Totalitarianism*, pt 3 (New York, 1951), pp. 151–2; R. Pipes, *Russia Under the Old Regime* (London, 1974), p. 302.

23 For a discussion of this see I. Lauchlan, *Russian Hide-and-Seek: The Tsarist Secret Police in St Petersburg, 1906–1914* (Helsinki, 2002), pp. 57–74.

24 I. A. Zybin, the head of the Okhrana's cryptology section, continued work in this area for the Soviets. General V. F. Dzhunkovskii, the Assistant Minister of the Interior 1913–15, was pressured into working briefly as a consultant for the Cheka. Henri Bint, the French head of the Foreign Agency's team of detectives in Paris, appears to have helped establish OGPU surveillance operations abroad.

25 S. P. Beletskii cited in C. Ruud and S. Stepanov, *Fontanka 16: The Tsars' Secret Police* (Quebec, 1999), p. 307.

26 M. K. Stockdale, 'Politics, Morality and Violence: Kadet Liberals and the Question of Terror', *Russian History*, 22, 1996, pp. 455–80.

27 S. A. Stepanov, *Zagadki ubiistva Stolypina* (Moscow, 1995), p. 34.

28 M. O. Gershenzon cited in D. Lieven, 'The Security Police, Civil Rights and the Fate of the Russian Empire' in O. Crisp (ed.), *Civil Rights in Imperial Russia* (Oxford, 1989), p. 262.

29 Cited in N. M. Naimark, *Terrorists and Social Democrats: The Russian Revolutionary Movement under Alexander III* (Cambridge, MA, 1983), pp. 33–4.

30 K. Tidmarsh, 'The Zubatov Idea', *American Slavic and East European Review*, 19, 1960, pp. 342–3.

31 See A. Geifman, *Entangled in Terror: The Azef Affair and the Russian Revolution* (Wilmington, DE, 2000); N. Schleifman, *Undercover Agents in the Russian Revolutionary Movement: The SR Party 1902–1914* (London, 1988).

32 Azef cited in B. Nicolaievsky, *Aseff: The Russian Judas* (London, 1934), p. 129.

33 Cited in A. Ascher, *The Revolution of 1905: Russia in Disarray* (Stanford, CA, 1988), p. 54.

34 A. P. Martynov, *Moia sluzhba v otdel'nom korpuse zhandarmov* (Stanford, CA, 1972), p. 24.

35 V. Chernov, 'Iz mira merzosti i zapusteniia', *Sotsialist-Revoliutsioner*, 2 (Paris, 1910), pp. 114 and 119.

36 See I. Lauchlan, 'The Accidental Terrorist: Okhrana Connections to the Extreme-Right and the Attempt to Assassinate Sergei Witte in 1907', *Revolutionary Russia*, 14(2), 2001, pp. 1–32.

37 A. Geifman, *Thou Shalt Kill: Revolutionary Terrorism in Russia, 1894–1917* (Princeton, NJ, 1993).

38 Hoover, Okhrana Collection, box 158, folder 10, S. E. Vissarionov, Police circular 5 Jan. 1910.

39 See K. Mitsit ('Martyn'), 'O pytkakh v Rizhskom sysknom otdelenii', *Byloe*, 13 (Paris, 1910), pp. 139–48.

40 Zubatov (1864–1917) was recruited by Moscow Okhrana in 1886, was exposed as a spy in 1887 and was soon after taken on as an officer in the same branch. In 1893 Zubatov became assistant head of Moscow Okhrana, and in 1895 head. He went on to become head of the Special Section from 1902 to 1903.

41 Rachkovskii (1851–1910) was intermittently a revolutionary and Third Section spy during the 1870s; from 1885 to 1902 he was head of the Foreign Agency, and from 1905 to 1906 head of the 'political section' of the Department of Police.

42 M. E. Bakai was recruited as an Okhrana spy in Ekaterinoslav from 1900 and soon after took up a position in the offices of Warsaw Okhrana. He began secretly

working for Burtsev while still employed at Warsaw, and was caught and exiled to Siberia in 1907. In 1908 he escaped from exile and went to work for Burtsev in Paris.

43 L. P. Menshchikov (1869–1932) was a member of People's Will until his arrest and recruitment into Moscow Okhrana's internal agency in 1887. In 1889–1902 he worked in Zubatov's office, and in 1902–6 in the Special Section. He was sacked in 1906 for sending a letter to an SR identifying party members as Okhrana spies. In 1906 he moved to France and began working for Vladimir Burtsev.

44 Harting worked as an agent of the Third Section and the Okhrana in the early 1880s under his original name of Gekel'man; he was forced to flee abroad after his exposure in 1884. In Zurich he began working under the name of Landezen for Rachkovskii; in 1900 he changed his name to Harting and became head of the Berlin branch of the Okhrana. In 1905 he worked with Rachkovskii in the Special Section and went on to become head the Foreign Agency from 1905 until his exposure in 1909.

45 W. Sablinsky, *The Road to Bloody Sunday: Father Gapon and the St Petersburg Massacre of 1905* (Princeton, NJ, 1976); Jeremiah Schneiderman, *Sergei Zubatov and Revolutionary Marxism* (Ithaca, NY, 1976).

46 Chernov, 'Iz mira merzosti', p. 116.

47 J. Schneiderman, 'From the Files of the Moscow Gendarme Corps: A Lecture on Combating Revolution', *Canadian Slavic Studies*, 2(1), 1968, p. 89.

48 Martynov, *Moia sluzhba*, p. 42.

49 Russiian, 'The Work', p. 24.

50 Lev Tikhomirov, one-time ideologue of People's Will who went on to work for tsarist censors, cited in R. Pipes, *The Degaev Affair: Terror and Treason in Tsarist Russia* (London, 2003), pp. 17–18.

51 A phrase used by V. Chernov.

52 A. A. Lopukhin, *Iz itogov sluzhebnogo opyta: Nastoiashchee i budushchee russkoi politsii* (Moscow, 1907), pp. 32–3.

53 M. Perrie, 'Political and Economic Terror in the Tactics of the Russian Socialist-Revolutionary Party Before 1914', in W. Mommsen and G. Herschfeld (eds), *Social Protest and Terror in Nineteenth and Twentieth Century Europe* (London, 1982), p. 67.

54 Cited in Nicolaievsky, *Aseff: The Russian Judas*, p. 163.

55 A. Volkov, *Petrogradskoe okhrannoe otdelenie* (Petrograd, 1917), p. 14.

56 W. C. Fuller, *Civil–Military Conflict in Imperial Russia 1881–1914* (Princeton, NJ, 1985), pp. 49, 144–53; J. Bushnell, *Mutiny Amid Repression: Russian Soldiers and the Revolution of 1905–1906* (Bloomington, IN, 1985), pp. 15–21; D. Rawson, 'The Death Penalty in Tsarist Russia: An Investigation of Judicial Procedures', *Russian History*, 11, 1984, p. 37.

57 R. B. McKean, *St Petersburg Between the Revolutions: Workers and Revolutionaries June 1907–February 1917* (London, 1990), p. 494.

5

Culture, patronage and civil society: theatrical impresarios in late imperial Russia

Murray Frame

There is a general consensus among historians of late imperial Russia that some form of civil society was beginning to emerge during the second half of the nineteenth century.[1] The 'Great Reforms' of the 1860s and 1870s stimulated an unprecedented degree of autonomous activity on the part of educated society (*obshchestvo*), notably by creating new institutions of local government (the *zemstva*), expanding educational provision to foster the professional classes, and relaxing censorship.[2] These developments were accompanied by increasing urbanisation, the rapid growth of commerce and industry, and the appearance, especially in Moscow, of a new business elite.[3] Based largely on these 'middling groups' and sitting incongruously with Russia's traditional estate structure, this proverbially 'nascent' civil society expressed itself through an extraordinary range of voluntary associations, learned societies and charitable organisations, all closely monitored by a deeply suspicious autocracy.[4] Yet, according to most historians of the period, Russia's emerging civil society posed little threat to the tsarist regime because it was underdeveloped, fragmented, and lacked a coherent identity. As R. B. McKean succinctly puts it:

> The emergent middles classes were politically splintered and socially fissured. The commercial and industrial middle classes never developed a common mentality, social consciousness, or political allegiance. Ethnic diversity and regional economic rivalries divided entrepreneurs and merchants. Finally, the professional middle class was numerically small, as well as being legally and economically dependent on the state.[5]

For these reasons, it is argued, civil society was ill equipped to mount an effective challenge to the autocracy, even after the 1905 revolution when, during the period of the 'constitutional monarchy', there was relatively greater scope for organisation in the public sphere. The implicit assumption is that a more cohesive and assertive civil society – or the co-ordinated mobilisation of the 'middling groups' – might have been able to appropriate substantive political influence from the tsarist regime, leading in turn to a more pluralistic and responsive political system, thereby avoiding revolutionary upheaval.[6] Consequently, the notion of civil society, and its weakness, is regarded as central to understanding the fate of late imperial Russia.

The historiographical emphasis on civil society's fragmentation and its debilitated relationship to the state, however, has obscured an equally important feature of the paradigm. According to Ernest Gellner, communities that resist central authority – and therefore appear to possess a robust civil society – do not necessarily guarantee the 'institutional and ideological pluralism' associated with civil society. Strong communities, for example, have the capacity to inhibit individualism and often demand adherence to a local culture and its traditions. Civil society, on the other hand, allows individuals to 'choose' their identities, and to move freely between them.[7] For Gellner, then, a really-existing civil society 'excludes both stifling communalism and centralized authoritarianism',[8] and its *sine qua non* is 'modular man', the individual who can enter into associations and form 'alignments and opinions', yet without these being totally binding.[9] Knowledge, convictions and allegiances in civil society are fundamentally flexible, and 'modular man' can shift between them without incurring the wrath of the community or its authorities. Political heterodoxy, for instance, will not be considered treasonous, religious beliefs will not be regarded as apostasies, and so forth. (The major exception is the 'macrocommunity' of the nation.) Therefore, in Gellner's final analysis: 'Civil Society is a cluster of institutions and associations strong enough to prevent tyranny, but which are, none the less, entered and left freely, rather than imposed by birth or sustained by ritual'.[10] Consequently, civil society must be understood in terms of its two distinct relationships, one with the state, the other with the individual. In both respects, the emphasis is on pluralism and flexibility, not only for institutions and associations, but also for ideologies and identities. The notion of a unified civil society therefore appears somewhat contradictory, because its very essence, and its unique strength, lies in its resistance to unity, and therefore its resistance to monopoly and manipulation.

This chapter provides an introduction to one prominent aspect of late imperial Russia's civil society – the patronage of theatre by members of the new professional and entrepreneurial elite – within the broad context of Gellner's amended definition. The aim is neither to critique the essential idea, nor to assess its validity, but rather to use it as a suggestive and experimental paradigm that offers a new perspective on civil society, repositioning the relational emphasis away from the state and towards cultural pluralism and flexibility of identity. The salient argument is that the patrons of commercial theatre in late nineteenth-century Russia are good examples of 'modular man' because their activities and interests, often pursued in their theatrical projects, testify to the growing strength of cultural pluralism and flexibility of identity, at least in

Moscow and St Petersburg, the geographical purview of the chapter. The most obvious example of this – and the one that will receive emphasis here – is the contrast between the modernity of the patrons and their interest in late sixteenth- and early seventeenth-century Muscovy. While this might be construed as a reflection of instability and confusion in a time of 'flux', or the need to find cultural and ideological anchors during a period of rapid change (as it was in the case of the state's 'rediscovery' of Muscovy at approximately the same time), it might also be regarded as evidence of an increasingly assured civil society, comfortable and confident with cultural pluralism and a flexible amalgam of identities and referents. Indeed, some of the new theatrical impresarios appear to have experimented with identities for themselves and, through their stage productions, for the wider community without considering this to be problematic in the way that historians tend to assume. The contrasting and flexible images, or the 'modularity', which they cultivated were not signs of confusion, but rather – and perhaps paradoxically – of certainties, of a civil society, in other words, that was sufficiently robust to avoid the monopolisation of cultural identity. None of this, of course, explains why imperial Russia's civil society failed to 'counterbalance' the tsarist state. However, it invites a more extensive consideration of the view that, in terms of cultural pluralism and flexibility of identity, civil society was a much healthier entity than is often assumed. This chapter undertakes a preliminary consideration of that idea, firstly by profiling three prominent theatrical impresarios of the late nineteenth century, and secondly by highlighting three of their major productions which, when placed in the context of the 1880s and 1890s, suggest a strong degree of 'modularity'.

Theatrical impresarios in late imperial Russia

The most important development in artistic culture during the late imperial era was its growing autonomy from the state or state-sponsored institutions. As the tsarist regime pursued a programme of modernisation following its defeat in the Crimean War, two interrelated developments began to alter the social and cultural landscape, namely the growing size and confidence of the public sphere, and the accumulation of vast personal fortunes by small but influential groups of entrepreneurs who benefited, directly or indirectly, from the government's reforms. Imperial Russia's *nouveaux riches* were enthusiastic patrons of art. Some of them collected Western art (for instance Sergei Shchukin and Ivan Morozov, who purchased the early paintings of Matisse and Picasso), while others supported native Russian painters. Notable amongst the latter was Pavel Tretiakov, who lavished his textile fortune on the works of the Itinerants, a group of artists who had rebelled against the Imperial Academy of Arts in 1863. Tretiakov, and others, provided the material support for such painters – who included Ilya Repin and Valentin Serov – as they developed a Russian artistic style and explored native themes that the Academy had prohibited them from studying. In 1892, Tretiakov bequeathed his vast collection to the city of Moscow, where it is still on display in the museum that bears his name.[11] This is merely one example of the broader impact that the steady modernisation of urban Russia was having on cultural life.[12]

Analogous developments occurred in the sphere of the theatre. In March 1882, Alexander III abolished the monopoly of the state-run Imperial Theatres on public performances in Moscow and St Petersburg. For the first time since the late eighteenth century, private – that is, non-state – commercial theatres could freely be established. Within two decades, the theatrical landscapes of Moscow and St Petersburg had been transformed almost beyond recognition. The two cities had possessed six Imperial Theatres between them in 1882. By 1901, the five remaining Imperials had been joined by fourteen commercial theatres in St Petersburg and twelve in Moscow.[13] Many of the new theatrical enterprises were ephemeral and insignificant, but several of the more durable ones made important contributions to late imperial culture, as well as to the development of civil society. The most famous was the Moscow Art Theatre (1898–present) of Konstantin Stanislavsky and Vladimir Nemirovich-Danchenko, the subject of many studies.[14] While its reputations for technical innovation and cultural prominence are deserved, the historiographical attention accorded the Moscow Art Theatre and its co-founders has tended to obscure the contributions of other prominent impresarios who established important theatrical ventures before 1898, some of which prefigured the reforms that were subsequently attributed to Stanislavsky and Nemirovich-Danchenko. Three prominent examples will be introduced here, namely the Korsh Theatre (Moscow, 1882–1917), the Mamontov Private Opera (Moscow, 1885–1904) and the Suvorin Theatre (St Petersburg, 1895–1917). As autonomous enterprises supported by private wealth, they contributed to the wider social trend that was gradually challenging the state as the curator of artistic culture and the arbiter of identity. The leading figures behind these theatres were all representatives of Russian modernisation: Korsh was a lawyer who had benefited from the 1864 judicial reform; Mamontov was a railroad magnate who had benefited from the state's economic policies; and Suvorin was a publisher who had benefited from the contemporaneous rise of the newspaper industry and the spread of literacy. But why did they establish theatres? We will consider each in turn.

Fedor Adamovich Korsh (1852–1923) was born in the Caucasus, the son of a doctor in the Georgian Grenadiers. After studying Oriental languages at the Lazarevsky Institute, he read law at Moscow University, where he acquired his passion for theatre. He indulged his interest by organising amateur dramatics and, according to one account, always ensured that the proceeds from such performances went to 'poor and indigent people'.[15] However, it cannot be assumed that Korsh was motivated by sympathy for impoverished Muscovites, since the only way to gain permission to stage amateur theatricals for ticket-paying audiences in Moscow before 1882 was to donate the proceeds to charity. After graduating in 1872, Korsh worked as a barrister, gaining a prominent status among the Moscow *advokatura*. The extent of his involvement in the theatre between 1872 and 1882 is unclear, but the rapidity with which he established his enterprise after the abolition of the Imperial Theatre monopoly suggests that he was relatively well-connected and involved at some level. Within a few months of the announcement on the 'freedom of the theatres', Korsh had organised a troupe of actors and actresses for what became the first permanent private theatre in Russia. It opened on 30 August 1882 under the official name of the Russian Drama Theatre, although it was popularly known as the Korsh Theatre. The date of the inaugural performance was significant because it corresponded with the traditional opening night of the Imperial Theatre season, signalling that Korsh's venture was to compete directly with the state-sponsored drama theatre in Moscow, the Malyi. Indeed, it was initially located only a few streets away from the Malyi, in the Liazanov House on Gazetnyi Lane (now the residence of the Moscow Art Theatre), subsequently moving to purpose-built premises on Bogoslovsky Lane.

Korsh formed his troupe from the remnants of a theatrical enterprise run by the actress Anna Brenko, who had gained special permission before the end of the Imperial Theatre monopoly to stage performances in Moscow between 1880 and 1882. Among the notable talents that Korsh inherited from Brenko were Modest Pisarev, Vasily Dalmatov and Vasily Andreev-Burlak. His initial suggestion that the new theatre be organised as a share-holding venture met with a negative response from the troupe, and he also failed to receive financial support from the Moscow duma (city council) or from business interests.[16] As a result, the new theatre was initially funded from Korsh's personal resources, and to a considerable extent this determined the nature of the repertoire, which, despite the aesthetic ambitions of the venture, concentrated on productions that were designed to ensure commercial success. Korsh later claimed that he was motivated by four main aims:

> 1) to give the Moscow public a stage that would satisfy its growing theatrical-aesthetic needs, 2) to give the most talented provincial artists the opportunity to work and perfect themselves in conditions more favourable and regular than in the provinces, 3) as far as possible to promote the well-being of dramatic literature by staging the works of new dramatists, 4) to make the best dramatic works of native and foreign authors as accessible as possible to the greatest number of the public and to the growing young generation by staging these works at generally accessible performances with prices reduced to a minimum.[17]

The repertoire of the Korsh Theatre included some notable firsts. Chekhov's first major play, *Ivanov*, was premièred there in November 1887, as was the first

Russian production of Ibsen's *Nora* (November 1891) and the first Moscow production of his *An Enemy of the People* (1892–93 season). Plays with historical themes figured prominently, but with varying degrees of popular success. They included Bukharin's *Izmail*, centred on the capture of the fortress of Izmail during the Russo-Turkish wars of the second half of the eighteenth century, and featuring national heroes like Rumiantsev, Suvorov and Potemkin; François Coppée's *The Jacobites*; and Pierre Berton's *A Marseille Beauty*, in which Petrovskii played Napoleon. But the repertoire, at least until 1907, was dominated by the Russian classics, especially the works of Alexander Ostrovsky, Nikolai Gogol, Alexander Griboedov and Denis Fonvizin, most of them brimming with comical and satirical characters. Indeed, Korsh insisted that: 'The key to the venture's success lies exclusively in the careful performance of pure comedy'.[18] In general, Korsh did not interfere in the artistic side of the theatre, content to provide the entrepreneurial energy for it. As one actress recalled: 'It seemed that he was always on the move, aspiration itself personified'.[19] Yet Korsh took a keen interest in literary work, successfully adapting and translating several foreign plays for the Russian stage, notably Victorien Sardou's popular comedy *Madame Sans-Gêne*, as well as writing a few himself, such as *The Matchmaker*.

The claim that the Korsh Theatre exercised 'a colossal influence on many other Russian stages' is probably an exaggeration.[20] But it was innovative in several important respects. First of all, its very durability confirmed that, by the 1880s, there was sufficient demand for a new theatre in Moscow. Secondly, Korsh pioneered the inexpensive matinée performance in order to attract young people and students to his theatre. At the Imperial Malyi, only approximately 130 seats out of 1,100 cost less than one ruble (30–60 kopeks). The Korsh Theatre had a capacity of 1,300, and during its matinée performances at least half the seats cost less than one ruble, with 256 seats costing as little as 10–35 kopeks.[21] Even if the intention was to ensure regular full houses, Korsh certainly succeeded in his professed aim of making performances 'generally accessible'. Thirdly, the Korsh Theatre was the first in Russia to be completely illuminated by electric lighting, although not, as claimed, the first in the world: London's Savoy Theatre beat it by several months.[22] Finally, the first production of a historical drama to strive for authenticity was staged at Korsh's theatre (see below).

Savva Mamontov (1841–1918), like Korsh, was not a native of Moscow. He was born into a Siberian family which had relocated to Moscow by the early 1850s. Mamontov studied law at Moscow University, again like Korsh, but instead of pursuing a legal career he joined the family business, predominantly railway construction, and largely at his father's prompting. But Savva's real interests lay in the arts. He had learned to sing when he was a child, and during the 1860s he became involved, much to his father's chagrin, with a Moscow student circle dedicated to theatre reform.[23] During the winter of 1872, while the Mamontov family was holidaying in Rome, they surrounded themselves with young artists and students, and on his return to Moscow the inspired Savva participated in the so-called Artistic Circle, originally founded in 1865 by, among others, Ostrovsky, N. G. Rubinstein and V. F. Odoevsky, and intended as a forum where writers, actors, musicians and fine artists could exchange ideas about the arts and organise lectures, exhibitions, musical evenings, and readings of plays for members. In addition to his vocal gifts, Mamontov also dabbled competently in acting, sculpture, writing and directing.

Mamontov's cultural tastes were a complex blend of traditionalism and modernism. He was reputedly fond of the Latin phrase 'Ars longa, vita brevis' (life is short, art endures),[24] and he displayed a keen interest in a variety of artistic styles without seeming to privilege one over the other. He established an 'artists' colony' at the country estate of Abramtsevo during 1872–73 where representatives of the Itinerants, among them Repin, Vasnetsov, Serov, Vrubel and Korovin, developed the 'Russian style' in art.[25] He and his wife also displayed an interest in old Russian folk crafts and, fearing their demise as the country modernised, promoted peasant crafts at Abramtsevo.[26] They also constructed an old-style church on the estate in 1882, after a design by Vasnetsov. But Mamontov's encouragement of traditional Russian styles in art and architecture was not dogmatic or exclusivist. His support for modernism, for example, was expressed in his sponsorship of Sergei Diaghilev's *Mir iskusstva* (*World of Art*) in 1898, to the tune of 12,000 rubles, almost half of the costs of the art journal.[27] Mamontov's generous sponsorship of the arts soon earned him the sobriquet of Moscow's Lorenzo Medici,[28] and his reputation is reflected in the fact that his portrait was painted by at least two of the great artists of the time, Vrubel and Repin.

Mamontov's passions for music and the visual arts found their natural expression in opera, which he was fond of producing on an amateur basis at his home. In 1884, however, he conceived the idea of establishing his own commercial opera theatre in Moscow. What were his motives? Financial motives can be dismissed. Mamontov was already very wealthy and, besides, he continued to pursue his other business interests. According to Rossikhina, who has produced the most scholarly history of the Private Opera to date, the immediate impetus to establishing the theatre derived from two events in 1884 which together persuaded Mamontov that he could offer the Moscow public something valuable. The first was a performance of N. S. Krotkov's opera *The Scarlet Rose* at Abramtsevo before a specially invited audience. The occasion was a great success and Mamontov sensed that the work he sponsored was starting to receive the 'serious, sincere approval of connoisseurs'.[29] The second event was a concert held in celebration of Rubinstein. Mamontov was invited to organise a performance of Robert Schumann's *Manfred* as part of the event; again his efforts were warmly received.[30] This lends credence to the view that

Mamontov's primary intention was to demonstrate the possibilities for opera, particularly through the application of modern art to its staging. Contemporaries commented that the Private Opera signalled a self-conscious break with traditional 'routines', meaning the production practices of the Bolshoi.[31] More broadly, Mamontov appears to have believed in the wider social responsibilities of art, and is reputed to have claimed that artistes, painters and poets are the 'property of the people [narod]' and that '[t]he country will be strong if the people are imbued with their understanding'.[32] He also firmly believed that it was the task of civil society to organise the arts. According to Gozenpud: 'Mamontov was convinced that industry and art could be developed in Russia only with the aid of private initiative'.[33]

The Private Opera Theatre duly opened on 9 January 1885. It was initially located in the premises of the Korsh Theatre on Gazetnyi Lane for its twice-weekly performances; when the Korsh moved in the autumn of 1885, the Private Opera remained there, although it subsequently relocated to the Solodovnikovsky theatre building.[34] Like Korsh, Mamontov devoted considerable energy and resources to his theatre but delegated artistic matters to others. The first director of the Private Opera was Krotkov, and although Mamontov's son later claimed that the enterprise was his father's 'favourite child',[35] there was some reluctance to publicise his involvement too openly: the playbill for the opening night made no mention of the theatre's owner, but described it as the 'Private opera troupe in Moscow of N. S. Krotkov'.[36] The inaugural production was Dargomyzhsky's *Rusalka*, the critical response to which foreshadowed the general reaction to the Private Opera for the next two decades: the scenery, especially for the underwater kingdom, produced from sketches by Vasnetsov, was well-received, but there was less enthusiasm for the singers and the musicians, who were merely adequate.[37] Nevertheless, the Private Opera soon gained a reputation for staging challenging productions, especially of works by Russian composers that the Imperial Theatres had generally neglected. It is true that the several Russian operas staged during the first season were the least well-attended,[38] but gradually the new theatre gained a reputation for promoting national music and the works of native composers. The financial fortunes of Mamontov's venture were mixed. It initially operated for two seasons, was temporarily liquidated in 1887, and then resurrected in 1896. It almost closed again in 1899 after Mamontov was implicated in a financial scandal involving his other businesses, but it was kept going until 1904 by some of the performers as the Association of the Russian Private Opera.[39]

The third and final impresario to be mentioned here, Alexei Sergeevich Suvorin (1834–1912), was born into a peasant family in the village of Korshevo in Voronezh province. In 1851, he graduated from the Voronezh military school, but soon abandoned an army career for primary school teaching and

journalism. In the early 1860s, he became a full-time journalist, moving to
Moscow and then St Petersburg. Suvorin gradually established a reputation for
himself as a journalist and writer, but suffered a personal tragedy in 1873 when
his wife was shot dead by her lover. Although he remarried two years later, he
devoted most of his energy to his work. In 1876, he raised the money to buy
the failing newspaper *Novoe vremia* (*New Times*), which he proceeded to revi-
talise into 'the nation's most powerful newspaper'[40] and which, along with his
major publishing house, secured his fortune.[41] Suvorin also gained a reputation
for his political views, initially flirting with liberalism in the 1860s, but subsequently transforming himself into a prominent, and notoriously anti-Semitic,
conservative who advocated strong central authority of the Hobbesian type.[42]

Like many public figures of the time, Suvorin indulged his predilection for
the arts, especially the theatre. He was a keen amateur dramatist – his notable
plays included *Tatyana Repina*[43] – and was well-connected in cultural spheres,
counting Chekhov, for example, among his regular correspondents.[44] Suvorin
was also an active member of the St Petersburg Literary-Artistic Circle, and it
was the success of the Circle's production of Gerhart Hauptmann's previously
banned *Hannele* that persuaded its members, notably Alexander Kugel, P. P.
Gnedich and P. D. Lensky, to establish a permanent theatre.[45] Suvorin emerged
as the principal investor and chief organiser but, like Korsh and Mamontov, he
delegated everyday artistic matters to others, inviting the provincial actor
Fadeev to form a troupe and to direct performances. He also invited Evtikhii
Karpov to work as a régisseur in the new theatre. According to his own
account, Karpov was surprised at the invitation because he was not personally
acquainted with the publishing baron and, more importantly, '[o]ur social
views were very different'.[46] However, Karpov was reassured by Gnedich, who
had approached him on Suvorin's behalf, that the aims of the new theatre were
purely artistic and that it would eschew any political tendency.[47]

The Suvorin Theatre opened on 17 September 1895 and quickly became the
most important private theatre in St Petersburg.[48] Suvorin appears to have
permitted his régisseurs a fair degree of independence. He himself was disin-
clined towards Ostrovsky and reputedly found Ibsen's plays 'cold . . . very intelligent',[49] yet the theatre's inaugural production was Ostrovsky's *The Storm* and
its second was Ibsen's *Nora*. Nevertheless, the repertoire often reflected his con-
troversial views, notably in 1900 when the theatre gained notoriety for its production of the blatantly anti-Semitic drama by V. Krylov and S. Litvin,
Contrabandists (*The Sons of Israel*). Yet the repertoire also contained relatively
progressive drama and the Suvorin Theatre regularly premièred works that
were neglected by the Imperials and even by other private theatres in Russia.
Among the notable premières were Lev Tolstoy's *The Power of Darkness* (1895),
Shakespeare's *Julius Caesar* (1897), A. K. Tolstoy's *Tsar Fedor Ioannovich*
(1898), Alexander Sukhovo-Kobylin's *The Death of Tarelkin* (1900) and S. A.

Naidenov's *Vaniushin's Children* (1901). *The Power of Darkness* had been banned, but Suvorin used his connections to persuade the censor to permit its production. The play was premièred on 16 October 1895, a few days before it was staged at the Imperial Theatre. The censor had expunged only Mitrich's scathing comments about the banking system in act three, but after five performances they were reinstated with the censor's permission.[50] With such influence wielded by its impresario, the Suvorin Theatre soon became something of a cultural authority in the imperial capital.

This brief introduction to three of the major theatrical impresarios of late imperial Russia suggests that, in establishing private theatres, Korsh, Mamontov and Suvorin were motivated not by politics or pecuniary gain but by an affection for the theatre. Their agendas were emphatically cultural, with very few apparent exceptions. Yet it is often suggested that members of Russia's new professional and especially business elites were drawn to the arts for a more fundamental reason than mere enthusiasm, namely the ostensible hostility within Russian culture to entrepreneurialism and the notion of 'vulgar profiteering'.[51] Although many Russians embraced and excelled at entrepreneurialism, social prestige did not necessarily result from such money-making in the manner that it did, for example, in nineteenth-century Britain. By contrast, the pursuit of intellectual and artistic crafts was regarded as an honourable endeavour because, in theory, they were concerned with truth-seeking rather than personal gain. Hence, it is argued, the number of businessmen who patronised the arts.[52] While there might be some truth in that view, it should be emphasised that the body of evidence relating to the impresarios discussed above contains no real indication that their theatrical patronage was a compensatory venture or a self-conscious bid for social status. In fact, Mamontov's reluctance to have his name on the playbills of his Private Opera suggests some degree of diffidence in openly declaring his patronage of the arts, despite the esteem that it meant for him in some circles. Whatever their real motives, the activity of the impresarios undoubtedly possessed wider importance as a significant and relatively high-profile dimension of civil society. Moreover, although they were largely devoid of political ambition, these vibrant, autonomous cultural institutions further undermined the tsarist regime's monopoly on identity by promoting – most likely unwittingly – a sense of cultural pluralism. This was particularly evident in their explorations of the Russian past and its folklore, to which we now turn.

Performing the past

As commercial enterprises, the theatres of Korsh, Mamontov and Suvorin were obliged to have repertoires that appealed to popular tastes, because although they received some financial backing from their wealthy patrons, none of them could afford to function as fully subsidised organisations like the Imperial Theatres. This meant that the repertoires of the Korsh and Suvorin theatres tended to be dominated by light comedies and the Russian classics, and when Mamontov needed to bolster his box-office takings he invited popular Italian singers to join his troupe. Occasionally, however, these three theatres experimented with genres and themes that were not guaranteed to enjoy popular success, even though they often attracted critical acclaim. Notable in this respect were the Korsh Theatre's production of *Tsar and Grand Duke of All Rus, Vasily Ivanovich Shuisky*, the Private Opera's production of *The Snow Maiden*, and the Suvorin Theatre's version of *Tsar Fedor Ioannovich*. Although the first two productions were not numerically significant in their respective theatre's repertoire, and although they were not commercial successes, they were arguably the most important works staged by Korsh and Mamontov because they established critical reputations for their ventures. *Tsar Fedor Ioannovich* likewise strengthened the reputation of the Suvorin Theatre, but unlike the other two productions it enjoyed a long run of commercial success. These three productions were important not simply because they coincided with an intellectual interest in history and folklore, but because they did so with a lavishness and extravagant attention to detail hitherto unseen in the Russian theatre. They stood out in bold relief from the mainstream repertoire as ambitious and studious explorations of Russia's heritage, not merely improvised spectacles intended to hypnotise audiences.

The new theatres' excursions into the Russian past are particularly intriguing because they occurred at a time when, after the accession of Alexander III in 1881, the state set out to promote Muscovite Russia as a model of stable autocratic government. This expressed itself in several ways, notably in the policy of Russification, attempts to strengthen the position of the Orthodox Church, and the construction of churches that imitated the Muscovite style, most prominently the Cathedral of the Resurrection of Christ (or the Saviour on the Blood), built on the spot where Alexander II was assassinated in St Petersburg. Perhaps the most famous example of the late imperial court's fascination with Muscovy was the St Petersburg winter ball in February 1903 when Nicholas II appeared as Tsar Alexei Mikhailovich.[53] Official interest in Muscovy was initially founded upon Alexander III's conviction that the gradual Westernisation of Russia, particularly during and after the reign of Peter the Great, was responsible for the revolutionary agitation that had resulted in the assassination of his father. According to Richard Wortman: 'Muscovite Rus' provided a model of an ethnically and religiously united people, ruled by an Orthodox tsar'.[54] But this model was derived from a carefully selected period of Muscovite history, namely the era following the Time of Troubles (1598–1613) when Muscovy had been torn apart by dynastic disputes, social unrest and foreign invasion, and prior to the accession of Peter the Great (1682 or 1689). Therefore:

The historical narrative of seventeenth-century Muscovy associated the origins of the Russian nation with the affirmation of monarchical authority after the breakdown period of 'Troubles' at the beginning of the seventeenth century. The seventeenth century was the paradigm for a recrudescence of state power that could reunite an administration divided in the previous reign by considerations of legality and institutional autonomy.[55]

In striking contrast to the regime's preoccupation with an ostensibly unified seventeenth-century Muscovy in which tsar and people lived in harmony, the new private theatres of the late nineteenth century revisited the Muscovy of the late sixteenth century and the Time of Troubles. The Korsh Theatre's production of *Tsar and Grand Duke of All Rus, Vasily Ivanovich Shuisky* dealt with an era of monarchical usurpation, while the Suvorin Theatre's *Tsar Fedor Ioannovich* depicted a period of weak rule and dastardly machinations behind the throne, hardly positive portrayals of Muscovy and its political attributes. Whether this contrasting view of the Russian past was pursued in deliberate opposition to the state's version is unclear, in fact unlikely. After all, most of the plays that had been written about Muscovy were understandably set amidst the events that were most conducive to gripping drama. Nevertheless, it confirms that the theatrical representations of Muscovy were not simply imitations of the state's agenda. Moreover, while the state evidently 'resurrected' Muscovy from a sense of insecurity and therefore for political reasons, the theatrical impresarios appear to have been motivated chiefly by an interest in Muscovite culture. This view is suggested by the performance reviews, which tended to draw attention to the producers' efforts to ensure historical authenticity in terms of costumes, scenery and atmosphere.

The Korsh Theatre's production of N. A. Chaev's *Tsar and Grand Duke of All Rus, Vasily Ivanovich Shuisky*, or *Vasily Shuisky*, was the biggest event of its second season, 1883–84. It was directed by A. A. Yablochkin, and the expenditure on sets and costumes was so enormous (35,000 rubles) that the production almost bankrupted Korsh. Furthermore, despite critical approval, *Vasily Shuisky* failed to attract consistently large audiences and there was no box-office return on the investment. Nevertheless, the production was one of the most significant theatrical events of the 1880s and 1890s, notably because it was the first to aspire to historical authenticity, sixteen years before the Moscow Art Theatre became famous for similar endeavours. The costumes were designed from historical drawings, the furniture and weapons were based on period originals held in the Kremlin armoury (where Chaev was a curator), and the make-up of the actor who played Shuisky was based on a rare portrait that the theatre had managed to track down abroad.[56] While such efforts might appear unsurprising by today's standards, they were innovative for 1883, particularly when compared to the lacklustre productions at the Imperial Theatres, which paid little heed to temporal or spatial accuracy.

The text of Chaev's play does not appear to have survived, at least in published form, and the reviews of performances at the Korsh Theatre reveal little about its structure except that it was a simple chronicle and that its interest for audiences lay in its production style, its 'historical kaleidoscope'.[57] Vasily Shuisky was a leading boyar who reigned as tsar between 1606 and 1610. He had been Boris Godunov's great rival before Godunov died in 1605, and had been plotting to remove his successor, the False Dmitry, before the latter was beaten to death by a mob in 1606. Most of Shuisky's reign involved a struggle between Moscow and a variety of rebellious movements, some supported by Sweden and Poland. When King Sigismund III invaded Muscovy and captured Smolensk, Shuisky was deposed and for the next three years Muscovy was governed by a boyar council. The opening night of *Vasily Shuisky* was described by one critic as 'an unquestionable and fully deserved success'. The parterre was 'completely full' and only a few of the boxes were empty. Moreover: 'In the sense of production and performance, nothing better could be wished for'. The performers were talented, and great expense had been lavished on the production. Both Chaev and Korsh, continued the reviewer, had made a 'prominent contribution' to society with *Vasily Shuisky*, immediately establishing the artistic importance of the new theatre. Statistics cited by the same critic indicate the scale of the production: there were thirteen different scenes with their own backdrops; 275 costumes; and 950 props, all designed on the basis of historical sketches. 'The audience ardently applauded after each scene . . .'.[58] Another reviewer reinforced the positive reception of the production, observing that: 'The scenery is all new and very effective'.[59] Particular praise was reserved for the carefully choreographed crowd scenes, as another observer remembered:

> The best scene of the play was 'At the Novgorod market'. This is the scene between the people and Mikhail Skopin-Shuisky, who is persuading the Novgorodians to stand up for Rus. Ivanov-Kozel'sky skilfully recited Skopin's monologue, but the first place undoubtedly belonged to 'the people'. The talented régisseur Yablochkin staged this scene wonderfully. His crowd 'lived', and when the action was reaching the execution of the traitor Tatishchev, the reality of the performance made the audience quiver.[60]

In contrast to *Vasily Shuisky*, Rimsky-Korsakov's opera *The Snow Maiden* was based on a traditional Russian folk tale, which Ostrovsky had popularised as a play, rather than historical events. Mamontov's production, however, drew upon authentic Russian costumes and architecture for several scenes, notably the depiction of Berendey's palace. Premièred at the Private Opera on 8 October 1885, *The Snow Maiden* is a blend of mythology, paganism and folk customs. The opera's eponymous character is the child of Father Frost and the Spring Fairy. Yavilo (the Sun), however, disapproves and withdraws his rays from her village, leaving it in a state of perpetual winter. To protect her from Yavilo, the Snow Maiden is kept hidden in a forest, guarded by a wood spirit.

She is eventually tempted out of the forest by the sound of humans at play. Mizgir falls in love with her, but the Snow Maiden does not reciprocate. Tsar Berendey then offers a reward to anyone who can win her hand. The Spring Fairy proceeds to use pagan magic to enable the Snow Maiden to fall in love. She falls for Mizgir, but just before their wedding Yavilo directs a ray of sun at her, and the heroine melts. The inconsolable Mizgir drowns himself.

The critical response to *The Snow Maiden* was almost unanimous in its verdict – the performance of the music by the singers and the orchestra was substandard, but the scenery and the props signalled a major turning-point in the application of the decorative arts in the Russian theatre. S. Kruglikov, for example, attacked the orchestra but wrote: 'The costumes and the scenery are fresh, distinctive and beautiful, even the magical transformations are not lacking in effect, despite the fact that they do not happen in time to the music. The direction is also meticulous, and all the folk [*narodnye*] scenes are observed with animation, intelligence and veracity.'[61] Another critic concluded that: 'The costumes and the sets are very good; evidently a lot of money has been spent on them'.[62] One reviewer, praising its originality, referred to the production as 'an epoch in the chronicle of our musical life',[63] while another remarked upon its 'wealth of imagination, style and splendour' and observed that: 'Since the time when the Meiningen troupe was resident with us, we have not had occasion to see anything similar in respect of artistic merit on any Russian stage'.[64]

The production of *The Snow Maiden* also allowed reviewers to wax lyrical about Russian art and music, even if they were relatively unimpressed by the technical aspects of the performance at the Private Opera. One critic pointed out that new operas with a 'Russian character' are a rarity and that 'it is impossible not to be ardently sympathetic towards the idea of serving Russian art'. He continued: 'to the lovers of patriotic art, one may recommend becoming acquainted with this work'.[65] Another asserted that: 'Of the latest composers, only Musorgsky can compete with Rimsky-Korsakov in the portrayal of everyday (particularly historical-everyday) scenes, but in the portrayal of magical elements perhaps no one nowadays is in a position to contend with him'.[66] The explanation for *The Snow Maiden*'s success lay in Mamontov's long-standing support for modern Russian artists and their work on folk culture, much of it carried out at Abramtsevo. The sets, for example, were based on sketches by Vasnetsov, and were worked on by, among others, Korovin and Levitan. Research for the production had been conducted in Tula province (although the playbills claimed that it was based on costumes from Riazan and Smolensk).[67] Like the Korsh Theatre before it, and the Suvorin and Moscow Art Theatres after it, the Private Opera had succeeded, albeit through a fairy tale, in conveying to audiences a sense of cultural veracity and of the possibilities of native Russian art.

The third and final production to be highlighted, the Suvorin Theatre's *Tsar Fedor Ioannovich*, was both an artistic and a commercial success. It was premièred on 12 October 1898, two days before the more famous Moscow Art Theatre version. During the 1899–1900 season, it was performed twenty-three times – a considerable number by the standards of the Russian repertoire, which tended to stage large numbers of plays and perform them infrequently – and by the spring of 1900 it had already reached its hundredth performance.[68] Tolstoy's play centres on the rivalries between the Shuisky family and Boris Godunov for influence over Tsar Fedor (reigned 1584–98), the frail successor to Ivan the Terrible and the last of the Riurikid dynasty. When Godunov has the supporters of the Shuiskys arrested, they incite a rebellion and seek to have Fedor divorced from his wife (Godunov's sister) so that they can proclaim Dmitry (another son of Ivan the Terrible) as tsar. Fedor is willing to relinquish the throne, but the idea of divorcing his wife sends him into a rage and he allows Godunov to deal with the Shuiskys. The Suvorin Theatre was permitted to stage a largely uncensored version of the play. The excisions related to religious figures such as the Metropolitan who, however, did not have significant parts in the story.[69]

The production was highly praised by the critics for its effective staging and performance. One reviewer claimed that during several scenes the audience was able to forget that it was watching a theatrical performance, and that the play 'transported them to the remote epoch of the reign of the "meekest" son of the Terrible tsar'.[70] In a more extensive review, the same writer recorded that the actor in the main role, Orlenev, had succeeded in portraying the various facets of Fedor's personality – his weak character and limited intelligence, as well as his 'elevated mental qualities', the 'pure soul of the ideal Christian'. The actor Tinsky was a 'genuine Godunov' who depicted the 'most important feature' of his character, namely 'his striving for a noble aim, for the good of the Russian land'. Moreover, in terms of the smallest details, it was 'historically faithful'.[71] According to another critic, the performance was a 'great success' and was a 'genuine triumph' for Orlenev: 'It can justifiably be said that Orlenev created the role of Tsar Fedor'. The critic also remarked favourably on the historical details and external effects, notably 'the horseman going at full speed across the stage, the departure from the church with the ringing of the bells, the breaking of the fence and so on'.[72] Like *Vasily Shuisky* at the Korsh Theatre and *The Snow Maiden* at Mamontov's Private Opera, *Tsar Fedor Ioannovich* was not typical of the mainstream Suvorin repertoire, despite its success. The repertoire at each of these theatres was dominated instead by works that were less expensive to stage and appealed to established popular tastes. The artistic significance of the productions highlighted here lay in their energetic and studious efforts to portray the Russian past in authentic visual detail, as well as in their sheer scale and critical impact.

Theatrical impresarios therefore made an important contribution to the development of late imperial Russia's civil society, but not merely because their enterprises augmented the growing number of private, non-state institutions that enjoyed reasonably high public profiles. Equally important, if not more so, were the cultural pluralism and flexibility of identity that the impresarios and their theatres appeared to reveal. As individuals, Korsh, Mamontov and Suvorin exemplified the new professional and entrepreneurial elites that the 'Great Reforms' of the 1860s and 1870s had created. They were good examples of the astute, university-educated businessmen of urban Russia who had benefited from, as well as contributed to, the ongoing process of modernisation in Russia. Yet their fundamental modernity did not act as a constraint on their cultural interests, rather it expanded them. Between them the impresarios identified with a variety of styles and tastes, and constantly seemed to resist uniformity, to defy neat classification according to cultural or even at times occupational identity. Simultaneously inhabiting the contemporaneous worlds of progressive ideas, conservatism, commerce and the professions, as well as dabbling in the curiosities of Muscovy and native Russian crafts, the patrons of private theatre appeared to possess composite identities, none of whose components dominated for any length of time. In other words, Korsh, Mamontov and Suvorin – as well as other impresarios whom space precludes discussion of here – arguably typified the 'modularity' that Ernest Gellner suggested is the essential precondition for an effective civil society. They did not allow their modernity to monopolise their identity, and nor, for example, was the state able to manipulate their approach to imperial Russia's Muscovite legacy. It might be suggested, therefore, that the activities of the theatrical impresarios of late imperial Russia simultaneously cultivated and exposed both the 'institutional and [the] ideological pluralism' deemed necessary for a healthy civil society. Of course, the observation of a perhaps superficial cultural pluralism does not in itself demonstrate the existence of a robust civil society. The examples highlighted in this chapter, however, collectively suggest that the state's capacity to influence cultural life was weakening as civil society advanced. This in turn suggests that there was a growing, and largely consensual, fragmentation of cultural identity, the measure of a vibrant civil society.

Notes

Research towards this chapter was carried out as part of a larger project on Russian theatre and civil society, generously sponsored by the Leverhulme Trust.

1 'Civil society', broadly understood, is the public sphere of associational activity that is separate from the state. It is defined by Ernest Gellner as 'institutional and ideological pluralism, which prevents the establishment of monopoly of power and truth, and counterbalances those central institutions which, though necessary, might otherwise acquire such a monopoly'. It therefore consists of 'that set of diverse non-governmental institutions which is strong enough to counterbalance the state

and, while not preventing the state from fulfilling its role of keeper of the peace and arbitrator between major interests, can nevertheless prevent it from dominating and atomizing the rest of society': Ernest Gellner, *Conditions of Liberty: Civil Society and its Rivals* (London, 1996), pp. 3–4, 5. (Gellner adds a significant caveat to this definition, discussed below.) See also D. E. Eberly, *The Essential Civil Society Reader* (Oxford, 2000) and A. B. Seligman, *The Idea of Civil Society* (New York, 1992).

2   On the 'Great Reforms', see B. Eklof, J. Bushnell and L. Zakharova, *Russia's Great Reforms, 1855–1881* (Bloomington, IN, 1994); W. Bruce Lincoln, *The Great Reforms: Autocracy, Bureaucracy, and the Politics of Change in Imperial Russia* (DeKalb, IL, 1990); W. E. Mosse, *Alexander II and the Modernization of Russia* (London, 1992).

3   See, for example, T. C. Owen, *Capitalism and Politics in Russia: A Social History of the Moscow Merchants, 1855–1905* (Cambridge, 1981) and A. J. Rieber, *Merchants and Entrepreneurs in Imperial Russia* (Chapel Hill, NC, 1982).

4   On late imperial Russia's civil society see, for example: H. D. Balzer, *Russia's Missing Middle Class: The Professions in Russian History* (London, 1996); J. Bradley, 'Russia's Parliament of Public Opinion: Association, Assembly, and the Autocracy, 1906–1914' in T. Taranowski (ed.), *Reform in Modern Russian History: Progress or Cycle?* (Cambridge, 1995), pp. 212–36; J. Bradley, 'Subjects into Citizens: Societies, Civil Society, and Autocracy in Tsarist Russia', *American Historical Review*, 107(4), October 2002, pp. 1094–123; E. W. Clowes, S. D. Kassow, and J. L. West (eds), *Between Tsar and People: Educated Society and the Quest for Public Identity in Late Imperial Russia* (Princeton, NJ, 1991); M. Raeff, *Understanding Imperial Russia: State and Society in the Old Regime* (New York, 1984); J. Walkin, *The Rise of Democracy in Pre-Revolutionary Russia: Political and Social Institutions Under the Last Three Czars* (London, 1963); D. Wartenweiler, *Civil Society and Academic Debate in Russia, 1905–1914* (Oxford, 1999).

5   R. B. McKean, *Between the Revolutions: Russia 1905 to 1917* (London, 1998), p. 7. Of the many reasons for the lack of 'middle-class' unity in Russia, one of the most important was the distrust between the entrepreneurial and intellectual classes. See V. T. Bill, *The Forgotten Class: The Russian Bourgeoisie from the Earliest Beginnings to 1900* (Westport, CT, 1959), especially chs 7 and 8.

6   R. B. McKean, for example, has expressed doubts about the long-term prospects for the constitutional monarchy on the basis of his study of imperial Russia's social fissures and its fragile civil society. See R. B. McKean, 'The Constitutional Monarchy in Russia, 1906–17' in I. D. Thatcher (ed.), *Regime and Society in Twentieth-Century Russia* (London, 1999), pp. 44–67, an expanded version of Robert B. McKean, 'Constitutional Russia', *Revolutionary Russia*, 9(1), 1996, pp. 33–42. It is interesting to note that, elsewhere, McKean provides a cogent argument for considering Russia after 1905 to be a 'proper constitutional monarchy' on the basis of comparisons with European equivalents: R. B. McKean, 'The Russian Constitutional Monarchy in Comparative Perspective' in C. Brennan and M. Frame (eds), *Russia and the Wider World in Historical Perspective: Essays for Paul Dukes* (London, 2000), pp. 109–25. Moreover, he has argued that the labour unrest between 1912 and 1914 had limited revolutionary potential: R. B. McKean, *St Petersburg Between the Revolutions: Workers and Revolutionaries, June 1907 – February 1917* (London,

1990), especially chs 8 and 10. Considered together, these studies – arguing that the constitutional monarchy had weak foundations but nevertheless conformed with the wider European experience and was not confronted with a revolutionary crisis on the eve of the First World War – present a challenging perspective on the period.

7   Gellner, *Conditions of Liberty*, p. 9.
8   Ibid., p. 12.
9   Ibid., p. 100.
10 Ibid., p. 103.
11 See J. E. Bowlt, 'The Moscow Art Market' in Clowes et al., *Between Tsar and People*, pp. 108–28; B. W. Kean, *French Painters, Russian Collectors: The Merchant Patrons of Modern Art in Pre-Revolutionary Russia* (London, 1994) [the first edition of this book (London, 1983) was titled *All the Empty Palaces*]; J. O. Norman, 'Pavel Tretiakov and Merchant Art Patronage, 1850–1900' in Clowes et al., *Between Tsar and People*, pp. 93–107.
12 For the growing diversity of late imperial commercial culture see, for example: C. Kelly and D. Shepherd (eds), *Constructing Russian Culture in the Age of Revolution: 1881–1940* (Oxford, 1998), especially part II; L. McReynolds, *Russia at Play: Leisure Activities at the End of the Tsarist Era* (London, 2003).
13 *Rossiiskii gosudarstvennyi arkhiv literatury i iskusstva*, Moscow, f. 641, op. 1, ed. khr. 2587 (list of theatres in Russia). These figures do not include the seventeen 'pleasure garden enterprises' in St Petersburg and the four 'summer enterprises' in Moscow which included theatrical entertainments.
14 For a good introduction, see N. Worrall, *The Moscow Art Theatre* (London, 1996).
15 D. D. Iazykov, *Kratkii ocherk dvadtsatipiatiletnei deialtel'nosti teatra F. A. Korsha* (Moscow, 1907), p. 12.
16 T. N. Pavlova, 'Antrepriza Fedora Korsha', *Moskovskii nabliudatel'*, 7–8, 1992, p. 50; E. G. Kholodov et al. (eds), *Istoriia russkogo dramaticheskogo teatra*, vol. 6, 1882–1897 (Moscow, 1982), pp. 241–2.
17 F. A. Korsh, *Kratkii ocherk desiatiletnei deiatel'nosti russkogo dramaticheskogo teatra Korsha v Moskve* (Moscow, 1892), p. 48.
18 Cited in Kholodov et al., *Istoriia russkogo dramaticheskogo teatra*, vol. 6, p. 243. Thirteen years later, Korsh still subscribed to that view: ibid.
19 A. Ia. Glama-Meshcherskaia, *Vospominaniia* (Moscow and Leningrad, 1937), p. 206.
20 Iazykov, *Kratkii ocherk*, p. 6. The marked similarity between this book and Korsh's *Kratkii ocherk* of 1892 strongly suggests that 'Iazykov' is a pseudonym, but corroborative evidence remains elusive.
21 Pavlova, 'Antrepriza Fedora Korsha', p. 50.
22 Iazykov, *Kratkii ocherk*, pp. 16–17; *The Oxford Companion to the Theatre*, 3rd edn, ed. Phyllis Hartnoll (London, 1967), p. 567
23 E. R. Arenzon, *Savva Mamontov* (Moscow, 1995), p. 23.
24 Ibid., p. 5; V. P. Rossikhina, *Opernyi teatr S. Mamontova* (Moscow, 1985), p. 64.
25 On Abramtsevo, see: N. V. Polenova, *Abramtsevo. Vospominaniia* (Moscow, 1922); G. Iu. Sternin et al., *Abramtsevo. Khudozhesvtennyi kruzhok. Zhivopis'. Grafika. Skul'ptura. Teatr. Masterskie* (Leningrad, 1988).

82   Murray Frame

26 J. E. Bowlt, 'Two Russian Maecenases: Savva Mamontov and Princess Ternisheva', *Apollo*, December 1973, pp. 447–8.

27 Ibid., p. 450.

28 Sternin et al., *Abramtsevo*, p. 45.

29 Rossikhina, *Opernyi teatr*, p. 41.

30 Ibid., p. 41.

31 See, for example, M. M. Ippolitov-Ivanov, *50 let russkoi muzyki v moikh vospominaniiakh* (Moscow, 1934), p. 94.

32 Rossikhina, *Opernyi teatr*, p. 25.

33 A. Gozenpud, *Russkii opernyi teatr XIX veka. 1873–1889* (Leningrad, 1973), p. 265.

34 Rossikhina, *Opernyi teatr*, pp. 71, 90.

35 V. S. Mamontov, *Vospominaniia o russkikh khudozhnikakh (Abramtsevskii khudozhestvennyi kruzhok)* (Moscow, 1950), p. 20.

36 Playbill reproduced in Bowlt, 'Two Russian Maecenases', p. 447. Bowlt explains the decision to name the theatre after Krotkov as follows: 'Mamontov felt that shareholders and fellow businessmen would be critical if his name were attached directly to such a light-hearted affair as a private opera' (p. 453, note 15).

37 V. Iakovlev, *Izbrannye trudy o muzyke. Tom 3: Muzykal'naia kul'tura Moskvy* (Moscow, 1983), p. 223.

38 Arenzon, *Savva Mamontov*, p. 92.

39 Rossikhina, *Opernyi teatr*, p. 42. Although Mamontov was acquitted – after a five-month spell in prison – his reputation was irreparably damaged and he had lost a lot of money: Kean, *French Painters, Russian Collectors*, pp. 73–75; Bowlt, 'Two Russian Maecenases', p. 450.

40 L. McReynolds, *The News Under Russia's Old Regime: The Development of a Mass-Circulation Press* (Princeton, NJ, 1991), p. 74.

41 For Suvorin's career, see D. Rayfield and O. Makarova, 'Predislovie', in A. S. Suvorin, *Dnevnik A. S. Suvorina* (London, 1999); E. Ambler, *Russian Journalism and Politics, 1861–1881: The Career of Aleksei S. Suvorin* (Detroit, 1972).

42 Rayfield and Makarova, 'Predislovie', p. xi.

43 See J. Racin (trans. and ed.), *Tatyana Repina: Two Translated Texts by Alexei Suvorin and Anton Chekhov* (Jefferson, NC, 1999).

44 See M. H. Heim (trans.) and S. Karlinsky (selection, commentary and introduction), *Letters of Anton Chekhov* (London, 1973), *passim*.

45 E. Karpov, 'A. S. Suvorin i osnovanie teatra literaturno-artisticheskogo kruzhka. Stranichki iz vospominanii "Minuvshee"' [Part I], *Istoricheskii vestnik*, 137, August 1914, pp. 449–51.

46 Ibid., p. 452. As a youth, Karpov had spent time in 'administrative exile' for political activity: E. Karpov, 'A. S. Suvorin i osnovanie teatra literaturno-artisticheskogo kruzhka. Stranichki iz vospominanii "Minuvshee"' [Part II], *Istoricheskii vestnik*, 137, September 1914, p. 892.

47 Karpov, 'A. S. Suvorin' [Part I], p. 452.

48 Its formal names were: from 1895, the Theatre of the Literary Artistic Circle (Teatr Literaturno-Artisticheskogo kruzhka); from 1899, the Theatre of the Literary-Art Society (Teatr Literaturno-Khudozhestvennogo obshchestva); and from 1912,

after the death of its leading figure, the Suvorin Theatre of the Literary-Art Society (Teatr Literaturno-Khudozhestvennogo obshchestva imeni A. S. Suvorina). However, it was also known as the Malyi Theatre because it used the premises of the old Malyi Theatre of Count Apraksin on the Fontanka Canal, or more commonly as the Suvorin Theatre after its majority shareholder and effective leader.

49   Karpov, 'A. S. Suvorin' [Part I], p. 461.

50   Karpov, 'A. S. Suvorin' [Part II], p. 880.

51   On the idea of antipathy to the market in Russian culture see, for example, S. A. Smith, 'Popular Culture and Market Development in Late-Imperial Russia' in G. Hosking and R. Service (eds), *Reinterpreting Russia* (London, 1999), pp. 142–55.

52   There are many more examples of new money patronising the arts besides the ones mentioned in this chapter. To cite two of them: Tchaikovsky was partly supported from the fortune made by the engineering and railroad magnate K. F. von Meck (d. 1875), via his widow, Nadezhda; and the Moscow Art Theatre was bankrolled in its early years by the wealthy tycoon Savva Morozov.

53   R. S. Wortman, *Scenarios of Power: Myth and Ceremony in Russian Monarchy. Volume 2: From Alexander II to the Abdication of Nicholas II* (Princeton, NJ, 2000), ch. 7, and for an account of the winter ball, pp. 377–9.

54   Ibid., p. 237.

55   Ibid., p. 256.

56   Iazykov, *Kratkii ocherk*, p. 24; B. A. Shchetinin, 'F. A. Korsh i ego teatr', *Istoricheskii vestnik*, 110, October–December 1907, p. 169.

57   *Moskovskiia vedomosti*, 3 December 1883, No. 335, p. 3.

58   *Novosti dnia*, 26 November 1883, No. 149, pp. 2–3.

59   *Moskovskiia vedomosti*, 3 December 1883, No. 335, p. 3.

60   Iazykov, *Kratkii ocherk*, p. 24.

61   *Sovremennye izvestiia*, 1885, No. 277, cited in Gozenpud, *Russkii opernyi teatr*, p. 271.

62   *Russkii kur'er*, 11 October 1885, No. 280, p. 4.

63   *Russkii kur'er*, 10 October 1885, No. 279, p. 3.

64   *Teatr i zhizn'*, 1885, No. 178, cited in Gozenpud, *Russkii opernyi teatr*, p. 271.

65   *Novosti dnia*, 10 October 1885, No. 275, p. 3.

66   *Russkii kur'er*, 11 October 1885, No. 280, p. 3.

67   Gozenpud, *Russkii opernyi teatr*, p. 270.

68   H. Dolgov, *Dvadtsatiletie teatra imeni A. S. Suvorina* (Petrograd, 1915), p. 37.

69   *Syn otechestva*, 17 (29) October 1898, No. 281, p. 2.

70   *Peterburgskaia gazeta*, 13 October 1898, No. 281, p. 3.

71   *Peterburgskaia gazeta*, 14 October 1898, No. 282, p. 4.

72   *Birzhevyia vedomosti*, 13 (25) October 1898, No. 279, p. 3.

6

Tugan-Baranovsky and *The Russian Factory*

Vincent Barnett

M. I. Tugan-Baranovsky (1865–1919) was undoubtedly one of the most profound economic thinkers that tsarist Russia ever produced. His reputation is (in part) built upon a major work in economic history, *Russkaia fabrika v proshlom i nastoiashchem* (*The Russian Factory in the Past and the Present*), first published in Russian in 1898. A second edition followed in 1900, and a third with minor alterations in 1907. The existing published volume was however only part of Tugan's proposed project, as he intended there to be a second volume to continue the story, but while a manuscript was apparently completed it was never published and now appears lost. A German translation of the published part was issued in 1900, and the third Russian edition was reprinted in 1922, 1934 and 1938. An English translation finally appeared in 1970. Richard Kindersley called this work 'the most considerable historical work produced by any Russian Marxist of the period',[1] while Alec Nove called it simply a 'masterpiece'.[2] In this chapter the first section provides an introductory account of some of the basic themes of *The Russian Factory*, while the following section discusses various criticisms of it that have subsequently been made.

In the preface Tugan explained that a basic aim of the work was to trace how the original merchant-owned factory was transformed into the gentry-owned factory, which then became the modern capitalist factory.[3] The impression conveyed was of an organic series of transformations in which the continuities were as important as the fractures, the abolition of serfdom being one of the most significant of the latter. In Russian studies circles today this is the book on which Tugan's reputation is based, although it should be kept in mind that among his contemporaries it was *Industrial Crises in Contemporary England of 1894* that first marked him out as an original thinker. Moreover *The Russian Factory* was part of the same general approach to understanding economic development as *Industrial Crises*, and Tugan no doubt saw them as two parts of a larger whole. It is also necessary to recognise that while ostensibly the work was a purely historical account of the development of the Russian factory, it also served a polemical purpose in that it attempted to counter other sharply divergent views about the role of industry in Russian development.

Eight themes of *The Russian Factory*

Various themes or leitmotifs reoccurred throughout *The Russian Factory* (and in Tugan's other works on Russian industrial development), eight of the most important being:

1 The simplistic opposition of state against private forms of economy with regards to Russian industrial development was a misnomer.
2 The Russian economy was without doubt becoming part of the world economy.
3 The Slavophile support for small-scale rural forms of economy was a dead-end.
4 The import of foreign capital was crucial to Russian economic development.
5 The growth of capitalism in Russia could in no way be hindered by a lack of overseas markets for Russian goods.
6 The idea of a linear scheme of industrial transformation, for example the replacement of small-scale *kustar* production (domestic handicraft) with the large capitalist factory, was an oversimplification.
7 The absence of the city in its West European form had important consequences for the form of capital prevalent in Russia.
8 Russian industrial fluctuations were being caused by the periodic creation of free loanable capital.

Each of these points will be discussed and expanded upon in turn.

Theme One – The state/private dichotomy

Tugan first questioned the relevance of this distinction in relation to Peter the Great. Many had labelled Peter's support for large-scale industry as artificial, given that prior to this time small-scale production had dominated in Russia. The origins of such a contrast between the natural order and an artificially stimulated one Tugan found in the work of the French physiocrats.[4] The physiocrats (F. Quesnay, A. R. J. Turgot) had introduced the idea of a 'natural order' to political economy in the third quarter of the eighteenth century, believing that laws of nature governed human societies.[5] In Russia this attitude took the form of contrasting 'natural' institutions such as the *obshchina* (peasant commune) and the *artel* (workers' collective) with unnatural bourgeois implants.

For Tugan such a contrast was fundamentally erroneous, as capitalist relations were just as 'natural' as feudal ones. There was not a single country in the world where capitalism would have developed without active state support, hence it had always developed 'artificially'. It followed that Peter's support for large-scale industry was just as 'natural' as such support in England or France.[6] At this point Tugan's analysis connected with Karl Marx's account of the historical development of capitalism across various countries. Marx had come to realise that the geographical extension of capitalist relations required the active intervention of the state, together with the circulation of capital to the region in question. For example in Russia after the 1861 reform, the rural population was dispossessed through government policies.[7] Hence even for Marx capitalist development was always a mixture of state and private activity.

While it seemed through this analysis that Tugan was at least in part advocating state support for industrial development, he qualified this impression as follows:

> In the first half of the 18th century the chief consumer of factory-made products was the state . . . Large-scale industry arose on the basis of direct state support, and in its early stages could not dispense with this support . . . In the 19th century the situation changed. Industry decidedly outgrew the state's demand. A new branch of industry, the cotton industry, arose without any state support (except tariff protection)[8]

Here Tugan gave the impression of adhering to the infant industries argument – state support was necessary only in the initial stages of the development of an industry. But at a more fundamental level he was questioning the simplistic idea of support for either purely state or purely private development of industry, seeing them as inextricably connected. The role of the state was to enable and encourage private industry, not necessarily to replace it. This becomes clearer in Tugan's analysis of exactly how Peter the Great fostered large-scale Russian industry. According to Tugan, the large-scale production that was established during Peter's reign was based on the (private) commercial capital that had been built up 'naturally' in pre-Petrine Russia. The great majority of the factory owners of the Petrine period were Russian merchants. Hence large-scale industry was in fact created in Russia by Petrine support for such industry, *in combination with* the commercial milieu of the great merchants that was the result of the preceding 'natural' history of the Muscovite state.[9]

Moreover Tugan explained that while those factories which Peter had deemed especially necessary – mines, munitions and textiles – had initially been set up by the government, they were then transferred to private individuals. The government had provided interest-free loans to entrepreneurs who were establishing factories, and even given all this the overwhelming majority of Petrine factories had been created privately, without state assistance. Hence the simplistic opposition of state to private forms of economy was misleading, and the idea that protectionism could create entire new branches of industry out of nothing was deceptive.[10]

Theme Two – Russian economic integration

Tugan's argument about Russia becoming part of the world economy was developed in part using ideas taken from his analysis of business cycles, in part from his debate with the Slavophiles. The abolition of serfdom in 1861 had marked a turning-point towards West European labour practices, the idea of the unprofitability of serfdom being inspired by Adam Smith.[11] According to Smith, the work done by slaves and bondmen was 'the dearest of all', as a person who could acquire no property had little incentive to work.[12] For Tugan serfdom had been a hindrance to improvements in labour productivity which held back Russian integration.

Tugan presented a series of graphs for the period 1860–99 to illustrate his argument about Russian integration. One regularity highlighted by Tugan was that while in the period 1860–81 the level of trade at the Nizhnii-Novgorod fair and the number of factory workers employed in Russia moved in parallel, after 1881 this similar motion disappeared. Tugan interpreted this as signifying that old archaic forms of trade were being replaced by more modern forms, such older trading forms dying out alongside ancient forms of economy such as the *obshchina*.[13] Moreover in recent times fluctuations in Russian and English industry had coincided. To prove this Tugan compared fluctuations in the number of Russian workers employed with movements in the value of exports from the UK.[14]

Tugan's analysis of increasing integration is confirmed by calculation of correlation coefficients for the periods in question. These are shown in Table 1.

Table 1 Correlation between number of Russian workers employed and English exports

Period	Correlation coefficient
1863–90	0.72
1863–80	0.55
1880–90	0.89

Source: Correlation analysis of data given in Tugan-Baranovsky, *The Russian Factory*, p. 254.

These coefficients show that the amount of correlation was substantially greater for the later period 1880–90 than for the earlier period 1863–80.[15] Tugan's argument was that fluctuations in the number of Russian factory workers paralleled that of English exports between 1880–90 because the causes of the former were no longer purely national in character. They had come to share a common cause. In contradistinction to the conventional wisdom of the harvest being the major determinant of conjunctural progress in Russia, Tugan believed recent history had shown that the opposite was the case. The industrial stagnation of the mid-

1870s coincided with years of good harvests, while the depression of 1882–86 and the crisis of 1899 also witnessed good harvests. For Tugan this demonstrated that the harvest was no longer king in Russia and that the same cause that generated cycles in more advanced capitalist countries was causing cycles in Russia – the periodic creation of new fixed capital.[16] This was an important indication that Russia was becoming part of the world economy.

While the first edition in book form of *The Russian Factory* was published in 1898, Tugan also published in 1898 a shorter account of related themes under the title 'Statistical Results of the Industrial Development of Russia'. This was a report Tugan had read at a meeting of the Imperial Free Economic Society on 17 January 1898, and the argument about Russian integration was pursued here also. This report differed from the third (1907) edition of *The Russian Factory* in that it presented data on the rye harvest in Russia compared to the average level, whereas the 1907 edition presented absolute data on the total harvest of grain in fifty provinces of European Russia. Tugan used this rye data to again dispute the idea that the harvest was the major determinant of conjunctural movements in Russia. Tugan outlined how the Russian industrial stagnation of the mid-1870s had coincided with better than average harvests in 1874, 1877 and 1878. The end of the 1870s and the beginning of the 1880s were an epoch of upturn in Russian industry, yet the 1879 and 1880 harvests were well below average. And the period 1882 to 1886 was one of depression yet in only one of these years (1883) was the harvest below the average level.[17] Tugan appeared not to consider the possibility that the influence of the harvest might be offset or mediated in some way.

Theme Three – The Slavophile dead-end

Tugan presented the Slavophile view of Russian industrial development as idealising small rural industry and the folk life of the peasantry.[18] In the 1860s this took the form of opposing the development of factories and advocating the preservation of the backward economic forms of serf Russia such as the *artel*.[19] Writers associated with such beliefs included I. V. Kireevskii and A. K. Korsak. However for Tugan such an approach was fatally flawed as it ignored the benefits of the factory, and if acted upon would lead to the suspension of industrial progress. The Slavophile view was linked to August von Haxthausen's idea that the Russian peasantry had achieved the communal utopia advocated by European revolutionaries.

According to Haxthausen, a sense of unity in nation, commune and family was the foundation of Russian society, the commune successfully mediating between the individual and society as a whole.[20] In Tugan's view such utopian notions were dangerous romanticism and were based on an overly simplistic view of the Russian economy. It should be recognised that in rejecting this idealised view of the peasant commune, Tugan was also rejecting the idea proposed by Marx towards the end of his life that socialism in Russia could be constructed upon such communal forms of economy. This idea had been expressed in 1882 in the foreword to the Russian translation of the *Communist Manifesto*.[21]

Theme Four – The importance of foreign capital

Tugan was concerned to highlight the necessary role of foreign (particularly English) capital in Russian industry. The founders and 'lords' of key branches of Russian industry such as cotton-spinning and weaving were foreigners, and the pioneer of the iron and steel industry in the Donets basin had been British. Moreover the more vigorously foreign capital flowed into Russia in the future the quicker would end the current condition of excess demand.[22]

In addition to the analysis of this question presented in *The Russian Factory*, Tugan wrote a short article, 'Foreign Capital', published in 1912, in which he highlighted the importance of such capital to Russian industrial progress. In this article he dismissed the idea that insufficient domestic demand was hindering Russian industry as superficial, instead arguing that it was the poverty of savings and hence insufficient capital which was the root cause of the lack of progress. The solution was to import capital from overseas. Tugan wrote:

> The huge growth of markets in Western countries has created a huge growth of social savings, social capital. Capital accumulates in the West in such proportions that it is abundant not only to nourish internal markets, but continuously streams overseas . . . the surplus from countries with an old capitalist culture is an exceedingly important factor in the development of capitalist industry in all the world. Without the flow of capital from overseas young countries could not energetically develop their own capitalist industry, as the indigenous capital in these countries is inadequate for this.[23]

According to Tugan, the accumulation of capital in Russia did not exceed several hundred million rubles in a year, this being absorbed by state credit to a significant degree. This level of domestic accumulation was insufficient for the task at hand and hence the import of foreign capital was necessary.

Theme Five – The irrelevance of foreign markets

Tugan's basic argument was that capitalist production itself created its own market, and hence the idea that the unavailability of foreign markets to Russian goods would be fatal to Russian industrial development was false. Tugan's important caveat, however, was that proportional distribution of any new production was required in capitalism, something that was certainly not inevitable. In fact while perfect proportionality was impossible to obtain, even the rough proportionality actually required was difficult to achieve; hence Tugan's view that capitalism created its own market internally was conditional.[24]

The difficulties of obtaining proportional distribution of production were however greatly diminished in one particular case – when capitalism grew in the midst of a natural, non-monetary economy. Tugan reasoned on this as follows. If all branches of newly created industrial production were intended for sale on the market, then a monetary balance of supply and demand between all new individual branches would be necessary. If, however, only some branches of new production were intended for sale, then monetary proportionality with new non-marketed branches would not be necessary, since proportionality could be achieved by varying the amount of the non-marketed produce exchanged naturally. In fact for Tugan the development of capitalism in the environment of a natural economy had two distinct advantages. The first was the possibility of increased commodity exchange even with static production, the second was a greater facility to expand production due to underutilised resources.

In Russia this could be seen clearly in that a new railway line opened up a whole new market for capitalist industry, whereas in England this would not be so. This advantage was the key to understanding the migration of capital from older to newer countries.[25] Tugan suggested that what was actually hindering the further development of capitalism in Russia was not a lack of overseas markets, but the *nekul'turnost'* (lack of culture) of the Russian people. This included the low level of labour productivity, the ignorance of the Russian worker, and the lack of entrepreneurship and business acumen amongst Russian capitalists as compared to their West European counterparts.[26]

In 1898 Tugan had reviewed S. N. Bulgakov's book *Concerning Markets in Capitalist Production* of 1897, a review which provided a more detailed account of his view of the importance of foreign markets. Tugan explained that the debate about the role of markets in connection with the possibility of capitalist development in Russia had begun following the publication of a book by V. V. (V. P. Vorontsov) titled *The Fate of Capitalism in Russia* in 1882. This book had proposed the thesis that capitalism could not develop in Russia beyond certain limits. No matter what measures were adopted by the government to assist capitalist development these measures would fail. This was because capitalism required foreign markets to develop, but these were closed to Russian goods. V. V. had suggested that if Russian fabrics could not triumph in competition with foreign fabrics even on domestic markets, then on the world market there was even less chance of success.[27]

Tugan accepted that, historically speaking, capitalism as it had developed in Western Europe was indeed based on foreign markets. He even went further by admitting that, for England, foreign markets were a necessity. However, this was true only because England also imported goods from overseas. In this case the portion of purchasing power which was spent on acquiring foreign goods was withdrawn from domestic markets. Two outcomes were possible in this case: a portion of domestic capital could flow overseas or a surplus of goods could flow overseas. Tugan wrote:

a foreign market is necessary for the development of capitalist production only in so far as the country needs to import foreign goods. England, receiving wheat for its population and raw materials for its fabric from overseas, undoubtedly required a foreign market. Russia, where the import of foreign goods has incomparably less significance, can dispense with foreign markets.[28]

Tugan explained that this conclusion was a development of the approach of the classical school of political economy concerning the impossibility of general overproduction. In making this connection with the classical economists Tugan was pointing to the origins of this idea, which was clearly formulated by James Mill in *Commerce Defended* of 1808:

> The production of commodities creates, and is the one and universal cause which creates a market for the commodities produced . . . Whatever be the additional quantity of goods therefore which is at any time created in any country, an additional power of purchasing, exactly equivalent, is at the same time instantly created; so that a nation can never be naturally overstocked either with capital or commodities.[29]

Mill thus argued that continued economic growth did not depend on the expansion of foreign markets, as the process of growth itself expanded domestic demand sufficiently.[30] Within this theme Tugan did not explicitly acknowledge that the growth of Russian capitalism might be hindered by a lack of foreign markets for primary produce if not for factory goods.

Theme Six – No linear scheme of industrial transformation

It was Tugan's view that large-scale industrial capital not only did not oppress and hence destroy small-scale industry, but in fact actually assisted in its development in the pre-reform period. In contrast to the widespread conception of the folk origins of the *kustar* expounded by writers such as V. V., sometimes it was the factory that gave birth to cottage industry and not vice versa. Tugan wrote: 'The cycle did not begin with the independent *kustari* developing through the putting-out system into the factory system but, on the contrary, from the factory through the putting-out system to the independent *kustar*'.[31] For example, *kustar* cotton printing sprang up as a result of the large cotton factories created by foreign capitalists at the end of the eighteenth century, and even contributed to the eventual dissolution of such large factories. One element of this was that in terms of the technology utilised, large-scale industry in pre-reform Russia was not significantly more advanced than small-scale industry.

The introduction of new types of machinery in the post-reform period led to the factory prevailing over the *kustar* in certain branches such as cotton weaving, because the *kustar* could not compete with factory weaving. For Tugan this meant that capitalism in Russia was entering its highest phase.

However, simultaneously this process led to the founding of new branches of *kustar* production in areas such as sheepskin-coat manufacture and some metal trades, and the general fragmentation of those *kustar* which had survived.[32] Tugan was concerned to stress that, against the romantic view of the *kustar* propagated by some writers, in fact it was a 'typical form of the so-called sweating system with all its horrors'.[33] He also suggested that industrial progress could be impeded in this context, intensified exploitation of workers being sometimes used as an equally valid means of maximising profits as increasing labour productivity.

A possible implication of Tugan's analysis of the *factory/kustar* relation was that all suggested linear schemes of progression (such as that from feudalism to capitalism to socialism perhaps?) were an oversimplification which did not fully represent the complexity of economic processes. An ongoing interrelation of all the elements in the economy over time was something that emerged from Tugan's analysis, although the rise and fall of dominant structures within a system was an important element highlighted. The significance of this approach was not lost on Soviet historians, one of whom described the idea in 1935 as 'an absolutely incorrect thesis that goes against the Marxist understanding of the process of the development of large industry'.[34]

Theme Seven – The absence of the West European city

One element in the industrialisation equation that Tugan did not discuss in detail in *The Russian Factory*, but one he believed was profoundly relevant, was the importance of the city. In his *Foundations of Political Economy* Tugan stated that the most important difference between the conditions of economic development in Russia and those in Western Europe was the absence in the former of the stage of municipal or urban (*gorodskoi*) economy. In Russian history there was no city in the sense there was in the Middle Ages in Western Europe; in Russia the city was so small that it 'drowned in the general mass of the countryside'. Moreover those cities which had existed had a very different character from those in the West. Western cities were centres of small industry, such industry working not for trading intermediaries but directly for consumers. In Russia, cities were mainly administrative and trading centres, industry being dispersed throughout the countryside.[35]

Because of this there was an essential difference between West European urban artisans and Russian rural *kustar* workers. The former worked for local inhabitants whereas the latter worked for distant markets, this necessitating the existence of trading intermediaries, which in turn created a need for various forms of trading capital.[36] The political predominance of Moscow was thus based on the fact that this city was a trading centre for a huge district, the industry of which found itself in direct submission to trading capital. The class that controlled this trading capital was, after the landed nobility, the most influential

class of old Rus'. The social class that played a large role in the history of Western Europe – free urban artisans – was absent from Moscow. Thus Russia did
not possess those 'harmonious and accomplished' organisations of small industrialists on which the civilisation and culture of the West arose.[37] For Tugan this
was a crucial difference which had affected Russian industrial development
profoundly.[38]

Theme Eight – Russian industrial fluctuations

While ostensibly a book about industrial organisation, *The Russian Factory*
also provided a sketch of various aspects of the progress of industrial crises in
Russia. Unsurprisingly Tugan applied his previously developed theory of crises
to the Russian economy, by suggesting that it was the periodic creation of new
fixed capital that caused the observed fluctuations in Russian industry.[39] Consequently it was a shortage of free loanable capital that led to a period of prosperity turning to depression. One mechanism specified by Tugan for the shift
to downturn was that within the gold standard system, an unfavourable trade
balance would produce a declining exchange rate, which in turn would provoke increased demand for specie, the curtailment of loans and then a fall in
stock prices.[40] As a consequence banks became much more cautious about
extending loans and liquidity was greatly reduced. Only after a definite period
of depression would sufficient free loanable capital be accumulated to launch
a new upturn.

Tugan gave a quantitative indication of the creation of new fixed capital
through data on new company creation in Russia between 1856 and 1889.
These indicated the cyclical character of the founding of new stock companies,
although the founding of new companies might not be thought to correspond
exactly with the idea of the creation of 'new fixed capital'. Tugan's view that
crises in Russia were being caused by the same factors as those in the West
dovetailed with his conviction that Russia was becoming integrated into the
world economy.

Criticisms of *The Russian Factory*

Given that the question of the development of capitalism in pre-revolutionary
Russia was a highly charged political question, *The Russian Factory* was unsurprisingly accused of being in error in a number of ways by various Soviet critics.
One accusation was that Tugan had dramatically exaggerated the number of factories that had existed in the period 1815 to 1861. Tugan had stated that the
number of 'factories' (*fabriki i zavody*) in the Russian Empire (excluding Poland
and Finland) had increased from 4,189 in 1815 to 14,148 in 1861. These figures
included all factories and mills, sugar-beet refineries and tobacco mills, but
excluded mines and wine/beer distilleries.[41] Tugan explained that the background

to his analysis was V. V.'s attempt to demonstrate that the number of workers in Russian factories had been declining in recent times.[42] Tugan's data on the development of the Russian factory between 1815 and 1861 are shown in Table 2.

M. F. Zlotnikov had noted that Tugan's figures appeared to contradict V. I. Lenin's assertion that the number of factories in European Russia was between 2,500 and 3,000 in 1866, around 4,500 in 1879 and had reached approximately 6,000 in 1890.[43] How could there be 14,148 factories in 1861 (according to Tugan) and yet only a maximum of 3,000 in 1866 (according to Lenin)? The answer of course for Zlotnikov was that Tugan's estimate was mistaken in that he had taken the pre-reform industrial statistics at face value, and had not made the necessary statistical corrections. Lenin had pointed out that statistics for 'factories' presented in the 1880s included all and every industrial and artisan establishment, without any rules for limiting the definition of factories to larger industrial institutions. According to A. M. Pankratov, Zlotnikov's revised estimate was 1,800 'manufactories' (*manufaktury*) in existence between 1825 and 1828, rising to 2,818 'factories' (*manufaktury i fabriki*) in the 1850s, although even this more accurate estimate was not conclusive.[44] One implication of Tugan's 'overestimate' might be that he had exaggerated the extent of industrial development in Russia before the abolition of serfdom. Zlotnikov appeared not to note the fact that Tugan's evaluation related to the Russian Empire, Lenin's to European Russia.

Zlotnikov also accused Tugan of exaggerating the number of Russian factories in the second half of the eighteenth century. Tugan had claimed there were 984 *fabriki i zavody* in 1762, rising to 3,161 in 1796. Zlotnikov argued that Tugan had inappropriately included in this measure all small, medium and large industrial enterprises. Zlotnikov's estimate was around 420 'manufactures' at the end of the 1760s, and around 1,161 *fabriki* in 1796, since in the latter Tugan had erroneously included around 2,000 small industrial units.[45] In a way this debate was in part a linguistic dispute over the meaning of the word 'factory'. If small enterprises could be classed as factories then Tugan's figures were reasonable, if not then Zlotnikov's figures were more correct. Olga Crisp's evaluation of Tugan's analysis of factory numbers was that 'it is unlikely that a man of his experience would have made such a fundamental error'.[46] Perhaps Tugan can be criticised for not being more explicit about exactly what he meant by 'factory'.[47]

In addition to disputing Tugan's factory estimates, Zlotnikov argued that Tugan had underestimated the number of Russian factory workers at the beginning of the nineteenth century. Tugan's estimate was 95,202 in total, of which 48 per cent were freely for hire and 52 per cent serf and possessional workers. According to Zlotnikov, the real figure was 224,882 in total, of which only 27.5 per cent were freely for hire.[48] In fact Tugan had admitted that the actual number of workers greatly exceeded that recorded in official reports.[49]

Table 2 The number of factories in the Russian Empire

Year	Number of factories	Workers per factory
1815	4,189	41.3
1816	4,484	41.7
1817	4,385	42.7
1818	4,457	40.0
1819	4,531	39.0
1820	4,578	39.2
1825	5,261	40.0
1826	5,128	40.3
1827	5,122	40.9
1828	5,244	43.0
1829	5,260	44.0
1830	5,450	46.6
1831	5,599	47.2
1832	5,636	48.3
1833	5,664	48.4
1836	6,332	51.2
1837	6,450	58.4
1838	6,855	60.2
1839	6,894	66.0
1840	6,863	63.5
1841	6,831	62.9
1842	6,939	65.7
1843	6,813	68.5
1844	7,399	63.4
1845	8,302	61.1
1846	8,333	61.0
1847	9,029	58.9
1848	8,928	54.2
1849	9,172	54.0
1850	9,848	50.9
1851	10,126	45.9
1852	10,388	45.3
1853	10,087	47.7
1854	9,948	46.2
1856	11,556	44.9
1857	10,856	47.3
1858	12,259	44.8
1861	14,148	36.9

Source: Tugan-Baranovskii, *Russkaia fabrika*, p. 63. The English translation gives '9,994' for the number of factories in 1854. One decimal place has been added to column 3.

Another element of this debate was the changing pattern identified by Tugan in the number of workers per Russian factory, this rising from 41.3 in 1815 to a maximum of 68.5 in 1843 and then falling back to 36.9 in 1861. Tugan explained the decline after 1843 as a consequence of the success of *kustar* industry.[50] Crisp suggested that where machinery was being introduced into Russian factories, Tugan acknowledged that the tendency towards dispersion was much less apparent.[51] Again Zlotnikov disputed Tugan's analysis of the number of workers per factory between 1815 and 1861. In general Zlotnikov claimed that Tugan used sources uncritically and therefore came to incorrect conclusions.

In fact at a discussion of his paper 'Statistical Results of the Industrial Development of Russia' which took place at the Imperial Free Economic Society in 1898, Tugan had admitted that up until the 1860s 'factories' (*fabriki*) were actually 'manufactories' (*manufaktury*). The latter did not utilise machinery and could not compete with the *kustar*.[52] At this discussion the estimates of the number of factory workers provided by Tugan were examined. V. P. Vorontsov explained that Tugan had characterised the official data on factory workers as inexact, and had considered it correct to increase this data in certain cases by 30 per cent. Vorontsov also suggested that if Tugan had compared data on factory workers in 1893 not with those on 1863 but with 1840, then the amount of growth would be between 80 and 100 per cent rather than 140 per cent.[53] Tugan responded that there was a basis to think that previous data on factory workers was exaggerated, owing to the inclusion of domestic workers.[54]

In *The Development of Capitalism in Russia* Lenin had actually given a partially positive review of Tugan's handling of the data on Russian factory workers. Lenin pointed out that establishments with an output of less than 1,000 rubles in a year had been categorised as 'large' in yearbook statistics, and that the task of showing how such data could not be compared with present-day statistics had been performed by Tugan. Tugan was also (according to Lenin) correct to point out the 'completely erroneous' character of the figures found in the *Military Statistical Abstract*. This source had exaggerated the number of workers employed in factories and works in European Russia by 50,000.[55] Tugan was somewhat mistaken, however, in asserting that the number of factories had declined between 1885 and 1891.[56] In fact Lenin quoted Tugan rather frequently in *The Development of Capitalism in Russia*, and later Soviet critics of *The Russian Factory* were clearly politically motivated.

Conclusion

Regarding Tugan's view of how industrialisation should best be further promoted in Russia in the future, he could be interpreted as 'advocating' state-assisted market-based industrialisation, in contrast to the state-led bureaucrat-controlled industrialisation eventually attempted by Stalin. Tugan rejected the idea that capitalist industrialisation was either state-led or market-led; it was this false dualism which much of Tugan's work in economic history was directed against. This approach conforms at least in part to the much more recent work on evaluating the successful industrialisation strategy pursued by the four newly industrialised economies (NIEs) – Korea, Taiwan, Singapore and Hong Kong.

According to Sanjaya Lall the East Asian experience provided evidence of the superiority of private-sector led, export-orientated industrialisation over the state-led, highly regulated import-substituting strategies adopted elsewhere.[57] Tugan also rejected the idea that capitalism inevitably progressed from small-scale to large-scale production. In fact in his view large-scale helped to engender small-scale (in certain instances) in an organic process of development. Tugan was quite critical of the ability of Russian entrepreneurs to act as industrial leaders, suggesting that they often lagged behind their Western counterparts in terms of skill and acumen. This was a reason for supporting the import of foreign capital over and above the physical shortage of Russian capital that Tugan had chronicled, as foreign capital usually brought with it foreign know-how and expertise.

One political question arises from the above account of Tugan's views – to what extent can he be called a 'Marxist'? In the literature he is usually labelled as a 'Legal Marxist', that is someone who adapted their socialistic writings so as they would pass the Russian censor. An entire chapter of *The Russian Factory* was devoted to worker unrest in possessional factories, which Tugan suggested was caused by cruel treatment, low wages, the imposition of fines and so on. Moreover Tugan stressed that the *kustar* system certainly involved exploitation, comparing it directly with what he called the English sweating system. Hence elements of Marxism were certainly present in Tugan's thinking, although perhaps they began to fade somewhat after 1900. However, Tugan also devoted much attention to overcoming simplistic conceptions of what capitalism actually was, even advocating its development in Russia as a desirable goal. He stressed that the state had a positive role to play in fostering capitalist development and that a straightforward rejection of capitalism was not a realistic option for Russia at the start of the twentieth century, although this attitude was explicitly directed against the regressive analysis provided by the Slavophiles. The idea that capitalism would or should be overthrown at any time in the near future was not something that Tugan's work on industrialisation stressed in much detail, although he did call the modern factory the 'highest phase of capitalism'.

In this sense Lenin's criticism of Tugan as turning from a sympathetic critic of Marx into a plain 'bourgeois' economist could appear at least in part to be vindicated. Even so, as Tugan's most famous pupil N. D. Kondratiev explained, Tugan did believe that capitalism should be consigned to history and replaced entirely with a more humane economic system, but that this would not happen inevitably.[58] All this might suggest that a deep-rooted contradiction was beginning to develop in Tugan's thinking, indeed in Russian Marxism in general. This conflict crystallised as the total rejection of all things capitalist as embraced by Bolshevism – something that Tugan distanced himself from – and a more ambiguous proto-reformism that Tugan sometimes appeared to support. Unfortunately the former current of thinking gained absolute ascendancy in Russia after 1917.

Notes

This chapter is part of a larger project investigating 'Tugan-Baranovskii and the Evolution of Russian Economics, 1890–1919', funded by the ESRC (grant number R000237778). I am grateful to the ESRC and to CREES, Birmingham University, for providing support. The helpful comments of a discussant, Professor Mark Harrison, at the SIPS seminar at which a version of this chapter was presented are also acknowledged, as are the comments of Professor Philip Hanson.

1   R. Kindersley, *The First Russian Revisionists* (Oxford, 1962), p. 175, fn. 3.
2   A. Nove, 'Tugan-Baranovsky' in *The New Palgrave Dictionary of Economics* (London, 1998), vol. 4, p. 705.
3   M. I. Tugan-Baranovsky, *The Russian Factory in the 19th Century* (Homewood, IL, 1970), p. xi.
4   Ibid., p. 5.
5   S. L. Brue, *The Evolution of Economic Thought* (Fort Worth, TX, 1994), p. 39.
6   Tugan-Baranovsky, *The Russian Factory in the 19th Century*, pp. 6–7.
7   J. D. White, *Karl Marx and the Intellectual Origins of Dialectical Materialism* (London, 1996), pp. 362–3.
8   Tugan-Baranovsky, *The Russian Factory in the 19th Century*, pp. 64–5.
9   Ibid., pp. 9–11.
10   Olga Crisp agreed with Tugan that what she called the 'autonomous growth stream' which had started in the eighteenth century was at least in part fostered by Peter's modernisation effort. See 'The Pattern of Industrialisation in Russia, 1700–1914' in *Studies in the Russian Economy Before 1914* (London, 1976), pp. 12–13. Moreover this autonomous stream was related to the state-induced stream in a number of ways: for example skills were sometimes disseminated between the two streams. Also the inducing policies of the 1880s and 1890s were operated by way of the market rather than in direct opposition to it. See ibid., pp. 52–3.
11   Tugan-Baranovsky, *The Russian Factory in the 19th Century*, p. 69.
12   A. Smith, *An Inquiry into the Nature and Causes of the Wealth of Nations* (Indianapolis, 1981), vol. 1, p. 387.
13   Tugan-Baranovsky, *The Russian Factory in the 19th Century*, pp. 252–3.
14   Ibid., p. 257.
15   The data for the period after 1890 may suggest that the regularities were changing again, although Tugan did not provide a complete data set for the period 1890–1900.

16 Tugan-Baranovsky, *The Russian Factory in the 19th Century*, pp. 258–60.

17 M. I. Tugan-Baranovskii, *Statisticheskie itogi promyshlennago razvitiia Rossii* (St Petersburg, 1898), pp. 9–10.

18 Tugan-Baranovsky, *The Russian Factory in the 19th Century*, p. 229.

19 Ibid., p. 421.

20 A. von Haxthausen, *Studies on the Interior of Russia* (Chicago, 1972), p. 288.

21 White, *Karl Marx and the Intellectual Origins of Dialectical Materialism*, pp. 308–9.

22 Tugan-Baranovsky, *The Russian Factory in the 19th Century*, pp. 295–7.

23 M. I. Tugan-Baranovskii, 'Inostrannye kapitaly' in *K luchshemu budushchemu* (St Petersburg, 1912), p. 202.

24 Tugan-Baranovsky, *The Russian Factory in the 19th Century*, p. 292.

25 Ibid., pp. 293–4.

26 Ibid., p. 306.

27 M. I. Tugan-Baranovskii, 'Kapitalizm i rynok', *Mir bozhii*, 6, 1898, pp. 118–19.

28 Ibid., p. 121.

29 J. Mill, 'Commerce Defended' in D. Winch (ed.), *Selected Economic Writings* (Edinburgh, 1966), p. 135.

30 R. Backhouse, *A History of Modern Economic Analysis* (Oxford, 1985), p. 51.

31 Tugan-Baranovsky, *The Russian Factory in the 19th Century*, p. 175.

32 Ibid., pp. 364–79.

33 Ibid., p. 396.

34 M. F. Zlotnikov, 'K voprosu ob izuchenii istorii rabochego klassa i promyshlennosti', *Katorga i Ssylka*, 1, 1935, p. 47.

35 M. I. Tugan-Baranovskii, *Osnovy politicheskoi ekonomii* (Moscow, 1998), p. 129.

36 In *The Russian Factory* the distinction between trading and industrial capital was connected directly to the *kustar* and the factory. See M. I. Tugan-Baranovskii, *Russkaia fabrika* (Moscow and Leningrad, 1934), p. 351.

37 Tugan-Baranovskii, *Osnovy politicheskoi ekonomii*, p. 130.

38 Adam Smith had suggested that the commerce engendered by towns introduced 'order and good government' as well as providing a ready market for country produce. See Smith, *An Inquiry into the Nature and Causes of the Wealth of Nations*, vol. 1, pp. 411–12.

39 Tugan-Baranovsky, *The Russian Factory in the 19th Century*, p. 268.

40 Ibid., p. 260.

41 Tugan-Baranovskii, *Russkaia fabrika*, p. 63.

42 Tugan-Baranovsky, *The Russian Factory in the 19th Century*, p. 298.

43 M. F. Zlotnikov, 'Ot manufaktury k fabrike', *Voprosy istorii*, 11–12, 1946, p. 32.

44 A. M. Pankratov, *Rabochee dvizhenie v Rossii v XIX veke* (Moscow, 955), vol. 1 part 1, p. 24.

45 Zlotnikov, 'K voprosu ob izuchenii istorii rabochego klassa i promyshlennosti', pp. 40–1.

46 O. Crisp, 'Mikhail I. Tugan-Baranovskii' in D. L. Sills (ed.), *International Encyclopedia of the Social Sciences* (London, 1968), vol. 16, p. 166.

47 A historical-etymological dictionary defined '*fabriki*' as an industrial enterprise with the capacity for production using machines. See P. Ia. Chernykh, *Istoriko-*

etimologicheskii slovar' (Moscow, 1993), vol. 2, p. 298. This then pushes the question to a definition of 'machine'. The current dictionary definition of '*zavod*' includes factories, mills and 'works'.

48   Zlotnikov, 'K voprosu ob izuchenii istorii rabochego klassa i promyshlennosti', p. 46.
49   Tugan-Baranovsky, *The Russian Factory in the 19th Century*, p. 251.
50   Ibid., p. 61.
51   Crisp, 'Mikhail I. Tugan-Baranovskii', p. 166.
52   *Leninskii sbornik* (Moscow, 1940), vol. 33, p. 436.
53   Ibid., pp. 435–6.
54   Ibid., p. 437.
55   V. I. Lenin, *Collected Works* (London, 1977), vol. 3, pp. 459–60.
56   Ibid., p. 463.
57   S. Lall, *Learning from the Asian Tigers* (London, 1996), p. 2. However, the superiority of export-orientated growth did not mean that simplistic Heckscher-Ohlin models of comparative advantage had been proved correct, since the evidence suggested that 'winners' were being picked by the NIEs at an industry level.
58   N. D. Kondratiev, 'The Life of Tugan-Baranovsky' in N. Makasheva, W. J. Samuels and V. Barnett (eds), *The Works of Nikolai Kondratiev* (London, 1998), vol. 4, p. 332.

7

Late imperial urban workers

Ian D. Thatcher

The rapid growth of a small but significant urban working class was a notable feature of industrialisation and urbanisation in the late imperial period. In the decades from the 1860s to 1914 Russia's population more than doubled; its major urban centres quadrupled (Moscow, St Petersburg, Warsaw), quintupled (Riga, Odessa), and even grew tenfold in size (Kiev). Such impressive growth was largely a consequence of in-migration. Late tsarist Russia has been described as a 'country of people on the move',[1] primarily in search of jobs, whether in the new factories and small workshops, or in the burgeoning service sector. Although much scholarly attention has focused upon the factory workers, it is best to remember that the majority of the urban workforce was employed outside of the super modern large industrial combines. Despite an influx of female workers into textile, tobacco and chemical plants, for example, the domestic and service sector remained the single largest source of employment for St Petersburg's women. More men and women worked outside than in the factories. The urban workforce was thus a diverse and stratified group, divided by occupation, gender, age, location and education, to name but a few of the major differences outlined by historians. Its emergence was also an indication that a still overwhelmingly peasant Russia was undergoing modernisation. The urban workers fascinated contemporary and subsequent observers for what they entailed as much as for what they were. Would this be a class that would save or ruin Russia? Certainly the upper orders looked upon the loose morals of the urban workers with horror. Socialist agitators welcomed the urban workforce, or at least its most advanced sections, as the harbinger of a new order. My intention is to outline the current state of knowledge about late imperial workers, their origins, work and everyday life. To what extent were urban workers a force for stability or instability in late tsarist Russia?

The majority of Russia's urban workers were of peasant origin. Many peasants retained links with their village. It was, after all, the village assembly that issued the passport necessary for a move to the towns – a passport that could be removed or not renewed if village community obligations were not met. Many urban workers would return periodically to the village whether on holidays, to help out on the farm, during periods of unemployment in the factories, or permanently. In any event, it was not unusual for the migrant to leave a family in the village, or to marry in the village and then to have any children raised in the village rather than in the town (urban infant mortality rates were much higher). Many workers could not afford the costs of lodging a whole family in the urban centres. This was a major reason why men tended to migrate, leaving women to tend the land. This should not obscure the not inconsiderable level of female migration. Nevertheless the urban workforce contained more men than women. This, as we shall see, has led some historians to focus upon the masculine aspects of the urban workers. Others have noted how male migratory and marriage trends had negative consequences for a single urban woman's courting and marriage opportunities.[2] Male workers were often under parental pressure to marry in the village, ensuring an additional pair of hands for the farm household. One St Petersburg worker, who was particularly interested in urban–village ties, surveyed his colleagues about connections with their villages: 'Eleven of the eighteen men were married, and all of their wives lived in the village. Only one of them had been visited by his wife recently, and before that she hadn't seen her husband in four whole years. One of them had lived there for five years without seeing his wife.'[3] A disrupted family life was thus one price many had to pay after migrating to the cities. That many were willing to pay this price is an indication of the advantages that a move to the towns entailed. There was a mixture of push and pull factors that attracted the peasants into the towns. Land hunger, lack of work in the village, rising rents and taxes against falling grain prices contrasted with the opportunities, both financial and cultural, of the urban environment. Peasants would naturally gravitate to the nearest urban centres. The land-hungry peasants of Tver province situated to the southeast of the capital, for example, headed to St Petersburg. The poverty-stricken villages of provinces located to the north and northeast of Moscow provided good recruitment for the businesses of Russia's second city. Of course, the railways enabled some migrants to travel further from home, even if it was a long trek to the nearest railway station; some workers moved long distances in search of new opportunities.

   The transition from countryside to town was often assisted by family and village networks. After all, the intention was that an urban income would supplement money made in the village. An initial choice of location and trade would depend upon contacts. These connections could also be very useful in adapting to an alien environment. Some peasants worried about their children being corrupted by urban life. Placing family via a village network was one way of trying to control offspring in the city. Apart from these concerns, establishing oneself in the towns was a difficult business. Above all one had to find work and accommodation. The memoirs of the metalworker S. I. Kanatchikov, for example, open with a description of being taken to Moscow by his father to begin an apprenticeship at the Gustav List engineering works. The job for the young Kanatchikov had been secured by a fellow villager, or *zemliak*, Korovin. It was Korovin who also arranged for accommodation and food. Kanatchikov's account of the boarding and lodge arrangement is typical of numerous memoirs of the time:

> We rented the apartment communally, as an artel of about fifteen men. Some were bachelors, others had wives in the village and ran their households. I was put in a tiny, dark, windowless corner room; it was dirty and stuffy, with many bedbugs and fleas, and the strong stench of 'humanity'. The room contained two cots. One belonged to Korovin, my countryman and guardian; the other I shared with Korovin's son Vanka, who was also an apprentice and worked in the factory's pattern shop.
>
> Our food and the woman who prepared it were also paid for communally. The food was purchased on credit at a shop; our individual shares were assessed twice monthly. Every day at noon, as soon as the factory's lunch bell rang, we would hurry back to the apartment and sit right down at the table where a huge basin full of cabbage soup was already steaming.
>
> All fifteen men ate from a common bowl with wooden spoons . . . After the soup came either buckwheat kasha with lard or fried potatoes. Everyone was hungry as a wolf; they ate quickly, greedily.[4]

The *artel* (workers' collective) would often become a substitute family for the newly arrived migrant. *Artels* could develop into close-knit communities, in which members would look out for one another. If someone became violent because of drink, for example, the other *artel* comrades would ensure that the drunk remained in bed until sober. An elder of the *artel* could be elected to take care of communal expenses such as shopping and cooking. The *artel* could also pool its resources to subscribe to a particular newspaper or journal. Literacy rates were much higher among the urban workers than peasants, and higher among men than women. Peasant families were far more willing to have their sons educated, seeing it as beneficial for their sons' eventual employment in the army or factory. The importance workers attached to being part of a safe and secure community is evident from the long distances some workers were willing to commute to factories rather than abandon their *artel* for a lodging closer to work.

Russia's urban infrastructure was not able to cope with the pace of population growth. The type of workers' accommodation varied according to one's place in the labour hierarchy, as well as other factors such as location. The highest paid and most skilled workers could manage to set up an independent home, if only in a rented room. Even then they would most likely seek to take in lodgers, to help pay for the high cost of urban living space. Others had to rely upon the accommodation provided by factory and workshop management, from sharing a bed in a workers' dormitory on a shift basis to bedding down on the floor of the workplace. The numerous domestic and service sector employees often had accommodation provided, for which deductions were made from meagre wages. Workers who depended upon their bosses for a roof as well as a job were much more constrained in all aspects of their lives than those able to live independently. The reminiscences of a factory textile worker, F. P. Pavlov, for example, recall a factory of some 5,500 workers, only 750 of whom resided outside the factory gates. Those on the inside were subject to the whims of the director, who exerted a profound influence over the lives of his employees. Pavlov points out that the director decided not only the length of the working day and the time of breaks. More importantly, the director provided and restricted a range of social services, including the type of living accommodation and how it would be used. There were restrictions regarding what time the workforce had to be in bed, how many residents could gather in one room and for how long, and so on. There was a corresponding assortment of fines for any transgressions. The director would also decide whose children would be educated in the factory school, what provisions would be sold in the factory shop, and which workers would have access to scarce entertainment resources, most notably the library and the theatre, whose content and productions were again controlled by the director. Pavlov concludes that 'I can only compare the discipline reigning at our factory with military discipline, and I believe that on the scales of authority, the power of our director will outweigh that of any commander of a brigade or regiment'.[5] The tyranny experienced by domestic servants may have made some urban workers feel even worse off than Pavlov. To have a room of one's own was thus a common aspiration, but one hard to achieve. In 1908, for example, only one-third of St Petersburg's single workers and less than one-half of its married workers could afford a single room.[6] One St Petersburg doctor calculated that the average room in a workers' quarter flat housed as many as twenty people. Whatever the differences in accommodation, however, most accounts agree that workers lived in appalling conditions: overcrowded, damp, dark, dirt-infected hovels. All workers suffered from a lack of adequate housing, with all of the negative consequences for privacy, leisure opportunities and so on.

Workers' accommodation was also often situated in the least desirable districts, suffering from a dearth of civic services. The workers lacked real clout in local politics. The franchise for the town and city dumas or councils was restricted largely to the most affluent property owners. This was a major reason why improvements to pavements, roads, street lighting, sewerage and water systems tended to be restricted to the central and most affluent districts. The workers' districts were starved of resources and their inhabitants suffered as a consequence, from inadequate and arbitrary policing to outbreaks of cholera. The mortality rates for the urban workers were higher than for peasants who remained in the villages. Each of the major urban centres had its most notorious workers' districts, the Vyborg in St Petersburg, the Shuliavka in Kiev, the Nakhalovka in Tiflis and so on. Of course workers could also be found outside specific workers' districts, but when they lived in the city centres they enjoyed the worst accommodation, in the cellars and basements for example. The dire state of the cities' dwelling quarters for the workers is evident from the testimony, for example, of the duma doctors who treated the sick.[7]

Of course the workers devoted most of their time not to tending a home, but to work. Numerous factors and variables stratified urban workers. There were, for example, skill and gender differentials from the mainly male metal-working complexes to the predominantly female cotton industry. Whatever the trade, men earned more than women. This was partly a reflection of skill differentials, that men moved up the labour hierarchy more than women. It was also a reflection of cultural beliefs that women were a weaker and more passive sex. Protective legislation, banning the employment of women for certain tasks, could be used to further bolster the male wage. It has been argued that female workers benefited least from the expansion of jobs in the towns and cities.[8]

Within trades and within sexes there was a hierarchy of occupations. Female bank clerks earned more than female shop workers and so on. The most sought-after skilled workers received the best rewards and benefits. They were paid fortnightly rather than daily, for example, and did not have to suffer the humiliation of being hired on a daily basis. At the bottom of the labour hierarchy was a range of apprenticeships that served as starter positions for many young people entering the urban labour force. The apprentices were the lowest paid and most abused section of the working class.[9] Their bosses could beat and scold with seeming impunity, as numerous memoirs testify. Conditions at work would depend not only upon the nature of the job and one's place in the labour hierarchy, but would also change from factory to factory and from workplace to workplace. Individual factory owners and employers enjoyed much leeway in setting the terms and conditions of employment. The legislative framework regulating the workplace was weak and underdeveloped. There were certain restrictions on the length of the working day at factories, particularly for certain categories of worker, women and children for example. But this left numerous jobs and trades that were not covered by legislation. Even legislation could be circumvented, as the reports submitted by the factory inspectorate reveal. At best a skilled worker could be restricted to a ten-hour working day, although eleven-and-a-half to twelve hours was the norm. At the other end of the scale a young apprentice in a shop or small workshop could be expected to labour for fifteen to seventeen hours a day, arriving before the rest of the staff to open up and staying later to clean the premises. The Russian working class was aware of its own divisions, from an aristocracy in

skilled positions to the unskilled labourers, and from those who had established themselves as more or less permanent fixtures in the urban landscape to
transitory workers who would return to the fields.

Status differentials within the working class were expressed in cultural patterns, such as dress and etiquette. It became popular to pour scorn upon the
rough manners of the peasant newcomers to the towns in jokes and vaudeville
skits.[10] The young Kanatchikov, recently arrived from the countryside, recalls
how the skilled workers 'looked down on me with scorn, pinched me by the ear,
pulled me by the hair, called me a "green country bumpkin" and other insulting
names'. After all, he was as he admits 'a typical village youth', with 'long hair that
had been cut under a round bowl, wearing heavy boots with horseshoes'. There
were some workers in the factory, described by Kanatchikov as 'patternmaker
peasants', whose style of dress and manners remained traditional. The skilled
workers to which Kanatichkov aspired, however, were distinguished by:

> The pattern shop was considered to be the 'aristocratic' workshop. Most of the
> patternmakers were urban types – they dressed neatly, wore their trousers over
> their boots, wore their shirts 'fantasia' style, tucked into their trousers, fastened
> their collars with a lace instead of a necktie, and on holidays some of them wore
> bowler hats. They cut their hair 'in the Polish style' or brush-cut. Their bearing
> was firm, conveying their consciousness of their own worth. They used foul lan-
> guage only when they lost their tempers and in extreme situations, or on paydays,
> when they got drunk, and even not all of them at that.[11]

Distinctions expressed by dress are found again and again in workers' memoirs. In an account of life in a textile factory P. Timofeev points out that 'only
foremen, foremen's assistants, and draftsmen carry rulers in their top pockets.
Ordinary workers put their rulers into the lower pocket of the jacket or in their
pants.'[12] Moreover, the better dressed a worker, the more likely that he would be
shown some respect. Writing about the tailor workers of Moscow E. A. Oliunina
noted that:

> Tailoring shop workers and subcontract workers shop quite differently. The
> former, especially those working in the center of Moscow, wear suits, shoes and
> different coats according to the season. The subcontract workers, on the other
> hand, wear quilt jackets and boots. In these workshops one can find half-dressed
> workers wearing nothing but a calico shirt, often torn and dirty, and a pair of
> faded pants or long underwear. They work barefoot. When they go out they cover
> themselves with a jacket.[13]

A range of other distinctions mirrored the divisions amongst workers
expressed by dress. Certain types of behaviour and language cemented patterns
of solidarity and division. Friendships were formed and reinforced through a
range of social intercourse. Recent research on the urban workers has emphasised how work mates could act as surrogate families. These families may have

been divided according to age, gender, behaviour ('advanced', 'backward'), but the sense of solidarity within and sometimes between these categories was nevertheless real. Some of the major areas of contentious behaviour included drinking, swearing and fist fighting.

An obvious and frequent form of bonding, although primarily for men, was through a ubiquitous drink culture. The tavern was mainly a man's world, in which women featured as barmaids, prostitutes, or of loose morals. There were numerous rites of passage, from being hired and completing an apprenticeship to promotion, in which the fortunate worker was expected to celebrate by standing a round of drinks. An exodus from the factories to the urban centres' numerous taverns and drinking establishments marked pay days and holidays. Excessive drinking was linked to the social ills of alcoholism, crime, domestic abuse, and fraught family circumstances. Nevertheless, women may not have begrudged their partners time in the taverns, but they did object to the whole family budget being spent on drink. It was not uncommon to see women waiting at the factory gates, trying to grab part of a partner's wages before he reached the tavern. The pervasive drinking culture among urban workers has been explained not only by a desire to escape a life of drudgery, although this undoubtedly played its part. The carnival atmosphere of the factory districts on pay days has been well documented. Group drinking was also how workers acknowledged and cemented friendships in an environment (the tavern) that they could call 'theirs'. To decline an invitation to imbibe in social drinking was taken as a rebuttal of an offer of friendship and could result in ostracism in a world where contacts counted for much. In drinking bouts men could prove their strength and virility through the consumption of large amounts of liquor. A small minority of 'advanced' workers, supported by socialist intellectuals and the socialist press, despaired at the drunken behaviour of 'backward' colleagues. The advanced workers were proud of sobriety, seeing it as an integral part of a civilised and cultured life dedicated to reason and the acquisition of knowledge. For them, drinking diverted workers from serious educational and political activities. How much stronger would the workers be, they bemoaned, if the money spent on alcohol could be diverted to workers' libraries and strike funds. Articles in socialist publications pointed out how the tsarist state budget depended to a large degree on the alcohol monopoly and thus the spread of drunkenness, how addiction to alcohol sapped the workers' morale and played into the hands of the bosses. Given the crucial social functions performed by alcohol, however, such cultured voices would remain a minority. A survey of 12,000 St Petersburg workers that was presented to a Congress of the Struggle Against Alcoholism, held in the capital over December 1909 and January 1910, found that 93 per cent drank. Most had begun the habit before their seventeenth birthday.[14]

A sense of shared identity was constructed and reinforced not only through drinking but also in swearing. Steve Smith, for example, has noted how a rich vocabulary of swearing was used, chiefly by male workers, to demonstrate and uphold a sense of male community. There were some women workers who broke the common perception of femininity and swore. However, swearing seems to have been one strategy by which male workers could assert their dominance over women workers, whose presence in the workplace may have been resented. Mouthing swear words or playing linguistic games with foul language served multiple purposes. Obscene talk and the rendering of jokes and stories through foul language could provide a sense of amusement and distraction from boredom at work; it could humiliate superiors and subordinates and help let off steam; but above all it expressed a male sense of acceptance and solidarity. Ubiquitous swearing was remarked upon by numerous memoirs. It was something that the 'advanced' workers protested against, arguing that this vile habit demeaned the user as well as the object of abuse. Clean and pure language was seen as cultured, representing human dignity and a worker's commitment to knowledge. Trade unions and meetings of factory workers, both male and female, would request management to refrain from abusing workers and for male workers to stop swearing at their female colleagues. It is unclear how much headway such protests made, however, when swearing was so interwoven into social relationships at the factory and beyond:

> For the majority of 'unconscious' workers, swearing, dirty jokes, and sexual boasting were ways of letting off steam and of demonstrating that you were one of the lads, a way of gaining acceptance from the group. More crucially, they were a way in which men sustained their manliness in the new environment of the capitalist workplace, which conspired to make them feel powerless in a way they had not felt when working the land.[15]

A culture of heavy drinking and swearing can be seen as part and parcel of a brutal and brutalised existence. Another feature of what some contemporaries called a 'hooligan' lifestyle[16] was the extension of village violence in an urban setting. It had been traditional for village men to engage in organised fist fights as part of the celebrations associated with popular holidays and festivals. The violence of everyday life, portrayed by some writers as a prominent and damning example of backward Russia, could also be observed in Russia's factories and small workshops. Directors, foremen, more experienced workers or apprentices could all beat up their immediate subordinates with seeming impunity, despite such beatings being outlawed. Some factory inspectors noted the harsh punishment beatings handed out as part of normal work relations.[17] Not only was such violence accepted within the workplace, it could also be used for recreation and entertainment. The metalworker Kanatchikov admits that he would join comrades from the Gustav List engineering works in fist fights with workers from the Butikov textile factory. 'In the evening,' he recalls, 'we would return home with our black eyes and our broken bloody noses.'[18] The practice of workers from different factories forming fighting teams was not uncommon, although teams could also be drawn from adjoining districts or other criteria. The fights had their rules, in which walls of men would fight over a disputed territory. It was not considered fair to hit someone when down or to use weapons. The fights could draw large appreciative crowds, with bets on teams or individual fighters. Fighting prowess could be used to assert a reputation amongst friends and colleagues, as well as being a cheap form of entertainment to enliven an otherwise dull free time.[19] Once again it was a pattern of behaviour that more 'advanced' workers frowned upon. A more suitable avenue for education and entertainment was no doubt provided, in the advanced workers' view, by the workers' education and cultural societies. Such societies were legalised after 1906, provided that they were registered with the police. For some workers they provided access to libraries, literacy classes, and organised series of lectures and trips to museums. Although catering to a minority of the urban workers (membership ranged from 100 to 500), the clubs did offer 'workers a public sphere within which to address educational needs, economic change and political ideals'.[20]

The opportunities for leisure and self-expression available to urban workers were not exhausted by drinking and swearing, sobriety and a clear tongue, hooliganism and violence, and a correct manner and reason. The cultural habits and interests adopted by the urban workers were as broad as the choices on offer. There was a variety of inexpensive pursuits for Sundays and holidays. The public parks with their occasional fairs were particularly popular. Others stuck to the old ways, most notably religion. The urban environment posed many problems for the Orthodox and other faiths. How could one ensure that there were sufficient churches in the 'new' workers districts, not to mention the priests to staff them? How could religion compete with other forms of belief and entertainment, from the tavern and prostitute to socialism? Several studies have highlighted the difficulties Orthodoxy faced in maintaining the loyalty of the urban working class. There can be no doubt that some workers took pride in consciously rejecting religion in forming a new, urban, scientific outlook. Others simply found religion boring and were more interested in other pursuits. Urban dandies, for example, followed fashion and the latest dances. There could be conflict within families, especially on holidays, between those who wanted to observe traditional religious rites and those who rejected them. Such arguments could have taken on a gendered pattern, with women more likely than men to remain tied to religious practice. More recently, however, some scholars have emphasised the extent to which urban workers, men as well as women, remained loyal to a religious faith.[21] Workers could pool resources, for example, to provide and upkeep religious iconography in the workplace.

On occasion a priest would attend the factory to hold a service there. The urban workers could even combine religious and other beliefs, when praying for the success of a strike when walking off the job, for example. Revolutionary songs could also combine religious sentiment with the urban workers' cause, evident in this excerpt from a famous protest song of the late 1890s onwards:

The enemy whirlwind is blowing above us
The forces of darkness and evil oppress
The enemy's started our fatal battle
Our unknown fate awaits us ahead.

But we shall raise up, proudly and bravely
The banner of struggle for a workers' rights
The banner of every nation's great battle
For holy freedom, and a better life.

To bloody battle, holy and righteous
March, forward march, working class!
To bloody battle, holy and righteous
March, forward march, working class![22]

For some workers a religious and socialist outlook could also be combined with national loyalties. Several of late imperial Russia's urban centres became sites for the discovery and flowering of a specific national culture. The multi-ethnic make-up of the Russian Empire became apparent as never before as different groups migrated to the cities. It was in the melting-pot of the urban environment that some urban workers first became conscious of themselves as having a national as well as a class identity. National languages spread and expanded, each having their own newspapers and bulletins. The city could become divided into particular districts noted for a particular national flavour, be it Yiddish, Polish, Armenian, Georgian, Lithuanian, German and so on. The ethnic diversity of some late imperial cities produced an array of anecdotes. These were rooted largely in bigoted stereotypes (greedy Jews, for example), but were a popular reflection of underlying ethnic tensions that could and did exist amongst the urban workers.[23]

Despite a variety of distinctions and divisions amongst the urban workers, there were factors that could unite them to take collective forms of action. There were, after all, numerous similarities that could make workers aware of themselves as a common group or class, not to mention the efforts of socialist intellectuals and 'conscious' workers in propagandising the notion of *a* working class. Some scholars have noted the increasing practice of workers to settle in the towns with their families, evident from the early 1900s but particularly after 1907 when poorer peasants may have abandoned the land altogether as a consequence of the Stolypin reforms. More stable urban worker communities fostered a shared sense of identity and purpose.[24] At work, whether one was at the top or bottom of the labour hierarchy, workers as a whole were subject to control by the managers and their representatives on the shop floor, the foremen. It was common for workers to share a sense of grievance against the arbitrary and harsh control exerted over them by the factory management. There was, for example, a whole range of fines that could be levied against the workers. Such fines covered lateness, unexplained absences, shoddy work, drunkenness and poor behaviour. The fines could often be arbitrary and unfairly and inconsistently applied. Foremen could be sympathetic to one worker and brutal to another. The workers were often treated with little respect, and resented being addressed in the familiar form of speech, but having to reply in a formal and respectful manner. As well as lacking rights and respect in the workplace, the workers were in an extremely precarious position should they fall out of work. Even the highest-skilled and best-paid workers suffered from dangerous and precarious conditions of work. There were numerous accidents in the workplace that could result in a temporary or permanent loss of employment, or the need to take a lower-paying job. Workers' songs often lamented a harsh lifestyle that affected their personal and physical fortunes. Who, asks one song, would wish to marry a cripple of a factory accident? Furthermore, even skilled workers could be sacked without notice, and there was no guarantee that their pay rates could not be altered without prior warning. Unfair dismissal and non-payment of wages were frequent complaints. With no security of tenure workers could be dismissed for a host of reasons. Some trades had particularly short career spans. Shop workers, for example, could be fired because they were no longer sufficiently young or attractive. There was, after all, a steady supply of labour to replace those workers already beaten and exhausted. Pregnancy could also lead to dismissal from domestic work and the factories. To make matters worse, tsarist Russia had no uniform private or state-sponsored system of insurance for temporary or permanent loss of work due to accidents, old age, ill-health, pregnancy, unemployment, and so on. In workers' memoirs periods of unemployment or illness are remembered as times when belts had to be tightened even further. One ate less and lower-quality food, one could change accommodation, and ultimately vital possessions had to be sold to make ends meet.

The tsarist state was well-aware of Russia's 'labour question'. It, along with employers, was unable to construct a coherent and adequate response. There was a series of *ad hoc* and half-hearted measures. All had serious deficiencies from the workers' perspective. A factory inspectorate, for example, had been established in the 1880s. It was charged with monitoring the implementation of certain basic requirements in the workplace, including a ban on child labour, a ten-hour day for adolescents, and a prohibition of night-time work for women. Even within this limited remit, however, the factory inspectorate's scope for interference in protection of labour was severely curtailed. Some (state-owned and artisanal) plants, for instance, lay outside its jurisdiction. The factory inspectorate had no independent power to insist upon improvements in the workshops. Nor could it reasonably maintain a regular and thorough policing function in the factories. The city and province of St Petersburg, for example, housed more than one-tenth of the nation's workers. Yet this area boasted only one senior inspector and twelve factory inspectors. Little wonder that workers looked upon the factory inspectorate as a feeble device, more concerned with defending the rights of state and employers over labour.

It took the authorities until 1912 to introduce a limited form of insurance, covering accidents and sickness. Funds were to be established from a combination of workers' and employers' contributions. The state was not to contribute to these schemes. The workers were entitled to elect representatives to the governing boards of the insurance funds, but their overall management would be the responsibility of the employers. The police and Insurance Boards were given special supervisory powers to ensure that insurance monies were not expended on anything other than their intended recipients and that the principle of workers' elections did not assume a political character. There were some advantages to the insurance scheme. Provision was made for medical treatment in the event of an accident at work, and rates for sickness benefits were established, with more generous payments going to workers with families. There could also be maternity payments and a death grant. The disadvantages were far greater, however. Once again the laws covered only a minority of the workforce. Important categories of workers as well as whole regions were excluded. There was no established uniformity of rights and benefits. Provision and payments varied from factory to factory, depending upon the make-up of the workforce and the meanness (or generosity) of the employers. Some workers were unwilling to commit to the upper limits of contributions because of low wages. Women workers were particularly vulnerable for this reason. The police and Insurance Boards used their powers of intervention to harass workers' representatives, some of whom were arrested, and to prevent funds from making payments, for example to unmarried mothers. By the time of its demise, there was still not coverage in imperial Russia for invalidity, old age, occupational diseases or unemployment. Indeed, there was a dearth of employment agencies. In most cases workers experiencing difficulties had to reply upon family help, or aid from a range of private and local council charitable agencies. The majority of institutions for aid to the needy were located in the urban centres. Some rural poor may even have gone to the cities in search of charity. But however impressive the aid given by individual citizens, and however much evidence private charitable organisations provide of an emerging civil society, there were simply insufficient resources to meet demand. As one historian of late imperial poverty has pointed out:

the neglect of the needs of the poor by the state and by most local governments probably contributed to popular alienation from both the state and . . . privileged society. The assistance that was provided was often punitive or degrading . . . Private charity offered an extensive and varied array of services and assistance, but they were still inadequate to the need. Moreover, even well-meant charity probably seemed condescending and offensive to a working population, especially in the cities, that was increasingly being exposed to socialist doctrines.[25]

The list of grievances that most workers could easily and readily construct, including poor and dangerous working conditions, a lack of rights and low pay, understandably resulted in friction between workers and bosses and ultimately between the labour force and autocracy. The institutions that were adopting the task of representing workers' demands to employers in a free labour market in the West, trade unions, also arose in Russia. However, the Russian trade unions faced numerous restrictions. It became possible to form trade unions legally only after the 1905 revolution. Even then trade unions were allotted limited functions and could be closed on any pretext. The tsarist state and the employers may have successfully inhibited the growth of a healthy and vibrant trade union movement. However, they were unable to wipe workers' associations out altogether and to prevent workers from striking.

In the absence of any serious attempt by government and employers to address legitimate workers' concerns via reform from above, there was an upsurge in strike activity in the late imperial period. Strikes tended to occur in waves, with times of intense strike activity interspersed with periods of relative tranquillity. An obvious periodisation for strikes in the late imperial period is the contrast between the fever of 1905–6 with the downturn of 1907–12, and the upsurge of 1912 onwards.[26] There were many facets to strike activity. There have been many studies examining the why, what, when and where of strikes. Were male metalworkers more prone to militancy than female textile operatives, for instance? Were literate workers more radical than the illiterate? Were workers more likely to strike during economic booms or recessions? Were workers' demands limited and specific or general and broad? How successful were strikes? And so on.

There were numerous reasons why workers would down tools. Strikes tended to focus upon economic grievances, both immediate and specific (the restatement of sacked colleagues), and longer-term and common objectives (the eight-hour day). Sometimes they protested against changes in working conditions, especially if the workers felt that their skills and wages were being undermined.[27] Strikes could be limited to one workshop or factory or they could spread. Workers would walk off the job at one factory to then seek the support of colleagues at other plants. Some workers were encouraged to organise and press their demands by the successful example of others. It was in November 1905, for example, that Moscow's servants first went out on strike and formed a trade union. The urban workers would also respond to the plight of colleagues elsewhere. In April 1912, for example, several hundred striking workers were shot upon and killed or wounded at the remote Lena goldfields. The miners raised over a dozen demands, many relating to their illegal working conditions. Workers across Russia's urban centres organised rolling one-day sympathy strikes that culminated in the largest May Day demonstrations witnessed for many years.[28]

Strikes would also raise issues of individual dignity, and political and civic freedom. Workers were troubled by often inhuman treatment at the factories, from the degrading body searches when leaving work to verbal and physical abuse. The concern to be treated as a human being was expressed in a range of documents, from the writings of worker-authors to specific demands and resolutions during strikes.[29] The workers also connected a desire for human recognition to the need for the rights and freedoms of citizens if they were to protect their interests. Resolutions passed by trade unions and other forms of workers' collectives regularly featured the call for the right to free association, freedom of the press, and equality before the law. Indeed, the autocratic regime in the factory could become linked with the autocracy itself. One could not democratise the factory without the democratisation of politics and society more broadly. Such linkages are clear in the petition that workers presented to the tsar in January 1905:

> The present position of the working class in Russia is totally unsecured by law or by those rights of individuality which would enable workers independently to defend their interests. Workers, like all Russian citizens, are deprived of freedom of speech, conscience, the press and assembly . . . In the light of the complete absence of personal rights and the support given by the police and governmental authorities to capitalist interests – which extends from arrest and exile to the encouragement by the security police of spying and provocation – and in the light of the unquestioned power which the capitalists wield, thanks to their advantage over labour on a world-wide scale, an advantage which is enhanced by the protection they receive from officials and by the legal defencelessness of the toilers, the workers are, in the full sense, serfs of the factory owners.[30]

Strikes were not only an opportunity to pursue demands, but also gave the workers a sense of power and fraternity, of their specific identity and worth. Some scholars have emphasised how divisions within urban workers could be softened during strikes. In 1905 and 1914, for example, it has been pointed out that workers would take temporary vows of abstinence. Such promises of sobriety were a means of showing commitment to the cause, as well as hurting the tsarist treasury through a loss of revenue. The demarcation between advanced 'sober' workers and backward 'drunkards' was thus not as clear as claimed in some of the literature.[31] Strikes could also turn the traditional world on its head. The increase in the hiring of female labour as part of the urban workforce, especially from 1905 onwards, has been explained by the relative cheapness of female labour and its more tranquil character. The latter assumption, if held, has not been borne out by gendered studies of strikes. If anything, there has been a suggested link between strike-prone industries and industries employing a higher percentage of women. After all, women felt themselves abused much more than men. The daily bodily searches to check for stolen items may have been humiliating for men, but for women they could be combined with sexual abuse. In work stoppages women would show themselves capable of formulating clear demands and of organising a strike. They could also violate codes of 'feminine behaviour' by violent acts, such as the smashing of machinery that was lowering their wages. Although male workers tended to view their female colleagues as more passive, it could be the case that men were the first to break strikes when women workers were holding out for more. In strikes, then, female labour could attack not only property, but also the world of male domination; it was a form of action that allowed women to 'articulate new gender concerns'.[32] Ultimately, it was strike action begun by women workers in the capital that started a series of demonstrations that resulted in Nicholas II's abdication. It was precisely the voices of 'passive women' that won the soldiers from a defence of the tsar to a defence of the revolution.

At their most frequent and radical, strikes could bring whole industries to a standstill. Workers proved themselves able to organise strikes not only at their own factory and workshop, but also across industries and on occasion across a whole town and city, or region and country. As well as trade unions, Russia's urban workers formed other bodies to help direct strike activity. It was in 1905, for example, that workers across the urban centres elected soviets, or councils, to co-ordinate their efforts and present their demands. The soviets were composed of delegates representing factories, with the principle of 1 delegate to 500 workers. They were dominated by male, skilled workers, although socialist intellectuals would also be allotted a consultative voice. Although the soviets and strikes were able to make an impact on an irregular basis, at times of national crisis that impact could be significant. It is generally acknowledged, for example, that in the year of revolution, 1905, it was the October general strike that wrestled the famous concessions to civil liberties contained in the October Manifesto. Socialists debated whether it would be through strikes, rather than a revolution in the streets, that autocracy would collapse. Such hopes were not realised in 1905, but strikes provided a constant thorn in the side of capitalists and government. The authorities responded with limited concessions, particularly in 1905–6, and reaction, most evident from 1907 onwards. The relative quiet of 1907–12 was shattered, however, by a new wave of labour militancy.

The extent to which late imperial Russia was destabilised by the strike activity of the urban workers is a major element of a general debate as to whether

Nicholas II would have been toppled by a popular revolution, even without the impact of the First World War. In a two-part article published in the mid-1960s Leopold Haimson argued that, already by 1914, urban workers were at one end of a polarised society that was heading for a revolutionary upheaval.[33] More recently, other scholars have noted the broad social sympathy for the plight of the urban workers. In the aftermath of the Lena Tragedy, for example, it has been pointed out that influential newspapers and politicians from across the political spectrum accepted that the workers were unfairly denied fundamental rights, and that working conditions had to ameliorated. Pressure from below, including some embarrassing moments for the government in debates in the national parliament, the Duma, led to some progressive measures in the workers' favour. Late imperial Russia was, even if slowly and with marked reluctance from the government, typical of many European societies that were making a transition from forms of autocracy or limited democracy to wider democratic norms. An alliance between workers and other social groups was in the offing and could have avoided the extremes of the eventual Russian Revolution. The workers were one aspect of Russia's growing civil society, a civil society that could have underpinned a different, democratic option for Russia's post-tsarist order.[34]

There are obvious problems with the liberal, consensual, evolutionary model outlined above. A broader consensus in the workers' favour may have been evident in the aftermath of such scandals as the shooting of unarmed workers. But even then it proved impossible to construct a programme of joint activity and resolutions backed by a political bloc from the socialists through to the liberals and left-minded conservatives. Russia's emerging civil society was fractured along social group and interest faultlines. Civil society was vibrant enough to spell the death-knell for tsarism; it was not sufficiently united to concur on a liberal, democratic option. If contemporaries compared Russian developments with conditions elsewhere in Europe, they may not have felt themselves part of common European processes. Russian workers most likely felt themselves worse off than their European equivalents. This may have been one reason why Russian urban workers were more receptive to a radical agenda, voiced in terms of class struggle and a remarkable record of strike militancy, especially in 1905–7, 1912–14 and 1916–17. The urban workers' most immediate political ties, expressed in trade unions and workers' clubs, were with various types of socialists. Of course the workers could also back reactionary political forces, such as the profoundly nationalist and anti-Semitic Black Hundreds. Worker participation in anti-Semitic pogroms has been well documented.[35] Despite the coexistence of progressive and reactionary outlooks, when the urban workers could make their political choices known, they predominantly backed socialist candidates. Indeed, it has argued that in 1917 and elsewhere, the popular programmes and revolutionary language of the urban workers ran ahead of the socialist parties.[36]

Workers often led a hard and brutal life. Such circumstances often resulted in a hard and brutalised workforce, evident in the prevalence of swearing, drunkenness and violence. At its worst the collective action of Russian workers meant involvement in pogroms and support for reactionary political movements. At its best, however, the workers promoted the deeply felt aspirations of the Russian liberation movement for a root and branch democratisation of the autocracy. In 1905 and 1912 it was the massacre of workers that pricked the conscience of the nation. In 1917 it was hungry and dissatisfied workers on the streets that brought the final crisis of autocracy to a head. Although the outcome of the First World War did much to further radicalise the urban workers against the tsar, there seems little reason to doubt R. B. McKean's conclusion that already before 1914 the cause of evolutionary reformism was lost:

> The historical verdict must be that the failure to fashion a sensible, logical, consistent and acceptable strategy of industrial relations rendered extremely doubtful the possibility of a legal labour movement taking root in Russia after 1907. The uncertainties and contradictions of labour policy made a significant contribution to industrial unrest. The combination of limited legality for workers' organisations with erratic and unpredictable repression particularly embittered workers, increased their discontent and their suspicion of and hostility to the authorities.[37]

Notes

Thanks are due to Steve Smith for comments on an earlier version of this chapter. Any errors are the author's responsibility.

1 P. Gatrell, *The Tsarist Economy 1850–1917* (Batsford, 1986), p. 97.
2 For an excellent account of female migrants see, for example, B. A. Engel, *Between the Fields and the City: Women, Work, and Family in Russia, 1861–1914* (Cambridge, 1996).
3 P. Timofeev, 'What the Factory Worker Lives By' in V. Bonnel (ed.), *The Russian Worker: Life and Labor under the Tsarist Regime* (Berkeley, CA, 1983), p. 79.
4 S. I. Kanatchikov, 'From the Story of My Life' in Bonnel (ed.) *The Russian Worker*, p. 40. For a broader analysis of Kantchikov's memoirs see R. E. Zelnik, '"Russian Bebels": An Introduction to the Memoirs of the Russian Workers Semen Kanatchkov and Matvei Fisher', *Russian Review*, 35, 1976, pp. 249–89 and 417–47.
5 F. P. Pavlov, 'Ten Years of Experience' in Bonnel (ed.), *The Russian Worker*, p. 119.
6 Iu. I. Kir'ianov, 'On the Nature of the Russian Working Class', *Soviet Studies in History*, 22(3), 1983–84, pp. 21–2.
7 See, for example, E. Slanskaia, 'House Calls: A Day in the Practice of a Duma Women Doctor in St Petersburg' in T. W. Clyman and J. Vowles (eds), *Russia Through Women's Eyes: Autobiographies from Tsarist Russia* (New Haven, CT, 1996).
8 For an excellent summary of recent research on female urban labour see, for example, J. McDermid and A. Hillyar, *Women and Work in Russia 1880–1930* (London, 1998).

9   For more on child labour see, for example, B. B. Gorshkiv, 'Factory Children:
    An Overview of Child Industrial Labor and Laws in Imperial Russia, 1840–1914'
    in M. Melancon and A. K. Pate (eds), *New Labor History: Worker Identity and
    Experience in Russia, 1840–1918* (Bloomington, IN, 2002).
10 See, for example, the vaudeville skit reproduced in J. von Geldern and L. McRey-
    nolds (eds), *Entertaining Tsarist Russia* (Bloomington, IN, 1998), pp. 183–6.
11 Kanatchikov, 'From the Story of My Life', p. 46.
12 Timofeev, 'What the Factory Worker Lives By', p. 84.
13 E. A. Oliunina, 'The Tailoring Trade in Moscow and the Villages of Moscow and
    Riazan Provinces: Material on the History of the Domestic Industry in Russia' in
    Bonnel (ed.), *The Russian Worker*, pp. 170–1.
14 A. K. Pate, 'Workers and *Obshchestvennost*': St Petersburg, 1906–14', *Revolutionary
    Russia*, 15(2), 2002, p. 67.
15 S. A. Smith, 'Masculinity in Transition: Peasant Migrants to Late-Imperial St
    Petersburg' in B. E. Clements, R. Friedman and D. Healey (eds), *Russian Mas-
    culinities in History and Culture* (Basingstoke, 2002), p. 99. For many of the points
    made in this paragraph see also S. A. Smith, 'The Social Meanings of Swearing:
    Workers and Bad Language in Late Imperial and Early Soviet Russia', *Past and
    Present*, 160, 1998, pp. 167–202.
16 J. Neuberger, 'Stories of the Street: Hooliganism in the St Petersburg Popular Press,
    1900–1905', *Slavic Review*, 48(2), 1989, pp. 177–94.
17 D. R. Brower, 'Labor Violence in Russia in the Late Nineteenth Century', *Slavic
    Review*, 41(3), 1982, pp. 429–30.
18 Kanatchikov, 'From the Story of My Life', p. 41.
19 Brower, 'Labor Violence', pp. 425–6; Smith, 'Masculinity in Transition', pp. 96–7.
20 Pate, 'Workers and *Obshchestvennost*', p. 62.
21 For more on workers and religion see the essays by Page, Herrlinger and S. L.
    Firsov in Melancon and Pate (eds), *New Labor History*.
22 Geldern and McReynolds (eds), *Entertaining Tsarist Russia*, p. 270.
23 For examples of 'ethnic humour' see Geldern and McReynolds (eds), *Entertaining
    Tsarist Russia*, pp. 206–8. The theme of ethnic rivalries in the urban environment
    recurs throughout M. F. Hamm (ed.), *The City in Late Imperial Russia* (Bloom-
    ington, IN, 1986). See, for example, the chapters on Warsaw (S. D. Corrsin), Riga
    (A. Henriksson), Tiflis (R. G. Suny) and Baku (A. Altstadt-Mirhadi).
24 See, for example, M. G. Meierovich, 'On the Sources from which Factory and Plant
    Workers Were Recruited in the Imperialist Era (Based on Data from Iaroslav
    Gubernia)', *Soviet Studies in History*, 19(4), 1981, pp. 43–77.
25 A. Lindenmeyr, *Poverty is Not a Vice: Charity, Society, and the State in Imperial
    Russia* (Princeton, NJ, 1996), p. 232.
26 For quantitative analyses of urban workers' strike activity see, for example, L.
    Haimson and C. Tilly (eds), *Strikes, Wars, and Revolutions in an International
    Perspective* (Cambridge, 1989), esp. chs 6, 7, 8.
27 See, for example, H. Hogan, 'Scientific Management and the Changing Nature
    of Work in the St Petersburg Metalworking Industry, 1900–1914' in Haimson
    and Tily (eds), *Strikes, Wars, and Revolutions*, pp. 356–79; L. H. Haimson, 'Struc-
    tural Processes of Change and Changing Patterns of Labour Unrest: The Case of

the Metal-Processing Industry in Imperial Russia (1890–1914)', in ibid., pp. 380–401.

28 For the most recent account of the Lena Tragedy see M. Melancon, 'Unexpected Consensus: Russian Society and the Lena Massacre, April 1912', *Revolutionary Russia*, 15(2), 2002, pp. 1–52.

29 For the worker-authors see, for example, M. D. Steinberg, 'Worker-Authors and the Cult of the Person' in S. P. Frank and M. D. Steinberg (eds), *Cultures in Flux: Lower-Class Values, Practices, and Resistance in Late Imperial Russia* (Princeton, NJ, 1994), pp. 168–84.

30 Cited in S. A. Smith, 'Workers and Civil Rights, 1899–1917' in O. Crisp and L. Edmondson (eds), *Civil Rights in Imperial Russia* (Oxford, 1989), p. 150. For an example of the range of demands raised by strikes in the late imperial period see, for example, G. L. Freeze, *From Supplication to Revolution: A Documentary Social History of Imperial Russia* (Oxford, 1988), pp. 261–8, 286–96.

31 L. L. Philips, 'Message in a Bottle: Working-Class Culture and the Struggle for Revolutionary Legitimacy, 1900–1929', *Russian Review*, 56(1), 1997, pp. 25–43.

32 S. Smith, 'Class and Gender: Women's Strikes in St Petersburg, 1895–1917 and in Shanghai, 1895–1927', *Social History*, 19(2), 1994, p. 161.

33 L. H. Haimson, 'The Problem of Social Stability in Urban Russia, 1905–1907', *Slavic Review*, 23(4), 1964, pp. 619–42 and *Slavic Review*, 24(1), 1965, pp. 1–22. Haimson has most recently returned to these articles in '"The Problem of Political and Social Stability in Urban Russia on the Eve of War and Revolution" Revisitied', *Slavic Review*, 59(4), 2000, pp. 848–75.

34 These arguments have been placed most recently and most strongly by M. Melancon and A. K. Pate in their above cited articles from *Revolutionary Russia*, 15(2), 2002.

35 See, for example, C. Wynn, *Workers, Strikes, Pogroms* (Princeton, NJ, 1992).

36 See, for example, S. A. Smith, 'Rethinking the Autonomy of Politics: A Rejoinder to John Eric Marot', *Revolutionary Russia*, 8(1), 1995, pp. 104–16.

37 R. B. McKean, 'The Bureaucracy and the Labour Problem, June 1907 – February 1917' in R. B. McKean (ed.), *New Perspectives in Modern Russian History* (New York, 1992), pp. 244–5.

8

Late imperial peasants

David Moon

Introduction

Did peasants become Russians – citizens who identified with a national political community – in late imperial Russia? The conventional view, that they did
not, was summed up in an essay published by Robert McKean in 1996. He
asked whether the peasantry 'remained particularistic down to 1917 – a distinct *soslovie* [legal estate], isolated from or at best incompletely integrated
with civil society and the body politic'. His answer was that the Stolypin
reforms of 1906–11 had failed to solve the problem of the exclusion of the
peasantry, and that the elections to the four Dumas after 1906 and the revolution in the countryside in 1917 strongly suggest that 'peasants were still largely
unconcerned with wider civil and political issues'.[1] This view, however, has
recently been challenged by a number of historians. They have considered the
question in the light of previously underused sources and current academic
literature on national identity. Most recently, in a book published in 2003,
Joshua Sanborn argued strongly that a decisive change occurred in the last
years of late imperial Russia, and that 'unbeknownst to urban intellectuals,
peasants had indeed become Russians'. For Sanborn, it was military service in
the reformed army that was the crucial factor.[2]

The question of peasant identities in various parts of the world in the nineteenth and twentieth centuries has been addressed by many historians. In his
influential book on France published in 1976, Eugen Weber argued that peasant identities were changed as a result of the development of the transport network and urbanisation, schooling, political participation, and military service
in a national conscript army. He argued that these acted as 'agencies of change',
which served as conduits that spread the emerging 'national' culture of the
Third Republic from Paris to the provinces, from the towns to the villages,
from bourgeois France to peasant France. He concluded that, between 1870
and 1914, these factors turned 'peasants into Frenchmen'.[3] Weber's book, while
widely praised, provoked a lively debate. Criticisms focused on four points:
Weber's unilinear model of 'modernisation' or, indeed, 'modernisation theory'
itself; the timing and extent of the changes (some argued they began long

before 1870); the lack of attention to social and political conflict; and, most fundamentally, the portrayal of peasants as largely passive assimilators of changes that came from outside. Writing nearly two decades later, James Lehning approached the question by moving from 'modernisation theory' to discourse, and stressed interaction and mutual perceptions. Weber's 'agencies of change' thus became 'sites' of 'cultural contact' on the landscape of 'the culture of the countryside'. Rather than the town conquering the country or urban France taking over rural France, Lehning suggested that the 'two Frances', 'peasant' and 'French', came together. The improved transport networks, village schools, mass electoral politics, and a national conscript army were the most important points of contact, interaction and negotiation between the nation-state and peasantry. Regardless of the debates inspired by Weber's book over when, how and why peasants became French, few historians dispute the importance of the factors considered by Weber, or deny that, by 1914, the majority of French peasants identified with the French nation-state.[4]

The debates concerning the French peasantry provide a useful lens through which to consider developments at the opposite end of Europe. Historians of late imperial Russia have examined the significance of the factors analysed by Weber, but have reached conflicting conclusions. A group of mostly American historians writing in the 1970s and 1980s argued that, rather than being changed – or perhaps 'nationalised' – by outside influences, Russian peasants played an active role in maintaining aspects of their society, economy and culture by adapting them to fit the changing world of which they were a part. Historians such as John Bushnell emphasised the extent to which peasants 'peasantised' the institutions, such as the army, which, in Weber's interpretation, transformed the peasantry of France.[5] The aim of this chapter is to review the arguments on the 'peasantisation' of Weber's 'agencies of change' in late imperial Russia in the light of more recent work on Russian peasants, such as Sanborn's, which suggests different conclusions.

The transport network and urbanisation

There were major developments in the transport network in late imperial Russia, in particular the construction of railways linking many parts of the vast empire. Railways facilitated greater contact between the villages and urban centres, and contributed to the movement of people from the villages to cities in Russia. The railway boom had an undeniable impact on large sections of the peasantry. Some peasants were hostile. The inhabitants of Sidorskaia township (*volost'*), in the north of the Don Cossack region, thought that 'railways in general are very harmful for mankind', and saw 'absolutely no advantage in them'. Their reaction was not just blind suspicion, however, but because a railway had been built which passed within a few miles of their village and had destroyed the carting trade on which they had relied.[6] Other peasants, however, saw possibilities to make use of the new communication links. Although most peasants, especially those who lived near urban centres or waterways, had long been engaged in some production for the market, the rapid growth of the rail network from the 1860s allowed an expansion of the market for agricultural produce, interregional trade and, therefore, greater regional specialisation. The growth in peasant involvement in the market was uneven. Richer peasants in the Central Non-Black Earth region around Moscow and, especially, the peripheral regions of the North-West, Baltic, Southern Ukraine and Siberia diversified into commercial production of grain, industrial crops such as flax, livestock and dairy produce. Poorer peasants and the rural populations of other regions, in particular the Central Black Earth region, where there were fewer opportunities for marketing agricultural produce, mostly persisted with largely subsistence-orientated grain farming. The improvements in transportation led also to an increase in the numbers of peasants working as migrant labourers (*otkhodniki*) in towns and cities.[7]

The increased contacts between rural and urban life allowed more urban ideas and factory-made products to find their way to Russia's villages. Changes in village life were noted by Olga Semyonova Tian-Shanskaia in her contemporary ethnographic study of a peasant community in Riazan' province in the Central Black Earth region at the turn of the twentieth century. She recorded that peasants who worked in Moscow returned to the villages with 'urban manners', for example addressing young women as 'miss', and brought back 'city clothes', including peaked caps, and wore boots instead of bast footwear. Younger peasants were starting to smoke cigarettes rather than pipes, and many peasants began to carry wallets. Historians writing in the 1970s and 1980s reached similar conclusions. Robert Johnson argued that peasant women who migrated to work in the cities adopted the predominant marriage pattern of the urban population: they married later than their mothers or sisters who had stayed in the villages, and a larger proportion never married. Barbara Engel investigated the lives of the peasant women who were left behind in the villages by male migrants. She showed that, compared with women whose menfolk stayed at home, such women enjoyed a higher standard of living, were more likely to be literate, and had gained greater control over their lives in their families and village communities.[8]

The culture of the Russian peasantry did not simply wither and die under competition from city fashions and urban behaviour, however, but was resilient and proved capable of adapting in order to survive. The main theme of Semyonova's study of village life was continuity rather than change. Peasant men who worked for a while in Moscow maintained the universal and early marriage pattern of peasant Russia. Peasant women who were left behind in the villages by migrant workers were, in Engel's words, 'more closely linked than men to a natural economy and traditional way of life and were far less exposed ... to modern sectors of society'. Furthermore, Anthony Netting showed that peasant craftsmen used new images from urban and industrial life, for example scenes from St Petersburg and paddle steamers, but incorporated them into traditional forms of peasant art together with images that had survived 'from the distant past'.[9]

Peasants who moved to towns and cities used the opportunity of working in urban Russia for their own objectives, which were linked more to the way of life the migrants came from than that of the towns and cities. Johnson raised the question of whether rural migrants in late nineteenth-century Moscow were peasants or proletarians. He argued that most migrants were 'nourished' by their lives and experiences from living in 'two worlds', and felt attached to both village and factory. Much migration, moreover, was 'circular'. Like first-generation urban inhabitants in many societies, the main aim of most peasants who migrated to towns and cities in imperial Russia in the late nineteenth century was to earn enough money to have a better life on their return to their native villages as peasants. The majority of migrants to urban areas left their families behind in the villages because they intended to, and did, return home after a few years. Young, unmarried male peasants who had worked and saved money in the cities were considered desirable partners by village women. John Bushnell argued: 'The tenacity with which peasants held on to their traditional social and economic practices [in the villages] may have had something to do with the increasing availability of by-employment, of migrant or short-term urban labour, of outlets for handicraft production'.[10] In this context, it is important to note not only the resilience and adaptability of Russian peasant society and culture in the face of urban influences, but the fact that the overwhelming majority of peasants chose to remain in the villages and therefore had no direct contact with urban culture. Even in the Central Non-Black Earth region, where migration was most widespread, only 20–25 per cent of villagers were working away from their home villages at the start of the twentieth century, and these included peasants who were working as seasonal agricultural labourers as well as urban workers. The view that change in late imperial Russia was not rapid has also been made by post-Soviet Russian historians. Avenir Korelin and Boris Mironov both argued that, given the rapid growth in the rural population and the extent of land hunger, the rate of peasant migration to cities at the turn of the twentieth century was low.[11]

Parallel to the impact of improved transportation and urban culture on the life of the villages, the rural population, to some extent, 'peasantised' the railways and the cities, and thus maintained their ways of life. Migrant labourers from the villages made up a significant part of the labour force that constructed many of Russia's railways. Peasants began to attach some of their aspirations to the new form of transport, and tried to use it for their own purposes.

The railway between Moscow and St Petersburg was used by peasants seeking to present petitions to the tsar in person. The growth of the railway network, in particular the Trans-Siberian Railway built in the 1890s and 1900s, contributed to the endurance of peasant society and culture by enabling millions of peasants to migrate to less densely populated rural areas beyond the Urals. With adjustments to their new environments, these migrants continued to live much as they had in their original homes.[12]

Peasant-migrants to urban areas took their rural attitudes and behavioural patterns with them, adapted them to city life and, in the short run, changed their new urban environments at least as much as they were altered by them. Travellers from Western Europe, together with members of Moscow's educated elite, had long felt that aspects of life in Moscow were more like those of a 'big village' than a city. From the mid-nineteenth century, moreover, the massive influx of peasant-migrants served to magnify this facet of Moscow. Johnson and Joseph Bradley noted that many of the work patterns and traditions of the Russian peasantry – regional loyalties and specialisations, *arteli* and aspects of rural culture – survived among peasant-migrants in Moscow through such institutions as *zemliachestvo* (district and village clubs or associations). Daniel Brower tentatively concluded that migrants' experiences in the cities were accompanied by an awareness of their 'separateness' on the margins of urban communities rather than a feeling that they were taking part in a 'process of integration of Russian society'. Bradley quoted the conclusion of the compilers of the 1902 municipal census that: 'The tremendous influx of peasants into the capital is more and more turning Moscow into a peasant city'.[13]

A case that urbanisation had a greater impact on peasant-migrants has recently been made by Evel Economakis. In a book published in 1998, he argued that peasant-migrants in St Petersburg were 'urbanised' and 'proletarianised' by their experiences. He paid attention to the growth in household divisions and land sales, and the impact of Stolypin's land reforms in the villages, all of which, he argued, contributed to the severing of ties between migrant workers in the capital city and their former lives as peasants. The growth in the female population of St Petersburg and the increase in the number of marriages between migrants in the city, the reluctance of many unemployed workers to return to their previous homes, and even the growth in ownership of bicycles and dogs, were all presented as evidence for the transformation of the identities of peasant-migrants. While Economakis can be criticised for not interrogating and elucidating his understanding of 'proletarianisation', he made a valuable contribution to the debate by pointing to the significance of migrants' backgrounds and the areas they came from. Thus, migrants who came from poor, agricultural provinces, such as Pskov and Tver', from which peasants were eager to escape, and from provinces that were located a long way from St Petersburg, making temporary return difficult, were more likely to make a break with their peasant identities and rural backgrounds.[14] Economakis focused on the idea of proletarianisation and class identities. What he did not consider, however, was the extent to which their experiences in the imperial capital transformed the peasant-migrants into citizens who identified with a Russian nation. The contrast between his conclusions about St Petersburg, a remote city in the northwest of the empire, and those of historians who considered peasant experiences in Moscow, in the heart of Russia, may suggest that St Petersburg was an exceptional case.

To the extent that peasants in late imperial Russia 'peasantised' the railways and cities more than they were transformed by them, an explanation is called for. A possible reason is suggested by the size of the railway network and the proportion of the population living in cities, both of which were far lower in the Russian Empire than in contemporary France, or indeed elsewhere in Western Europe. In 1914, the Russian Empire had 48,000 miles of railways, a considerable increase on the 17,000 miles in 1885 and, most dramatically, the mere 850 miles in 1855. The total length of France's rail network in 1914 was 41,000 miles, which had increased from 11,000 miles since 1870. Relative to the areas of the two states, however, the French network of railways was much more extensive than the Russian. Furthermore, France had a network of branch lines and good trunk and local roads, all of which were virtually absent in large parts of Russia. Consequently, rural France was substantially better served with transportation links than rural Russia.[15]

There were also considerable differences in the urban populations of the two countries. The proportion of the population of European Russia who lived in cities with over 100,000 inhabitants was only 5 per cent in 1900, and a tiny 1.5 per cent in 1850. In France, however, by the same criterion, 15.4 per cent of the population lived in urban centres in 1900, and 5.8 per cent had done so in 1850. Figures for the urban populations of Russia and France based on broader, but not comparable, definitions, put the percentages on the eve of the First World War at 13–20 per cent and 44 per cent respectively.[16] Not only was Russia's urban population relative to the total population considerably smaller than France's, but much of it was of more recent origin. Migrants from rural areas formed the majority of the population of most of Russia's towns and cities in the late nineteenth and early twentieth centuries as urban centres were deluged by a tidal wave of arrivals from the villages. McKean has demonstrated that: 'At no point . . . between 1881 and 1910 did the native-born inhabitants of [St Petersburg] comprise more than 32 per cent of the population'. In other words, over two-thirds of the population was made up of peasant migrants. In Moscow, throughout the last two decades of the nineteenth century, migrants constituted almost three-quarters of the city's population, and two-thirds were members of the peasant estate.[17]

The massive, and largely transient, populations of peasant-migrants living in Russia's rapidly expanding towns and cities were closer to swamping Russia's tiny urban culture, especially in Moscow, than becoming part of it. In the short term, only a small proportion of peasant-migrants assimilated to urban culture. Moreover, most of the minority of the total peasant population who spent a few years working in a city may have adopted some of the superficial aspects of urban culture, such as urban fashions and manners, and certainly seemed different to their fellow-villagers when they returned home. But how far peasants who had taken advantage of the improved transport networks and had spent time in the Russian Empire's growing towns and cities had changed their attitudes, and begun to consider themselves part of a wider, national community, rather than peasants concerned mainly with their villages, is, at least in the short term, open to question.

Schools

Another important factor in Weber's interpretation of the 'nationalisation' of the French peasantry was schooling. In late imperial Russia, as in contemporary France, village schools served as points of cultural contact and interaction. In the short term, however, Russian peasants seem to have maintained their ways of life and 'peasantised' the schools to a greater extent than formal education transformed them. In the 1890s and, especially, with the laws of 3 May 1908 and 22 June 1909, the Russian state and elites had overcome their long-standing reluctance to make provision for educating peasants, lest they learned to question their station in life, and instead the state came to see illiterate peasants as a greater danger than literate villagers. In the words of Ben Eklof, the author of a study of Russian peasant schools that appeared in the 1980s, the provincial *zemstva* and the Ministry of National Education began to consider schools as important sources of 'military strength, national integration, economic productivity, labour discipline, and political stability'.[18] The government in St Petersburg seems to have been aware of the connection between mass education and the development of a sense of national identity among peasants, and that in the non-Russian parts of the empire this was potentially harmful for the regime. David Saunders has made a strong case that one of the reasons for the severity with which the imperial government tried to stamp out the Ukrainian written language in the second half of the nineteenth century was the fear that Ukrainian intellectuals would be able to use literature in their native language in primary schools to turn Ukrainian peasants into Ukrainian nationalists.[19]

Peasants in late imperial Russia seem to have recognised the value of acquiring literacy and numeracy, and of adapting their ways of life to accommodate and make use of these skills, before the Russian state was prepared to pay for village schools. From the 1860s to the 1890s, the main initiative for building schools and hiring teachers in rural areas came from peasants themselves. Once the *zemstva* and Ministry of National Education began to take over the provision of primary education in the villages, however, peasants were anxious to limit their children's involvement in the schools. Many peasants took their children out of school after only two winters, once they had grasped basic skills, but before they completed the curriculum and received their leaving certificates. Only a very small proportion of peasant children went on to receive secondary education. Peasants were worried their children would be socialised into the culture of educated Russia and would cease, or refuse, to be useful members of their households and village communities. Peasants seem to have recognised that reading, writing and arithmetic are important skills that peasants can acquire and incorporate into village life without substantially changing either the newly literate and numerate peasants or peasant culture. On the other hand, peasants also appear to have realised that it is regular and long-term attendance at formal schools, rather than the acquisition of certain skills, that transforms peoples' attitudes and values. Eklof readily acknowledged that peasants seem to have anticipated conclusions reached by himself and other modern specialists on literacy and education. He concluded:

> Peasants recognized that their children had to learn how to read, write, and count in order to survive in a world increasingly crowded with written documents, but they had no use for the cultural baggage that accompanied basic instruction. Educators wanted to civilize the peasant; villagers wanted to produce children in their own image.

In the late nineteenth century and at the start of the twentieth century, it seems it was peasants who were largely successful in this struggle for the hearts and minds of the village children.[20]

Eklof's conclusions were also anticipated by Semyonova. In her study of a peasant community at the turn of the twentieth century, she wrote that the average peasant was sent to school at the age of ten. She recorded some peasants' comments on literacy: 'He'll be better paid if he can read and write'; 'In Moscow it is more important than here to know reading and writing, and you are judged by your knowledge of it'; and 'It is harder to cheat a literate person'. She also noted, however, that boys forgot their grammar, spelling, history and geography after leaving school, and concluded: 'school fails to change the peasants' view of the life around them'.[21]

Russian village teachers did not match up to the image of 'missionaries' of modern, urban, national culture or 'agents' of the regime that Weber attributed to their French counterparts. According to Eklof, Russian village teachers were 'moderately well prepared for their limited tasks', but enjoyed little respect in the villages and 'did not play an influential role in village culture'. In the 1870s, the Minister of National Education, Count Dmitrii Tol'stoi, had been eager to recruit and train peasants as teachers to avoid the 'contamination' of the villages by urban life. The state was suspicious of village teachers and feared that, rather than providing basic instruction and inculcating feelings of loyalty to tsar and fatherland, they would take advantage of their positions to spread revolutionary ideas.[22]

Whereas Eklof stressed the cultural and social gulf that separated most village teachers from the peasants, and understated the extent to which teachers contributed to the radical politicisation of the peasantry, Scott Seregny took a different line. He argued that, during the 1905 revolution, a minority of teachers and peasants acted together in the political mobilisation of the villages against the regime and in transmitting the peasants' demands to the national stage.[23] Seregny took up directly the issue of whether education transformed 'peasants' into 'Russians' in a recent case study of adult education organised by the *zemstvo* in Ufa province during the First World War. He reached carefully measured conclusions:

> peasants were not transformed into citizens; the foundation of schooling was too shaky, the period of the war was too short, and the adult education audience was too unstable. But it would be difficult to deny that something remarkable was underway. Peasants responded to the zemstvo's campaign in a massive way and this alone should make historians skeptical about stereotypes of the isolated, parochial, static, inward-looking village.[24]

In the years prior to the outbreak of the First World War, there is no question that more Russian peasants than ever before had attended primary schools and could read and write. Jeffrey Brooks's research opened up the rich and exciting world of Russian popular fiction in this period. He identified a strand in this literature that presented new ideas about Russia as a nation and an empire.[25] In spite of Brooks's conclusions, however, it is not certain that peasants were reading this popular literature and, if they were, that they were absorbing the ideas presented.[26]

In spite of Seregny's and Brooks's more positive conclusions about the impact of education and literacy on both children and adult peasants, rural schooling in Russia does not seem to have had the same impact as in France. This may well have been due to the difference in the availability of formal education. In 1914, 51 per cent of the school-age population (aged 8–11) of the Russian Empire attended primary schools. Although this was a considerable increase over the preceding decades, the level of school attendance in imperial Russia in 1914 was well below that of France half a century earlier. The state in late imperial Russia had lagged a long way behind the various regimes of nineteenth-century France, and indeed other Western European states, in legislating and providing the resources for a national network of schools. Primary education in France had been compulsory, and funded, since the 1880s. Moreover, Russian primary schools were less effective, from the state's point of view, than their counterparts in France. Many scholars have concluded that in France, as in other Western European countries, by 1914 primary schools had succeeded in imparting to rural pupils an awareness of a wider society outside their villages and feelings of patriotism. The extent to which, in the short run, this had been achieved in late imperial Russia, however, is open to question.[27]

Political participation

If an argument can be made that the growing transport network and urban areas, together with the increasing numbers of rural schools, were, to some extent and in the short term, 'peasantised' in late imperial Russia, the same cannot be said about politics. The heading of this section is, therefore, a slight misnomer since the point of the following is to stress the extent to which peasants in late imperial Russia were largely excluded from participation in a national political culture. There were no national elections in the Russian Empire until after the 1905 revolution as the tsars sought to retain their autocratic powers. In late imperial Russia, moreover, the hierarchical social structure persisted, surviving the abolition of serfdom in 1861 and the other 'great reforms' of the 1860s and 1870s. Until the downfall of the imperial government in 1917, peasants had a distinct and inferior social status, and were tainted by legal disabilities that prevented them from participating in national politics on the same terms as other sections of the population.[28] In contrast, in France, adult males had had the right to vote in national elections since 1848, and, in time, French peasants began to feel that they could have some impact on national politics.[29]

There seemed little prospect of this in late imperial Russia, but changes were taking place. The long-term objective of the abolition of serfdom and parallel reforms of other categories of peasants had been to create a landed peasantry that was partly responsible for its own self-government rather than subject to the patrimonial authority of noble landowners. The provisions of abolition allowed for the *eventual* merger between the peasantry and other social estates (*sosloviia*). In the meantime, however, peasants were subjected to segregated *soslovie* administration, and the Ministry of Internal Affairs assumed 'stewardship' (*opeka*) over them.[30] Thus, the peasantry continued to have its own, separate systems of local administration and justice after the reforms of the 1860s and 1870s. At local level, peasants administered their own affairs in their village and township (*volost'*) communities. But, ultimately, peasants and their institutions were subordinate to the local administration. In 1889, moreover, the new post of 'land captain' (*zemskii nachal'nik*) gave the local nobility a formal role in supervising peasant affairs.[31]

There were, however, institutions at the local level that did give peasants opportunities to take part in politics with members of other social groups.

In 1861 the government appointed 'peace arbitrators' (*mirovye posredniki*) to supervise the process of undoing the ties that had bound former serfs to their former owners and to mediate between them. This had important implications. As Roxanne Easley, writing in 2002, has concluded:

> The arbitrators . . . brought together peasants and landowners, formerly isolated by a chasm of social, legal, and cultural differences, to resolve crucial issues of property and to redraw their political relationship. The arbitrator invited or compelled each group to articulate its own program of interests in the disputes that he adjudicated. Landowners could no longer automatically rely on social privilege or the immediate satisfaction of their demands, and peasants could no longer depend on the myth of the passive and ignorant muzhik to achieve their aims. Instead, the two estates, brought to nearly the same legal level, had to rely on their ability to communicate and to compromise.

Although the post of peace arbitrator was abolished in 1874, the institution had 'nevertheless opened a new public arena of competing factions, communication, and negotiation. The state could blight this growth, but it could not uproot it.'[32]

Peasants also interacted with wider society through the law. This has been the subject of much research in recent years which, amongst other things, suggests interesting conclusions about peasant identities. Despite the fact that peasants had their own, separate system of justice and *volost'* courts, peasants could, and did, appeal to higher bodies. (Indeed, this was part of a centuries-old tradition of peasant petitions and complaints to the authorities.) In a detailed analysis of peasant appeals in the years 1891–1917, Gareth Popkins has recently suggested that while, on the one hand, 'an appeal might be an attempt to co-opt state power on local terms for personal local ends . . ., [a]t the same time, in their contacts with the [provincial] boards and congresses [of land captains], villagers were engaging with a system far outside the village and the *volost'*'. Other historians of peasant legal culture have taken the argument a stage further. Jane Burbank argued that the extent of peasant participation in the system and processes of *volost'* courts enabled them to 'acquire an identity as citizens'.[33]

Another arena for peasant involvement in local politics with members of other groups in society was the elected district and provincial councils (*zemstva*) set up after 1864. Peasant representatives sat down with nobles and others in the *zemstva*, took part in discussions, and sought to protect their interests, especially insofar as taxation by the new councils was concerned. Peasants, however, were grossly under-represented relative to their numbers due to the deliberate weighting of the franchise heavily in favour of nobles. Peasant under-representation was increased further by the 'counter-reform' of 1890. Thus, in practice, the *zemstvo* served to protect the predominance of the nobility in local affairs. In the words of Dorothy Atkinson: 'The *zemstvo* presented an unparalleled opportunity to integrate Russian society and to integrate state and society, but the principles on which integration might have been possible were contradictory to those on which the social and political systems rested'.[34]

At the same time as some peasants were struggling to make the most of the limited opportunities for them to take part in politics, there was considerable discussion within the central government concerning the long-term problem of the peasantry's exclusion from the emerging political culture of post-reform Russia. Francis Wcislo, in a book published in 1990, argued that bureaucratic reformers wanted to work for the gradual transformation of Russia from an autocratic state governing a 'particularistic society of estates (*sosloviia*)' to a 'national state governing a civil society'. Wcislo attributed the failure of attempts to reform the administration of rural Russia to two factors. Firstly, there was a conflict between reforms aimed at promoting the values of civic culture in rural public life and the political culture of the autocracy and of a society of estates. Secondly, reforms foundered in the face of staunch traditionalist opposition from advocates of ministerial police power who feared the consequences of reforms, and from conservative provincial nobles who retained a particularistic outlook and wished to preserve their place in the social and political order.

In the view of many officials, however, peasants were not yet 'ready' 'to assimilate the responsibilities of civil freedom' or 'for life in civil society'. Left to themselves, it was believed, they would cultivate their land but shirk public responsibilities. The Kakhanov Commission of the early 1880s was critical of the *soslovie* system of administration for the peasantry because it perpetuated their isolation from the rest of the society and failed to provide adequate supervision. The Commission proposed the retention of the commune, but its conversion into an all-*soslovie* administrative institution. The members of the Commission concluded that the peasantry still needed special 'protection'. They were, however, 'optimistic' about the prospects for 'acculturation' of the peasantry, believing that the necessary changes could be fostered by improving peasants' civil rights and the structure of rural administration. Rather less optimism was expressed by the opponents of the Kakhanov Commission's proposals, and by bureaucratic opponents of rural civil and political reform in the second half of the nineteenth century. These opinions were part of the motivation behind the creation of the post of 'land captain' in 1889. David Macey argued that the majority of members of the State Council in the early 1890s believed, in effect, that peasants did not possess free will, but were dependent on custom and culture. They therefore believed that it would be impossible to implement radical changes. At the very end of the nineteenth century, Sergei Witte began to see that the way ahead lay in bringing peasants 'up' to the cultural level of educated Russians to pave the way for their incorporation into national political life.[35] Thus, in a sense, government officials in the late nineteenth century anticipated the debate by historians a century later over whether peasants were becoming 'Russians'.

A further reason for the continued segregation of the peasantry by the government was financial. In 1858 the government committed itself to a landed abolition of serfdom with compensation for the landowners. In early 1859 the government was considering extending considerable monetary assistance to finance part of the redemption operation. In the wake of the serious banking crisis of 1859, however, financial aid had to be abandoned, and the entire cost put on the shoulders of the peasantry. The peasants were thus burdened with massive, long-term debts in redemption payments to the government and remained tied to the land, through their village communes, until they had paid these debts.[36] A major factor determining government policy towards the peasantry in the late nineteenth century was, therefore, a concern to make sure peasants kept up with their redemption payments. Moreover, since the peasant population produced most of the agricultural produce in Russia, for both domestic consumption and export, and was a major source of tax revenue, the government was very concerned lest any reform inadvertently led to the impoverishment of agriculture or threatened receipts of redemption payments or taxes. The government was caught between two stools. The rate of population growth made agrarian (i.e. land) or agricultural (i.e. the techniques of farming) reform an ever more pressing issue as land hunger and the perception of rural poverty grew. On the other hand, fears that agrarian reform could lead to the creation of a class of impoverished, landless labourers and could thus threaten fiscal stability were arguments against change. Until the first decade of the twentieth century, the government responded to this dilemma by supporting the existing rural institutions and communal land tenure. The members of village communes remained collectively responsible for their redemption payments until 1903, and the payments themselves continued until 1907. Until 1906, moreover, peasants needed internal passports when they travelled beyond their home villages.[37]

When political change at the centre did take place in the wake of the 1905 revolution, and after the redemption payments came to an end on 1 January 1907, peasants were still discriminated against as, at best, second-class citizens. The electoral law of December 1905 granted fairly broad adult male suffrage, but divided the population into curias with the aim of greatly reducing the weight of the votes of the peasantry and other low-status groups. The vote of one nobleman was the equivalent of those of fifteen peasants. The government was being extremely cautious since it initially assumed that peasants would vote for candidates loyal to the tsar. This proved to be wrong. At the elections to the first two Dumas, peasants voted overwhelmingly for candidates who were opposed to the government. This was one of the reasons for Stolypin's 'coup d'état' of June 1907, when he issued a new electoral law that further diluted the weight of peasant votes. Wcislo concluded:

Even officials who hoped that facilitating the evolutionary development of Russian society would allow a reformed autocracy to survive the demands of the twentieth century cautiously trod the line that divided civil progress – which state power, law, and institutions could control and supervise – from the unaccultur- ated world of peasant 'land and liberty' that potentially threatened to explode the civic culture whose isolation these reformers felt so acutely. To that extent, reformist initiatives, far-reaching as they were, hesitated to go too far toward the mass politics that were beginning to dominate Europe in the early twentieth cen- tury. The paradox of Stolypin – a statesman dedicated to the social and political reconstruction of autocratic Russia, who undertook a coup d'etat to effect such change – testified most poignantly to the self-imposed constraints of the reformist perspective.[38]

The government in late imperial Russia was continually concerned not only that the world of peasant 'land and liberty' would erupt and upset their plans for cautious change, but that the growing revolutionary movement, consisting mostly of intellectuals, would succeed in making common cause with the mass of the peasantry and the growing urban population against the autocratic regime in both its pre- and post-1905 forms. Early efforts by radical opponents of the regime to win the peasantry over to the side of the revolution were bedeviled by intellectual preconceptions about the peasants' allegedly low cul- tural level. The Decembrists did not try to explain their objectives to the mass of the population, not even to the peasant-soldiers in their own regiments. Historians have long claimed that peasants did not understand the Populists who 'went to people' in 1870s, and handed them over to the police. They attrib- uted the peasants' 'refusal to respond' to the Populists' preachings in part to the '[vast] cultural and social chasm' between society and people (*narod*). Recent work on the Populist 'movement to the people' has suggested, however, that the educated radicals met with rather more resonance among the peasants than has previously been argued. Daniel Field, moreover, denied that peasants handed them over to the police. In the early twentieth century, moreover, the SRs – with their programme of socialisation of the land – managed to estab- lish closer links with peasants than their Populist predecessors.[39]

In spite of the caution of the electoral law of 1905, and the decision of the SRs to boycott the first elections, the votes of the peasantry ensured that the majorities in both the first two Dumas were in favour of an extension of the franchise, an end to the system of voting by curia, and the compulsory trans- fer of land owned by the nobility, the state and the church to the peasantry. However, their demands were rejected and the first two Dumas dismissed. Instead, Stolypin curtailed the franchise and imposed his more conservative land reform. Instead of a wholesale distribution of non-peasant land to the peasantry, the main part of Stolypin's reforms envisaged a redistribution of land within peasant communities with the aim of effecting gradual change in the social structure of the countryside. Stolypin's reforms allowed peasants to withdraw from their village communes and consolidate their land allotments. He hoped, in time, to create in rural Russia a class of independent, prosperous husbandmen and loyal citizens who would have a stake in the existing order and be a force for stability.[40]

In a recent monograph, Judith Pallot has pointed to many examples of peasants seeking to subvert the Stolypin reforms by recourse to customary peasant 'weapons of the weak'. For example, whole villages carried out community-wide consolidations of their land in order to prevent a few peasants from breaking away. Other communes took steps, including intimidation, to prevent members from separating, or tried to undo enclosures by removing boundary markers and symbolically re-possessing the land. Many of those who did separate from their villages did so for reasons other than those envisaged by Stolypin. Some saw opportunities in separating. Under the communal and repartitional land tenure that prevailed in much of central Russia, households that had lost members, for example through death or the departure of married sons, also lost entitlements to shares of the communal land. It made sense, therefore, for such households to use the reform to acquire the full titles to all their existing land before parts were taken away from them. Likewise, households with disproportionate shares of better-quality land had an incentive to separate. A number of households acquired the titles to their land in order to sell it before moving to a city or Siberia. Thus, Pallot's conclusions seriously undermine arguments for the potential success of the reforms based simply on numbers of peasants who separated. Pallot's explanation for the peasants' responses to the reform lies in the gap between the reformers' conviction in the incontrovertible benefits of enclosure and 'farm modernisation', compared with what they saw as the 'backward' traditions of the 'ignorant' peasantry, and most peasants' equally strong beliefs in the efficacy of the customary ways in which they held and cultivated their land. There was no serious attempt by the reformers to seek the views of the peasants on the proposed measures before they were implemented. Pallot concluded: 'Conceived as a broad measure to modernize peasant farming and create a loyal peasantry, the final verdict on the Stolypin Reform must be that it was too narrowly conceived to be able to deliver this result'.[41] This must also serve as the verdict on the extent to which the reform contributed to the process of transforming peasants into 'Russians', thus supporting the argument made by McKean quoted in the introduction to this chapter.

In the years after 1907, most peasants became increasingly indifferent to a 'constitutional regime' in which they had very limited representation and that had not addressed their grievances in the way they wanted, and seemed unlikely to do so in the future. It was not that peasants were unaware of national politics or did not want to take part – Russian peasants had long had a good sense of what was going on in national politics and had tried to articulate their interests by the limited means available to them.[42] Nor did peasants lack the necessary experience – they had served on district and provincial *zemstva* since the 1860s. Rather, peasants in late imperial Russia, as in earlier periods, were excluded from participating in politics at national level in any meaningful way.[43]

Military service

The government of late imperial Russia may have prevented peasants from playing a meaningful part in national politics, but it was very keen to conscript young peasant men into its armed forces. Sanborn recently noted the need to engage in 'mass politics in order to achieve mass mobilization', but pointed out that the Russian state did not do this before 1914.[44] The system of conscription into the Russian army underwent major reforms in the late nineteenth century. The ranks of the army prior to the reform of 1874 were filled by men from only the lower social estates (chiefly the peasantry). In the first half of the nineteenth century men were drafted for terms of 20–25 years. Legally, recruits ceased to be members of their old social estates and became part of a separate caste of soldiers. Although the hierarchical structure of the army – with noble-officers and peasant-soldiers – mirrored that of Russian society at large, military training was fairly effective in converting peasant-recruits into soldiers. Moreover, only a few soldiers who completed their terms of service returned to their villages and resumed their old lives as peasants. Conscription was a significant drain on the rural population, especially in wartime when extra levies were raised, but in peacetime under 1 per cent of all male peasants was drafted each year. Peasants dreaded the prospect of conscription, looked on military service as a life sentence to penal servitude, and did anything they could, including self-mutilation, to evade it.[45] Thus, the pre-reform system of recruitment served to alienate the mass of the peasantry from the state.

Russia's humiliating defeat in the Crimean War in the mid-1850s convinced the authorities of the need to reform the army and, in particular, a system of recruitment that did not make provision for a significant trained reserve that could be called up when needed. Dmitrii Miliutin's military service reform of 1874 ended the principle of conscripting only the lower orders, and made all male subjects, regardless of their social estates, eligible for military service in the ranks when they reached the age of 20. The term of active service was reduced to six years with an additional nine years in the reserve. The period of active service was reduced in stages to three years by 1906, but the time spent in the reserve was increased. Men remained members of their original social estate during their military service, and most returned to their previous lives afterwards. Men were entitled to serve for shorter terms if they had received formal education or could read and write. For example, at the top end of the scale, university graduates served for only six months. This was a concession to the nobility, who resented their sons having to serve alongside the lowly peasants who made up the overwhelming majority of rank-and-file soldiers. William Fuller has argued that Miliutin also intended this measure to spur peasants to educate their sons. Eklof has suggested that it succeeded. In general, Miliutin hoped that, together with the other 'great reforms' of the 1860s and 1870s, his reform of military service 'would make all Russians equal subjects of the Tsar and citizens of a united Russia' and that the army would become the 'school of the nation'.[46]

The reformed Russian army may have encouraged peasant literacy and education, but, at least in the short term, it was less successful in socialising the Russian peasantry into a national culture. In contrast to France, where from the introduction of universal conscription in 1889 most young men were called up, only just over a quarter of 20-year-old Russians were drafted into the army each year. The 1874 law in Russia allowed liberal exemptions on grounds of ethnicity (some ethnic groups, e.g. Finns and Central Asians, were originally excluded), and on account of family circumstances (for example, only sons and sole breadwinners were exempt). In addition, men of draft age drew lots to decide who would go into the army and who would remain at home. As well as a genuine concern not to alienate some ethnic groups or to ruin peasant families, the state simply did not have the resources to conscript and train the entire male population. By 1905, only 20 per cent of adult males aged over 27 had served in the army and returned to civilian life. Financial constraints also meant that the classes envisaged by the law of 1874 to instruct recruits in basic literacy were dropped in the 1880s. Fuller has made a case that, after 1881, the Russian government preferred to spend its money on railways and investment in industry than its military forces.

The 1874 reform did not end the peasantry's customary reluctance to serve in the army. Peasants were all too well aware that the new recruitment system still favoured the nobles and emerging middle classes. General Golovin believed that the continued inequities of the recruitment system 'made it impossible to inculcate a sense of the duty of every citizen to defend his fatherland'. Allan Wildman argued that Russian peasants 'remained unmoved by the idea of a "nation at arms"'. He compared Russians' patriotic motivation to serve unfavourably with that of the populations of France, Britain and Germany, and concluded that, at the turn of the twentieth century, the Russian army:

> lacked the supportive institutions and attitudes of the society as a whole. It served
> primarily as an instrument to preserve the outmoded autocratic system, and the
> social classes upon which it increasingly depended to service its various functions
> could not but look upon it as an alien growth.[47]

In an influential article published in 1980 tellingly titled 'Peasants in Uniform', Bushnell argued that in the late nineteenth century and early years of the twentieth century, peasant-conscripts to some extent 'peasantised' the reformed Russian army in much the same way that peasant-migrants transformed the growing cities and peasants assimilated the village schools. He investigated the extent to which the army of late tsarist Russia acted as a 'modernizing institution', asking whether army service was 'a qualitatively new experience for peasants', which brought them 'into contact with a world beyond their villages'. Peasant-recruits were certainly disorientated by their first few months in the army, during which it was impressed on them that they had to 'speak, look, turn and move with military precision'. Once basic training was completed, however, soldiers spent most of their time working to support the regimental economy. Wherever and whenever possible, regiments grew and cooked their own food and made their own uniforms. Some soldiers were sent to work as labourers in the civilian economy to earn money for the regimental coffers. Officers used soldiers as servants and lackeys. Some noble officers treated their men in a manner similar to the way their forebears had treated their serfs. Bushnell argued that, down to 1905 and beyond, the officers and men in the Russian army were, and remained, representatives of 'two Russias' with two different, conflicting, and mutually uncomprehending cultures. The soldiers ran their own lives through *arteli* of *zemliaki* (men from the same or neighbouring villages). Thus, life in the reformed army for most peasant-soldiers replicated their experiences of peasant life in the villages or as migrant labourers to such an extent that Bushnell concluded: 'it is scarcely credible that military service could have done much to reshape peasant mentality', and 'the world of the Russian soldier bore a strong resemblance to the world of the Russian peasant.'[48]

In Bushnell's interpretation, therefore, the Russian army was less successful than its French counterpart in creating the conditions for the emergence of a new national culture. After the reforms of 1874 in Russia and 1889 in France, a much smaller proportion of the respective populations served in the Russian army than in the French army. The differences were, in part, a result of the relative underfunding of the Russian army. Fuller has shown that while the proportion of Russian state expenditure allocated to the army fell after 1881, in France it remained fairly constant. Overall, Russia's outlay on its army was roughly the same as France's, but since the Russian army was almost twice as large, the Russian state spent less per soldier than the French.[49]

A different interpretation has recently been put forward by Sanborn, who saw the military service reform of 1874 as the start of a long-term process that led eventually to the 'drafting of the Russian nation'. Military officers and state bureaucrats, as well as conscripts and their families, contributed to a transformation of the status of soldiers from pariahs at the bottom of the social heap to citizen-soldiers who were held up as 'paragons' for their service in defence of their families and fatherland, and who, in return, received 'rights' and 'benefits'. Military modernisers in late imperial Russia believed that 'only nations could win modern wars', and therefore advocated 'an inclusive, multiethnic, multiclass army that would grow inclusive over time'. To this end, in spite of conservative opposition, conscription was in time extended to previously exempt ethnic groups. Sanborn stressed the importance of mass conscription and state-sanctioned, organised violence by conscripts in a mass national army in contributing to a change in the identities of Russian peasant-soldiers and the construction of a national identity. He gave a particular emphasis to the role of the First World War in accelerating these developments. On the basis of his analysis of letters from soldiers and civilians during the war, in which they insisted on 'fairness' and 'equality' in the application of conscription in the nation as a whole, he suggested that 'traditional egalitarianism corresponded rather nicely with the idea of equality of citizens that lay at the heart of national ideology'. He concluded that 'peasant consciousness' had broadened from the parochial to the national, and that 'peasants had indeed become Russians'.[50]

Sanborn's book deserves much praise and prompts many questions. A critic might ask how far the peasants and soldiers protesting about conscription during the First World War were taking advantage of a national situation and using national language to pursue their own goals as peasants, e.g. the return of a son, husband or brother from the army. Over half a century earlier, during the Crimean War, thousands of serfs sought to take advantage of the state's need for manpower by seeking, illegally, to volunteer for service in short-term militia. Analysis of the 'volunteer phenomenon' of the mid-1850s suggests that the would-be militiamen were hoping to attain exemption from the long term of conscription into the regular army and freedom from serfdom.[51] Over a generation earlier, moreover, at the end of the Napoleonic Wars in 1814, demobilised militiamen refused to return to their former, servile status, in the belief or hope that they had earned freedom by their military service to the state.[52] Thus, peasants had a tradition of using military service in wartime as lever to extract concessions from the state. In particular, peasant-soldiers demanded that their status be raised to that of other members of the population. A potentially interesting line of enquiry would be to ask whether these earlier generations of peasants were anticipating their descendants' demands for equality as citizens of a nation-state? If it can be demonstrated that they had a national rather than particularistic sense of identity, then can the origins of the changes Sanborn identified be traced back to the early nineteenth century, long before the military service reform of 1874?

Alternatively, were Sanborn's peasants simply continuing to conduct themselves in ways their forebears would recognise? A recent article by a Russian historian, A. B. Astashov, who also examined soldiers' letters, as well as censors' reports on letters, to some extent supports this view, but also provides evidence for change. In analysing themes in the letters, Astashov looked back to pre-war peasant culture as well as forward to new developments. Thus, he identified striking parallels between soldiers' views on the seasonality of military campaigns and the seasonality of agricultural work. He also saw older peasant views in soldiers' attitudes to the tsar, to their home villages, to drinking, and also in the growth of desertion. In addition, however, Astashov detected the start of new attitudes over the course of the war. By 1917, soldiers were linking the defence of the 'motherland' against the external enemy with the need to defend the revolution and 'freedom' against the 'internal enemy', often identified as the 'bourgeoisie'.[53] Thus, Astashov reached more measured conclusions than Sanborn from a similar body of evidence. Other recent historians, moreover, have continued to find evidence for the limited development of a sense of national identity during the First World War. Hubertus Jahn, who investigated Russian popular culture during the war, concluded that: 'Most Russians did not see themselves as loyal subjects of the empire', and there was 'no functioning integrative ideology of a common nation'.[54]

Conclusion

Thus, historians have continued to put forward different views of the extent to which peasants in late imperial Russia changed, and whether they developed a sense of citizenship and identity with a Russian nation. In this chapter, attention has focused on the role of the four factors which Eugen Weber considered as 'agencies of change' in contemporary France: improved transport networks and urbanisation, the development of schooling, political participation, and military service in a national conscript army. A number of historians, writing mostly in the 1970s and 1980s, put forward arguments that peasants in late imperial Russia transformed or 'peasantised' these factors rather more than they were changed by them. More recently, however, some scholars have started to put forward a case for change in peasant attitudes and culture in the last decades of imperial Russia. While some historians, for example Economakis, have paid attention to class identities, others have focused directly on national identities. Steve Smith, who is one the scholars putting forward a case for change and the emergence of identity with the nation, has made the suggestion, well worth deeper investigation, 'that [in 1917] class identity ultimately proved ephemeral, whereas Russian national identity proved to be surprisingly robust'.[55]

The emerging debate between the older view of 'peasantisation' and the newer argument for the emergence of national identities is not beyond resolution. The older interpretation that emphasised the persistence of peasant culture is not impervious to adaptation to deal with the arguments for change.

One approach to resolving the two sides in the debate, not undertaken in this chapter for reasons of space, would be to consider regional differences. It is possible that changes were more rapid among peasants in regions closer to big cities than in more remote regions. However, Seregny's study of adult education in Ufa province, in the far off southern Urals region, cautions against too simple conclusions in this regard. A further approach is to disaggregate the peasantry by generation. It is clear from the analysis presented above that it was the younger generation of peasants which was most affected by, and played the largest part in, the changes in late imperial Russia. The older generation, in contrast, was more likely to remain in the villages, less likely to have the opportunity for formal education (notwithstanding opportunities for adult education), and those of the older generation of men who had served in the reformed army had long since returned home. This approach leads to a consideration of patterns in the attitudes of the rural population over time. A distinction can be made between the short term, until the turn of the twentieth century, and the longer term, up to and including the more dramatic developments of 1914–17. It can be argued that, in the short term, peasants maintained and adapted aspects of their culture in response to the changing world of which they were a part. In the longer term, however, peasants began to alter or transform their culture as increasing numbers travelled more, spent more time in towns and cities, attended schools, learned to read, started to learn from reading, took what limited opportunities they had to take part in political life, and served as conscripts in a national army. This approach can be developed further to tighten the focus on the First World War. Some of the recent research, both on peasants serving in the armed forces and on peasants in the villages, suggests that the experience of the war accelerated and developed tendencies which can be noted in the pre-war years. Finally, the debate over whether Weber's 'agencies of change' were 'peasantised' or indeed imparted a sense of national identity on peasants may be based on a false premise. Sanborn made the important point, drawing on Lehning's argument for 'cultural contact' in contemporary France, that '"peasantization" [should not] preclude the building up potential national energy', and that '[t]hough institutions may have been "peasantized" in Russia, this does not imply that they were thereby rendered nonnational'.[56]

In conclusion, the older view – that Russian peasants 'peasantised' the 'agencies' which for Weber 'nationalised' the French peasantry – suggests a sharp contrast between Russia and France in terms of the evolution of national political communities that incorporated the rural population in the late nineteenth and early twentieth centuries. More recent interpretations significantly modify this contrast. Lehning argued that 'peasant' and 'French' identities were not in conflict but came together. This idea has informed some of the newer work on the Russian peasantry, such as Sanborn's, which sees processes of change in the identities of peasants as they interacted with the outside world. The contrast between peasants in Russia and France, and indeed peasants in other parts of the globe, seems not to be as great. Thus, towards the end of imperial Russia, peasants did start, slowly and gradually, to construct newer, wider identities as they sought to adapt to and deal with the changing world of which they were a part.

Notes

The author would like to thank Frank Cass publishers and the editor of the journal for permission to reprint revised sections of his article: 'Peasants into Russian citizens? A Comparative Perspective', *Revolutionary Russia*, 9, 1996, pp. 43–81.

1   R. B.McKean, 'Constitutional Russia', *Revolutionary Russia*, 9, 1996, pp. 33–42.
2   J. A. Sanborn, *Drafting the Russian Nation: Military Conscription, Total War, and Mass Politics, 1905–1925* (DeKalb, IL, 2003), quotation from p. 38. See also J. A. Sanborn, 'The Mobilization of 1914 and the Question of the Russian Nation: A Re-examination', *Slavic Review*, 59, 2000, pp. 267–89; J. A. Sanborn, 'More Than Imagined: A Few Notes on Modern Identities', ibid., pp. 330–5. For another approach, analysing the meaning of local festivities, see C. J. Chulos, *Converging Worlds: Religion and Community in Peasant Russia, 1861–1917* (DeKalb, IL, 2003).
3   E. Weber, *Peasants into Frenchmen: The Modernization of Rural France, 1870–1914* (Stanford, CA, 1976).
4   J. R. Lehning, *Peasant and French: Cultural Contact in Rural France during the Nineteenth Century* (Cambridge, 1995). See also C. Tilly, 'Did the Cake of Custom Break?' in J. M. Merriman (ed.), *Consciousness and Class Experience in Nineteenth-Century Europe* (London, 1979), pp.17–44; R. Magraw, *France 1815–1914: The Bourgeois Century* (London, 1983), pp. 18, 92, 106, 108–14, 141–55, 312–32, 345–50; J. Merriman, Review, *Journal of Modern History*, 50, 1978, pp. 534–6; P. McPhee, *The Politics of Rural Life: Political Mobilization in the French Countryside 1846–1852* (Oxford, 1992), esp. pp. 16–17, 227–42, 260–76. For a discussion of Weber's book by Russian and Western historians, see V. V. Babashkin, 'Sovremennye kontseptsii agrarnogo razvitiia: teoreticheskii seminar', *Otechestvennaia istoriia*, 2, 1997, pp. 39–60.
5   For examples of this work, including Bushnell's article, see B. Eklof and S. Frank (eds), *The World of the Russian Peasant: Post–Emancipation Culture and Society* (London, 1990). For a recent survey of the literature, see A. Karagodin, 'Velikorusskii pakhar' at the Global Village: Comparing Methods and Approaches in Western and Russian Historiographies of the Post-Emancipation Russian Peasantry', *Revolutionary Russia*, 15, 2002. For a broader discussion of continuity and change in peasant society in this period, see D. Moon, *The Russian Peasantry, 1600–1930: The World the Peasants Made* (London, 1999), pp. 325–55.
6   I. Timoshchenkov, 'Sidorskaia volost' (Ust'–Medveditskogo okruga). Statistichesko-etnograficheskii ocherk', *Sbornik Oblastnogo Voiska Donskogo Statisticheskogo Komiteta*, 5, 1905, p. 76.
7   See P. Gatrell, *The Tsarist Economy 1850–1917* (London, 1986), pp. 128–40; E. Melton, 'Proto-Industrialization, Serf Agriculture and Agrarian Social Structure:

Two Estates in Nineteenth Century Russia', *Past and Present*, 115, 1987, pp. 69–106; J. Metzer, 'Railroad Development and Market Integration: The Case of Tsarist Russia', *Journal of Economic History*, 34, 1974, pp. 529–50.

8 O. Semyonova Tian-Shanskaia, *Village Life in Late Tsarist Russia*, ed. D. L. Ransel (Bloomington, IN, 1993), pp. 37, 55, 141–2, 146; R. E. Johnson, *Peasant and Proletarian: The Working Class of Moscow in the Late Nineteenth Century* (Leicester, 1979), pp. 56–61; B. A. Engel, 'The Woman's Side: Male Out-Migration and the Family Economy in Kostroma Province' in Eklof and Frank (eds), *The World of the Russian Peasant*, p. 74. See also B. A. Engel, *Between the Fields and the City: Women, Work and Family in Russia, 1861–1914* (Cambridge, 1994).

9 Johnson, *Peasant and Proletarian*, pp. 56–61; Engel, 'The Woman's Side', p. 74; A. Netting, 'Images and Ideas in Russian Peasant Art' in Eklof and Frank (eds), *The World of the Russian Peasant*, pp. 169–88.

10 Bushnell, 'Peasant Economy and Peasant Revolution at the Turn of the Century: Neither Immiseration nor Autonomy', *Russian Review*, 46, 1987, p. 82; Johnson, *Peasant and Proletarian*; J. H. Bater, 'Transience, Residential Persistence, and Mobility in Moscow and St Petersburg, 1900–1914', *Slavic Review*, 39, 1980, pp. 239–54.

11 A. P. Korelin, 'The Social Problem in Russia, 1906–1914: Stolypin's Agrarian Reform' in T. Taranovski (ed.), *Reform in Modern Russian History: Progress or Cycle?* (Cambridge, 1995), pp. 143, 158; B. N. Mironov, *Sotsial'naia istoriia Rossii (XVIII–nachalo XX vv.)*, 2 vols (St Petersburg, 1999), vol. 1, p. 247.

12 See D. Moon, *Russian Peasants and Tsarist Legislation on the Eve of Reform, 1825–1855* (London, 1992), pp. 145–6; D. Moon, 'Peasant Migration and the Settlement of Russia's Frontiers, 1550–1897', *Historical Journal*, 30, 1997, pp. 859–93; S. G. Marks, *Road to Power: The Trans-Siberian Railroad and the Colonization of Asian Russia, 1850–1917* (Ithaca, NY, 1991).

13 See J. Bradley, *Muzhik and Muscovite: Urbanization in Late Imperial Russia* (Berkeley, CA, 1985) (quotation from p. 347); D. R. Brower, *The Russian City between Tradition and Modernity 1850–1900* (Berkeley, CA, 1990), esp. pp. 75–91; J. Cracraft, *The Petrine Revolution in Russian Architecture* (London, 1988), pp. 20–6, 33–7, 255–7; Engel, *Between the Fields and the City*, pp. 3, 44, 98–9; Johnson, *Peasant and Proletarian*; Semyonova, *Village Life in Late Tsarist Russia*, pp. 55, 145.

14 E. G. Economakis, *From Peasant to Petersburger* (London, 1998).

15 See Magraw, *France 1815–1914*, p. 318; H. Rogger, *Russia in the Age of Modernisation and Revolution* (London, 1983), p. 105; Engel, *Between the Fields and the City*, p. 1.

16 Tilly, 'Did the Cake of Custom Break?', pp. 26–7; R. Price, *A Concise History of France* (Cambridge, 1993), p. 154; Rogger, *Russia in the Age of Modernisation and Revolution*, pp. 125–6, 131.

17 R. B. McKean, *St Petersburg Between the Revolutions: Workers and Revolutionaries June 1907 – February 1917* (London, 1990), p. 16; Bradley, *Muzhik and Muscovite*, p. 4.

18 B. Eklof, *Russian Peasant Schools: Officialdom, Village Culture, and Popular Pedagogy, 1861–1914* (Berkeley, CA, 1986), esp. pp. 70–119, 471–82 (quotation from p. 472).

19 D. Saunders, 'Russia's Ukrainian Policy (1847–1905): A Demographic Approach', *European History Quarterly*, 25, 1995, pp. 181–208.

20 Eklof, *Russian Peasant Schools*, esp. pp. 70–119, 471–82 (quotation from p. 476). On the relatively small number of peasants who had received secondary education in 1897, see D. Moon, 'Estimating the Peasant Population of Late Imperial Russia from the 1897 Census: A Research Note', *Europe–Asia Studies*, 48, 1996, p. 145.
21 Semyonova, *Village Life in Late Tsarist Russia*, pp. 44–5.
22 Eklof, *Russian Peasant Schools*, pp. 179–248, 480–1.
23 S. J. Seregny, *Russian Teachers and Peasant Revolution: The Politics of Education in 1905* (Bloomington, IN, 1989).
24 S. J. Seregny, 'Zemstvos, Peasants, and Citizenship: The Russian Adult Education Movement and World War I', *Slavic Review*, 59, 2000, pp. 313–14.
25 J. Brooks, *When Russia Learned to Read: Literacy and Popular Literature, 1981–1917* (Princeton, NJ, 1985), pp. 214–45.
26 See Seregny, 'Zemstvos, Peasants, and Citizenship', p. 290.
27 See Eklof, *Russian Peasant Schools*, pp. 55, 70–96, 291–3, 419–20, 474–82; Seregny, *Russian Teachers and Peasant Revolution*, pp. 7–8, 207–8; Lehning, *Peasant and French*, p. 136.
28 See G. L. Freeze, 'The *Soslovie* (Estate) Paradigm and Russian Social History', *American Historical Review*, 91, 1986, pp. 11–36; D. Moon, *The Abolition of Serfdom in Russia, 1762–1907* (London, 2001).
29 See E. Weber, 'Comment la politique vint aux paysans: A Second Look at Peasant Politicization', *American Historical Review*, 87, 1982, pp. 357–89.
30 F. W. Wcislo, *Reforming Rural Russia: State, Local Society, and National Politics, 1855–1914* (Princeton, NJ, 1990), p. xv; G. Yaney, *The Urge to Mobilize: Agrarian Reform in Russia, 1861–1930* (London, 1982), p. 175.
31 Mironov, *Sotsial'naia istoriia*, vol. 1, pp. 461–86.
32 R. Easley, 'Opening Public Space: The Peace Arbitrator and Rural Politicization, 1861–1864', *Slavic Review*, 61, 2002, pp. 730–1.
33 G. Popkins, 'Peasant Experiences of the Late Tsarist State: District Congresses of Land Captains, Provincial Boards and the Legal Appeals Process, 1891–1917', *Slavonic and East European Review*, 2000, pp. 113–14; J. Burbank, 'A Question of Dignity: Peasant Legal Culture in Late Imperial Russia', *Continuity and Change*, 10, 1995, pp. 391–404. A less positive interpretation has been put forward in T. V. Shatkovskaia, *Pravovaia mental'nost' rossiskikh krest'ian vtoroi poloviny XIX veka: opyt iuridicheskoi antropometrii* (Rostov-on-Don, 2000).
34 D. Atkinson, 'The Zemstvo and the Peasantry' in T. Emmons and W. S. Vucinich (eds), *The Zemstvo in Russia: An Experiment in Local Self-Government* (Cambridge, 1982), pp. 79–132 (quotation from p. 125).
35 See Wcislo, *Reforming Rural Russia*; D. A. J. Macey, *Government and Peasant in Russia, 1861–1906: The Prehistory of the Stolypin Reforms* (DeKalb, IL, 1987), pp. 14, 23–4, 29–30.
36 S. Hoch, 'The Banking Crisis, Peasant Reform, and Economic Development in Russia, 1857–1861', *American Historical Review*, 96, 1991, pp. 795–820.
37 See Gatrell, *Tsarist Economy*, pp. 128–40, 200–2; B. Mironov, 'The Russian Peasant Commune After the Reforms of the 1860s', in Eklof and Frank (eds), *The World of the Russian Peasant*, pp. 7–43; D. Atkinson, *The End of the Russian Land Commune*,

   1905–1930 (Stanford, CA, 1983), pp. 3, 22, 36, 391; B. V. Anan'ich, 'Iz istorii zakon-
   odatel'stva o krest'ianakh (vtoraia polovina XIX v.)' in V. V. Mavrodin (ed.),
   Voprosy istorii Rossii: XIX-nachala XX v. (Leningrad, 1983), pp. 34–45.

38 See Wcislo, *Reforming Rural Russia*, quotation from pp. 306–7.

39 See W. B. Lincoln, *The Great Reforms: Autocracy, Bureaucracy, and the Politics of
   Change in Imperial Russia* (DeKalb, IL, 1990), pp. 192–3; D. Field, 'Peasants and
   Propagandists in the Russian Movement to the People of 1874', *Journal of Modern
   History*, 59, 1987, pp. 415–38; D. Hardy, *Land and Freedom: The Origins of Russian
   Terrorism 1876–1879* (London, 1987), pp. 29–45; D. Moon, 'Decembrist Rebels,
   Tsars, and Peasants in Early Nineteenth-Century Russia', *New Perspective*, 2, 1996,
   pp. 8–12; M. P. Perrie, *The Agrarian Policy of the Russian Socialist-Revolutionary
   Party from its Origins through the Revolution of 1905–1907* (Cambridge, 1976).

40 See G. A. Hosking, *The Russian Constitutional Experiment: Government and Duma
   1907–1914* (Cambridge, 1973), esp. chs 2–3.

41 J. Pallot, *Land Reform in Russia 1906–1917: Peasant Responses to Stolypin's Project of
   Rural Transformation* (Oxford, 1999), quotation from p. 247. See also R. B. McKean,
   'Introduction' in R. B. McKean (ed.), *New Perspectives in Modern Russian History*
   (Basingstoke, 1992), pp. 8–10.

42 See A. V. Buganov, *Russkaia istoriia v pamiati krest'ian XIX veka i natsional'noe
   samosoznanie* (Moscow, 1992); M. M. Gromyko, 'Kul'tura russkogo krest'ianstva
   XVIII-XIX vekov kak predmet istoricheskogo issledovaniia', *Istoriia SSSR*, 3, 1987,
   pp. 39–60; Moon, *Russian Peasants and Tsarist Legislation*, pp. 2–3, 126, 167–9;
   M. Perrie, *The Image of Ivan the Terrible in Russian Folklore* (Cambridge, 1987).

43 See Smith, 'Citizenship and the Russian Nation', p. 327.

44 Sanborn, *Drafting the Nation*, p. 97.

45 See J. C. Curtiss, *The Russian Army under Nicholas I 1825–1855* (Durham, NC,
   1965); E. K. Wirtschafter, *From Serf to Russian Soldier* (Princeton, NJ, 1990).

46 See A. J. Rieber (ed.), *The Politics of Autocracy: Letters of Alexander II to Prince A. I.
   Bariatinskii* (Paris, 1966), pp.17–29; J. Bushnell, *Mutiny amid Repression: Russian
   Soldiers in the Revolution of 1905–1906* (Bloomington, IN, 1985), pp. 7–9 (quotation
   from p. 8); A. Wildman, *The End of the Russian Imperial Army. Vol. 1: The Old
   Army and the Soldiers' Revolt* (Princeton, NJ, 1980), pp. 25–8; Moon, 'Estimating the
   Peasant Population', p. 144; W. C. Fuller, *Strategy and Power in Russia 1600–1914*
   (New York, 1992), p. 285; Eklof, *Russian Peasant Schools*, p. 125.

47 Wildman, *End of the Russian Imperial Army*, vol. 1, pp. 26–40 (quotations from pp.
   27, 40.) On the financial constraints, see W. C. Fuller, *Civil–Military Conflict in
   Imperial Russia 1881–1914* (Princeton, NJ, 1985), esp. pp. 47–74, 259.

48 J. Bushnell, 'Peasants in Uniform: The Tsarist Army as a Peasant Society' in Eklof and
   Frank (eds), *The World of the Russian Peasant*, pp. 101–14 (quotations from pp. 102,
   103, 107); Bushnell, *Mutiny amid Repression*, pp. 1–23 (quotation from p. 19).

49 Fuller, *Civil–Military Conflict*, pp. 47–54.

50 Sanborn, *Drafting the Nation*, p. 38.

51 See Moon, *Russian Peasants and Tsarist Legislation*, pp. 113–64.

52 V. Babkin, *Narodnoe opolchenie v otechestvennoi voine 1812 goda* (Moscow, 1962),
   pp. 207–9.

53 A. B. Astashov, 'Russkii krest'ianin na frontakh pervoi mirovoi voiny', *Otechestven-naia istoriia*, 2, 2003, pp. 72–8.
54 H. F. Jahn, 'For Tsar and Fatherland? Russian Popular Culture and the First World War' in Frank and Steinberg, *Cultures in Flux*, pp. 131–46 (quotation from p. 146). See also H. F. Jahn, *Patriotic Culture in Russia during World War I* (Ithaca, NY, 1996).
55 S. A. Smith, 'Citizenship and the Nation during World War I: A Comment', *Slavic Review*, 59, 2000, p. 329.
56 Sanborn, 'Mobilization of 1914', p. 283.

9

Late imperial revolutionaries

Geoffrey Swain

Foundations

The Russian Social Democratic Labour Party (RSDLP) was founded in March 1898, formalising developments already well under way. Until the 1896 St Petersburg textile workers' strike Marxist ideas had been predominantly 'the plaything of intellectuals', but in the course of that strike working-class leaders too came to adopt Marxist ideas. It was the 1890s generation of intellectuals, epitomised by Vladimir Lenin and Iulii Martov, who achieved this, arguing that workers learned through struggle, and that every factory dispute provided agitational material from which workers could benefit.[1] By June 1896, 19 factories were affected by the strikes and 16,000 workers were involved; this success could be linked to delegate meetings organised by social democrat activists.[2]

Some working-class leaders felt that these strikes had become too politicised. Workers had gained much practical experience, recruiting new activists, keeping the books, and, as strikes became more frequent and more widespread, handling considerable sums of money accumulated in strike funds. Since the law allowed workers to collect money to establish funeral funds, these worker activists argued that such funds could serve as a cover for trade union style activity. They felt that the politicised slogans of 1896 had diverted the workers from their true concerns. It was views such as this that Lenin heard when, in February 1897, paroled from prison to gather the essentials needed for Siberian exile, he listened as worker activists proposed that in future the heart of the labour movement should be the funds rather than the underground. Before leaving for Siberia, Lenin made a speech condemning such proposals as 'Economism'. And for the next few years Economism dominated the labour movement. The constant arrest of intellectuals had left the movement in the hands of the workers, who had established a network of committees based on the numerous factory-based funds and those people elected to run them.[3] Between 1898 and 1902 the journal *Rabochaia mysl'* was produced, for much of the time in St Petersburg itself, and it mixed a diet of reports from the factories with articles which stressed 'the struggle for economic betterment' as the primary task.[4]

It was to combat this Economism that Lenin and Martov, released from their exile early in 1900, decided to launch the newspaper *Iskra*, as a vehicle for organising a Second Congress of the RSDLP which would condemn the Economist heresy and give the party clear organisational principles. This agenda was outlined more fully in Lenin's treatise *What Is To Be Done?*, which, in a striking image, condemned those who followed at the tail of the working class, and called on professional revolutionaries to give the working class a lead. The issue of just how that lead was to be exercised was debated when the Second Congress met in August 1903; it split the party in two. The congress accepted a centralist organisational structure, but then fell apart over the definition of a party member when presented with different proposals advanced by the former allies, Lenin and Martov. Both Martov and Lenin wanted only conscious workers in the party. However, Lenin wanted to restrict membership to those workers who personally participated in party cells; Martov wanted to include those second-level activists who did not participate in secret cell meetings but did run risks distributing newspapers and leaflets. Lenin was defeated and a pamphlet war ensued between his Bolsheviks and Martov's Mensheviks.

The programme adopted by the RSDLP at the Second Congress caused no controversy. It was orthodox Marxist in content, and saw the only revolutionary class as the proletariat, with the peasantry, the vast majority of Russia's population, condemned as 'petty bourgeois' small property owners who at best could give the proletariat wavering support. The Socialist Revolutionary party, founded at the end of 1901 from the merger of two pre-existing organisations, had a very different approach to the peasantry. The party's ideas were most coherently expounded by its undisputed leader, Viktor Chernov. For the SRs, the working class was everyone who was exploited, not just the industrial working class. Peasants might own small plots of land, but they laboured for their living and were exploited in the market place when they sold their meagre product to agricultural traders. Although in differing ways, workers and peasants were equally exploited and therefore equally revolutionary. The SRs' programme was not formally adopted until the First Congress in January 1906, but was discussed in 1902 and a draft circulated in 1904.[5] For peasants it called for 'socialisation of the land': private property in land would be abolished; all land would then be administered by democratically elected bodies drawn from local and central government; and all land would be used on an egalitarian basis by those who worked it.[6]

Chernov was, like Lenin, a law student in the 1890s who got caught up in the revolutionary movement. His experiences when exiled in Tambov province between 1895 and 1899 convinced him that organisational work among the peasantry was possible, if approached in the right way; he had some success in organising peasant revolutionary 'brotherhoods'. When he emigrated in 1899 he found it difficult to persuade other peasant socialists of what could be achieved, but the outbreak of peasant disturbances in Ukraine and the Volga in 1902 convinced the SRs that organisational work among the peasantry, however difficult, was feasible. The party launched a Peasant Union in November 1902 with the specific task of organising both peaceful forms of struggle such as rent boycotts and illegal pasturing, and traditional forms of resistance such as arson. Peasant Unions soon existed in Saratov, Kharkov, Ekaterinoslav, Penza and Kherson provinces, and as peasant unrest continued to spread, there was a good correlation between peasant disturbances and the presence of SR propaganda.[7]

The other substantive difference between the SRs and the RSDLP was the SRs' commitment to terror. Even before the formal founding of the party the Minister of Education was assassinated by the SRs in February 1901. This was followed by the killing of the Minister of the Interior in April 1902, the wounding of the Governor of Kharkov in June 1902, the killing of the Governor of Ufa in May 1903 and then by the party's two great terrorist successes: in July 1904 the party assassinated V. K. Plehve, the Minister of the Interior, and in February 1905 Grand Duke Sergei, the Governor-General of Moscow. These well-chosen targets brought the party a great deal of support. However, the SRs were keen that terrorism should not become indiscriminate, and disciplined those who campaigned to develop 'agrarian terrorism', attacks on local landlords and officials.[8]

The revolution of 1905

The split in the RSDLP meant that just as the Russo-Japanese War began in January 1904, the party found itself unable to focus on growing industrial discontent. In August 1903 the Russian Orthodox priest Father Gapon established an Assembly of St Petersburg Factory Workers. Despite the fact that Gapon included known Marxists among his advisers, the Assembly was recognised by the St Petersburg authorities in February 1904 and by March it had drawn up an eclectic programme of revolutionary and reformist demands.[9] Its branches soon had considerable authority among St Petersburg factory workers. When, under liberal pressure, the tsar gave permission for a congress of provincial assemblies to be held on 6–8 November, that congress called on all provincial assemblies to send petitions to the tsar demanding constitutional change. On 20 November liberals started to organise a series of large-scale banquets, all of which resolved to send similar petitions to the tsar. Activists within the Assembly began to discuss the possibility of sending in a petition from the workers. Although rejected at the end of November 1904, the idea of a petition did not go away, but got caught up in the campaign to reinstate four Assembly activists who had been dismissed from the Putilov works. From the end of December the 20,000-strong Assembly began preparing for a demonstration to be held on 9 January 1905, a demonstration which would present the tsar with a workers' petition.[10]

When on 9 January some of the demonstrators reached Palace Square, the army opened fire and then opened fire in other parts of the city. In all 96 died, with a further 43 later succumbing to their wounds.[11] The government's immediate response to this 'Bloody Sunday' was the decision to call a commission of enquiry, led by N. V. Shidlovskii, a member of the State Council and the Senate. Workers would be allowed to take part in the work of this commission by delegating electors. Any factory employing more than one hundred workers would be entitled to send an elector, and in big factories there would be one elector per 500 workers; the electors would then chose 50 representatives to join the commission. In all 372 electors were delegated from 208 factories, representing 145,259 workers. Social democrats claimed that 20 per cent of the electors were linked to the party and that some 40 per cent more were said to be sympathetic to them; 35 per cent were Gaponists. Such figures, pointedly ignoring the presence of SRs, merely underlined the very modest influence of the social democrats at the start of 1905. When these electors met for the first time on 16–17 February and demanded the re-opening of Gapon's Assembly, which had been closed on 11 January, the dominant figure was G. S. Nosar, a liberal lawyer who gained admission by posing as the textile elector P. A. Khrustalev.[12]

It was the government itself that allowed social democrats to assert control over the labour movement. The refusal of the authorities to re-open the Assembly removed a powerful rival to the RSDLP while Shidlovskii's refusal to guarantee that workers demanding political change would not be arrested meant that the worker electors voted to boycott his commission. In the strike waves which followed, instigated for a variety of economic and political motives, those worker electors became increasingly involved in social democratic and SR activity, serving as factory elders. When the St Petersburg Soviet was set up in October 1905, it was based on the same elective principle as the Shidlovskii Commission; many of the same activists were involved.[13] The Soviet was a Menshevik initiative. On 10 October they summoned a 'revolutionary workers' council of self-management'. It met for the first time on 13 October as the General Workers' Committee of St Petersburg and called for a general strike. On 14 October its first full meeting took place, attended by 100 delegates, and on 17 October the title 'Soviet' was formally adopted. By the second half of November the Soviet comprised 562 delegates from 147 factories, 34 workshops and 16 trade unions. Although dominated by the Mensheviks, there were sizeable Bolshevik and SR fractions, and the Soviet always gave due representation to the SRs.[14]

Despite the SRs' peasant orientation, they had always agitated among the working class as well. In 1904 the party informed the Socialist International it had workers' groups in twenty-four towns; in the capital it had established a St Petersburg Committee in 1902 and was well represented in some of the major plants, in particular the Obukhov works in Neva District. Reflecting this, the Soviet leadership was balanced. Khrustalev-Nosar was chosen as chairman precisely because he was a figurehead and had no party affiliation. Leon Trotsky, then a Menshevik, was one of the two vice-chairmen, while the other was the SR N. D. Avksentiev. Police reports suggested that the ratio of social democrats to SRs was about two to one, and the SRs had a dominant position in the Railway Workers' Union.[15] Joint work in the Petrograd Soviet, and the soviets formed in other cities during 1905, brought close collaboration between the SRs and the RSDLP, particularly in the armed militias established to defend the soviets. When in December 1905 the Moscow Soviet staged an insurrection, the military side of the operation was largely the work of the local SRs.[16]

Peasant disturbances followed quickly on the heels of the strikes which followed Bloody Sunday. This unrest continued throughout 1905 and into the first half of 1906 in a series of waves that suggested very little in the way of organisation, and with a level of violence which went beyond SR guidelines. Yet it was equally clear that the SRs invested great energy in trying to direct these disturbances, and on more than one occasion the unrest began with the appearance of SR propaganda; in July 1905 disturbances reached a peak in Saratov, where the SRs were strongest. Much of this work was carried out by the SRs' Peasants' Union, which was well represented in the two congresses of the liberal-sponsored All-Russian Peasant Union held in May and November 1905. The political agenda of the SRs was made clear in an article published in July 1905. This argued that the SRs 'should not restrict the scale of the revolution in advance for the benefit of the bourgeoisie, but on the contrary they should turn it into a permanent one'. In other words, the SRs would pursue their own agenda, without concerning themselves about the fate of the liberal opposition to the tsar.[17] Their stance did not change when the tsar issued his Manifesto on 17 October 1905 and an era of quasi-parliamentary politics dawned in Russia.

First and Second State Dumas, 1906–7

By the time the SRs gathered for their First Congress in January 1906 it had become clear that the tsar's proposals for a State Duma would not introduce anything resembling genuine constitutional democracy. So the SRs resolved to boycott the Duma. Not all party activists accepted this decision. At the First Congress some argued that the time had come to establish an open, legal party and to oppose the use of terror. The most vociferous of these left the party in spring 1906 to establish the Party of Popular Socialists, which offered immediate help to the peasant deputies elected to the First Duma who had formed themselves into the Trudovik group. The SRs, quick to realise that the boycott had been a mistake, made the same offer.[18] The RSDLP, which had also decided to boycott the First Duma, similarly voted to change its mind, but for the social democrats this about-turn was caught up in continuing tension between the Bolshevik and Menshevik wings of the party.

The new era of more open Duma politics meant that the issue of defining party membership ceased to have its former importance. The distinction between the committee member and the rank-and-file activist, which had so concerned Martov, was now a thing of the past. Lenin had organised a Third RSDLP Congress in April 1905 which the Mensheviks refused to attend. This congress duly accepted Lenin's definition of party membership.[19] Then, over the summer of 1905 many of the separate Bolshevik and Menshevik organisations reunited, a trend formalised at the Stockholm Congress of May 1906. This congress gave victory to the Mensheviks, but the issue of membership was not re-opened. The congress accepted Lenin's definition of party membership without demur. Organisation no longer lay at the heart of the Bolshevik–Menshevik dispute. The new area of disagreement was one of Duma tactics, whether or not to side with the liberals or the SRs.

When the First Duma opened on 27 April, there were over one hundred Trudoviki, representing 19.7 per cent of the votes cast. Since the liberals had won 37.4 per cent of the vote, the tsar was faced with an assembly with a clear opposition majority. The crux issue was that of land reform and three proposals emerged from the opposition: the liberals proposed a scheme for the expropriation of some of the landlords' land, with compensation coming both from the peasant and the state; the Trudoviki proposed the expropriation of land without compensation; and some 33 Trudovik deputies, members of the SR party who had ignored the instruction to boycott the election, demanded the socialisation of the land. These three schemes were debated in a Duma commission, and it was the liberal proposal which finally emerged. The social democrats, with their Menshevik-controlled Central Committee, were determined to try to influence this clash between the tsar and his Duma. In six provinces of Russia the Duma elections were held late and in these provinces, one in Siberia and five in the Caucasus, the social democrats put up official candidates. Among the Trudoviki there already existed several deputies from working-class backgrounds sympathetic to the social democrats, and so an eighteen-strong social democratic fraction was created, a fraction that was instructed to support the liberals' call for a Duma ministry. Such a ministry seemed a distinct possibility when the liberal leader Paul Miliukov was invited for talks with the government. As rumours circulated that Miliukov might be given the post of Minister of Foreign Affairs, it seemed plausible that a ministry responsible to the Duma might be formed; but these talks broke down and the Duma was dissolved on 9 July.[20]

Bolshevik opposition to this pro-liberal policy centred on St Petersburg, where the St Petersburg Committee remained a Bolshevik bastion. The Bolsheviks argued that the Menshevik love-affair with the liberals blinded them to the potential offered by the Trudoviki.[21] When in May the St Petersburg Committee discussed the Central Committee's instruction to the Duma fraction, it accepted a resolution drawn up by Lenin.[22] From mid-May onwards the Menshevik press campaigned in favour of a 'responsible ministry' as the 'first indispensable task', while the Bolsheviks countered by arguing that the proletariat should never allow itself to be used by the bourgeoisie to carry out a deal with the bureaucracy.[23] As the Bolsheviks started persuading more and more workers' meetings to pass resolutions critical of the Menshevik Central Committee, the Central Committee passed a resolution banning all public agitation against its decisions. In response, the Bolsheviks argued that there should be complete freedom of criticism within the party for any policy not endorsed by a party congress.[24] The Mensheviks countered that the decision to ban factional agitation had been taken unanimously and should be accepted by all.[25] On 21 June the factional strife reached its climax when a conference of the St Petersburg social democrats was held and the Bolsheviks again emerged victorious.[26]

This dispute continued after the tsar dissolved the First Duma and summoned the Second Duma. Determined to have control over the elections in the capital, in October 1906 the Central Committee asserted that it would establish an electoral commission in the capital and allow only one representative of the St Petersburg Committee to sit on it; the St Petersburg Committee declared that this was against party rules.[27] At the All-Russian Party Conference in mid-November 1906 the row continued as to whether or not to follow a Bolshevik 'Left Bloc' strategy in the elections, identifying the Trudoviki as the preferred ally, or accepting the Menshevik principle of the 'defence of the revolution', opening the way to deals with the liberals. The conference came down on the side of the Mensheviks, but the Mensheviks still did not control St Petersburg. When the St Petersburg party organisation held its conference on 6 January 1907, it was a bitterly fought affair, but the Mensheviks just failed to capture control.[28] In frustration, the Menshevik delegates walked out in protest and decided to boycott future meetings.[29]

This factional dispute was both vitriolic and petty. It was scarcely surprising that when the Second Duma elections took place in the capital's workers' curia in January 1907 it was the SRs who polled best. The SR Council had decided at the end of October 1906 that it would participate in the elections to the Second Duma, leaving the question of whether to take up any seats won to the Second Congress in February 1907; participation was duly agreed.[30] For much of 1905 and into 1906 SR propaganda in the factories had been radical in the extreme. They had co-operated with the Bolsheviks during the Moscow uprising in December, and many party activists had become convinced of the benefits of economic terror in the factories, assassinating factory owners or oppressive managers. The party had accepted as part of its immediate minimum programme the socialisation of land; however, the socialisation of the factories was left to the future and confined to the maximum programme. In the course of 1906 a radical group broke away from the party to form a Union of SR Maximalists committed to both economic terror and the socialisation of the factories. The police succeeded in ending the activities of this group by the end of 1906, and thereafter SR labour activists trod a more familiar path. By 1907 there were SR groups in half of the St Petersburg trade unions and a quarter of those unions were under SR control.[31] The election campaign in the workers' curia involved some fierce confrontations, particularly in the Neva District, always an SR stronghold; two meetings there in December 1906 attracted audiences of over 1,000 each. Overall the SRs won 45 per cent of the vote, the Mensheviks 24 per cent and the Bolsheviks 13 per cent.[32]

Both Bolsheviks and Mensheviks recognised that their defeat in the workers' curia had been due to the bitter factional squabbling, but the Bolsheviks could at least draw comfort from the fact that a vote for the SRs was a vote against co-operating with the liberals.[33] They drew similar comfort from their victory at the St Petersburg party conference in March 1907.[34] The problem for the Mensheviks was that the politics of the Second Duma revealed that the 'Left Bloc' policy was far more fruitful than that of supporting the liberals. The social democrat deputies decided to consider all Duma alliances on their merits, and this guideline soon worked out to favour Bolshevik rather than Menshevik perceptions.[35] In the debates over procedural rules, the social democrats, SRs and Trudoviki found themselves co-operating to the exclusion of the liberals. A pattern began to emerge. The social democrats and the Trudoviki clashed with the liberals on famine relief, while on another occasion the liberals prevented the SRs and social democrats putting down a motion of no confidence. To the embarrassment of the Mensheviks, when the debates on land reform opened in mid-March, the liberals destroyed any chance of a common approach by attacking the Trudoviki. The liberal line was clear: only their proposal stood a chance of gaining acceptance, so the other proposals should be withdrawn. Repeatedly the entire social democratic fraction found itself firmly aligned against the liberal deputies.[36]

When the Fifth Congress of the RSDLP met in London in May 1907 it gave a slender victory to the Bolsheviks. The congress condemned the slogan of 'a responsible ministry' and favoured the concept of the Left Bloc. Two weeks later, when it rejected the government's plans for land reform, the Second Duma was dissolved on 3 June 1907. In violation of the constitution, the electoral law was changed in the absence of a Duma and a Third Duma summoned, to be elected on 1 September by a completely new franchise which drastically reduced the representation of workers, peasants and other oppositional groups like parties representing the national minorities. The revolutionary upheaval that had begun in November 1904 was over.

Years of reaction

Although the main ideological dispute between the Bolsheviks and Mensheviks during the years 1906–7 related to the question of electoral alliances, there was a secondary issue which took on greater significance when the Third Duma was summoned, that of the trade unions. The government's provisional regulations, under which trade unions were made legal, were made public on 4 March 1906. Under them the trade union movement grew apace. By mid-May 1907 a total of 245,555 workers had joined trade unions, 3.5 per cent of the workforce. In the country as a whole 904 unions were registered between March 1906 and December 1907. This process was far from easy. Although work began on organising the St Petersburg Metal Workers' Union in May 1906, it was not until 15 May 1907 that the union was formally registered. The St Petersburg Print Workers' Union was not registered until April 1907, while the St Petersburg Textile Workers' Union was only registered in September 1907. The registration process was helped by the Central Bureau of St Petersburg Trade Unions, an organisation specifically banned by the provisional regulations which prohibited both national trade union federations and inter-union confederations. In 1907 the social democratic Duma deputies co-operated closely with the St Petersburg Central Bureau of Trade Unions.[37]

Mensheviks threw themselves into this trade union work with enthusiasm. The SRs, having abandoned factory terror, gradually turned to trade union affairs. Bolsheviks were far less certain. It was only after the SRs' strong showing in the workers' curia in January 1907 that the St Petersburg Committee resolved 'to convene a meeting of Bolsheviks working in the trade unions' because 'this side of affairs has been ignored and is being used by the Mensheviks to win over the masses'. In Moscow, however, this realisation had come about much earlier; since August 1906 a local Bolshevik had been social democrat representative on the Central Bureau of Moscow Trade Unions and had done much to involve Bolsheviks in trade union work, helping to organise a regional conference of textile workers. At the London Party Congress he lobbied the Bolsheviks to take trade union affairs seriously, and won Lenin's support.[38] But before the Bolsheviks could begin serious trade union work, the government staged its 3 June coup and launched an assault on the trade unions. In 1907, 159 unions were closed down, in 1908 it was 101, then 96 and 88 in 1909 and 1910 respectively. During the years 1907–11, 604 unions were refused registration and 206 trade union activists were either imprisoned or exiled.[39]

Despite this continuing persecution, a legal labour movement survived. More than that, as early as January 1908 it became clear that after 1905 there were other 'legal possibilities' for labour activists. In January 1908 the authorities allowed the People's Universities to hold a national congress. A workers' delegation attended this gathering, headed by the leaders of the St Petersburg Metal Workers' Union and St Petersburg Textile Workers' Union; they found the congress provided a platform for socialist agitation. The RSDLP was ambivalent about this development. By the end of 1907 the Central Committee had fled abroad, leaving behind its Russian Bureau. This had been lukewarm about the policy of workers attending the Congress of People's Universities, but the success of the group meant it had no hesitation in endorsing the proposal to send a workers' group to the Cooperative Congress in April 1908.[40] The activities of the Russian Bureau at this congress led to its arrest.

The arrest of the Russian Bureau left the affairs of the capital under the control of the St Petersburg Committee, which was still in the hands of not only the Bolsheviks but 'Recallist' Bolsheviks. In July 1907 the Third RSDLP Conference had voted to take part in the Third Duma elections, despite the narrowing of the franchise. Many Bolsheviks had accepted this decision very reluctantly and argued that the experience of the first weeks of the Third Duma had proved how ineffective it was in preventing the assault on the labour movement, so the deputies should be recalled. This hard-line stance spilled over into trade union work and that of labour representation at legal congresses. As one Recallist noted: 'The impossibility of founding legal trade unions puts us almost back in the position we were before the revolution [of 1905], puts back on the shoulders of the party the task of leading economic struggle'.[41] By summer 1908 Recallists had such a grip on the St Petersburg Committee that it had virtually ceased to work in the trade unions. Those committee members who did undertake trade union work were as likely to be disruptive as positive in their contribution. Bolshevik trade unionists, on the other hand, found themselves in the awkward position of being bad mouthed by the leaders of the faction with which they identified. Relations were particularly bad during the Congress of Women's Organisations, held in December 1908, where the activities of the trade union sponsored 'group of working women' were derided by the St Petersburg Committee.[42]

This development proved a dilemma for Lenin. If during 1906–7 the split between Bolshevism and Menshevism revolved around the attitude to be taken towards the liberals, for the next few years it again revolved around the question of organisation. Lenin's problem was this: the new breed of legal activists emerging in Russia as trade unionists participating in legal congresses were not organisationally linked to any committee of the RSDLP. Worse, the fact that what remained of the party hierarchy was in Recallist hands meant that these legal activists were unlikely to move nearer the surviving committees. Some Mensheviks were keen to exploit such feelings for their own purposes. When the Russian Bureau had been arrested, some émigré Mensheviks had proposed abolishing the Central Committee and replacing it with an 'information bureau' which would simply co-ordinate the work of legally operating labour activists within Russia. When this proposal, tantamount to a return to Economism, was discussed in August 1908, it met with little support; a conference of St Petersburg Mensheviks countered that what was needed was not the abolition of the Central Committee and its committee structure, but a mechanism whereby the legal activists were given a greater say in party affairs. Bolshevik legal activists made precisely the same point. Proposals for a joint conference of legal activists and the underground were put to the Fifth Party Conference in Paris in December 1908, but were rejected. Lenin accused those who advanced this proposal of planning to 'liquidate' the party.[43]

However, the idea for a joint conference did not go away. It was not, after all, an unreasonable proposal. The police believed that half the membership of the St Petersburg Metal Workers' Union, some 1,500 workers, identified themselves as social democrats. If the same were true of the members of the other trade unions in St Petersburg, then 2,500 social democrats were active in St Petersburg factories in 1909; at the same time the most optimistic figure for underground activists was 500.[44] So there were five times as many social democrats in the factories as in the remaining underground cells, a reality which existing hierarchies did not reflect and which was made worse by the fact that throughout 1908 and 1909 the secretary of the St Petersburg Committee was a police agent.[45] Yet the work of legal activists went from strength to strength. In 1909 there was a revival of the Central Bureau of St Petersburg Trade Unions, which was again in contact with the social democratic deputies. What brought this collaboration to the fore was the government's proposals for social insurance legislation, which began their extended progress through the Duma in 1909. The Central Bureau issued its 'Theses on Insurance' in March.[46]

In June 1909 Lenin organised a meeting in Paris of the Bolshevik ruling group. The delegates from Russia dutifully expelled the Recallists, as Lenin asked them to do, but then returned to Russia determined that they should be the first to organise a congress of legal activists.[47] In September 1909 worker delegates to the planned Temperance Congress drew up plans for reviving the social democratic organisation of the capital. Sixty representatives attended this meeting and only six of them supported the proposal that the Central Committee should be liquidated. The majority wanted to retain a social democrat organisation, but replace 'outworn forms of organisation sullied by provocation'. At a second meeting in November 1909 legal activists met with local underground activists and decided to unite into one illegal social democratic party.[48] The Congress of Handicraft Trades, held in January 1911, was preceded by a further conference of legal activists, which again resolved to encourage co-operation between legal activists and the underground.[49] The party leadership in emigration could no longer ignore this pressure and in January 1910 the Central Committee met in

Paris to agree that any legal activists who formed themselves into a 'social dem-ocratic group' would be invited to attend the next party conference.[50] This con-ference would be called by a newly constituted Russian Bureau. That Russian Bureau was not a success. It was arrested in May 1910, reformed and arrested again in March 1911. Legal activists remained outside the party.[51]

However, if the legal activists were outside the party hierarchy in 1911, so too were underground activists, for after 1910 there was no generally recog-nised St Petersburg Committee, although occasionally groups adopted that name. Towards the end of March 1911 it was the Duma deputy for St Peters-burg, a former member of the St Petersburg Soviet, who organised a meeting of representatives of the city's social democratic organisations which estab-lished the General City Group, a group which survived for much of the summer of 1911 and was in looser contact with the Neva, Narva and Moscow districts where social democrat organisations existed, but kept their distance for fear of provocation. After October 1913 the strongest social democratic organisation in the capital was the Inter-District Group, established by another social democrat deputy and a Bolshevik activist in the Metal Workers' Union.[52]

The impact of the years of reaction on the SR underground was broadly similar. The organisational hierarchy was decimated by the police, as had hap-pened with the RSDLP, and there was no equivalent to the RSDLP Duma deputies with whom local party activists could identify because at its Third Council in July 1907 it voted for a boycott, a view confirmed by the First Party Conference in August 1908. Reports to the Socialist International in 1910 and 1914 showed that grass-roots organisations continued their activities through-out the years of reaction and beyond – in 1910 there were active peasant organ-isations in ten provinces uniting Ukraine, the Volga Basin and the Urals[53] – but that contact with the leading groups abroad were ephemeral.[54] Many SR activists responded to the trade unions in a similar way to the Bolshevik Recal-lists. Although the Third Council produced a lengthy resolution on trade union affairs, and the St Petersburg Committee established a trade union bureau in August 1907, there was little response. The party's message was that it was 'incorrect' to become diverted from the political struggle, and the SR press con-sistently ridiculed the reformist work of Menshevik trade union activists. SRs deliberately either took no part in such organisations, or played a disruptive role, forming an alliance with Recallists in 1909,[55] and pilfering union funds for party activities.[56]

However, as with the Bolsheviks themselves, other SR activists became actively involved in trade union affairs, maintaining a shadowy but widespread organisational existence. Such activists accepted that the party should agitate to keep alive its ultimate revolutionary goals, but that did not mean boycotting the 'legal possibilities'. The party conference in 1908 heard Chernov call on SRs not to ignore the trade unions,[57] and when the issue was debated at the Fifth

Council in Paris in May 1909 it was resolved that the party would establish trade union groups, closely bound to the territorial party hierarchy. These groups would establish party cells in the legal labour movement, which would retain their ideological distinctiveness while working for the greater good of the union. Although the party in St Petersburg established a 'workers' bureau' in 1909 to co-ordinate this work,[58] in 1910 Alexander Kerensky, the Trudovik deputy and SR member, complained that the party's work in the legal labour movement was 'paltry'.[59] Paltry or not, the SRs had a marked presence in the Metal Workers' Union from the end of 1907 onwards. If in 1908 several of those elected to positions of authority did not take their task seriously, in 1910–11 one of its vice-presidents was an SR, who briefly assumed the post of acting president. Individual SRs took part in the workers' groups to the Co-operative Congress, the Women's Congress and the Temperance Congress.[60] At the end of 1909 the workers' bureau in St Petersburg retained contact with the eight working-class regions.[61]

As with the emergence among the social democrats of the Central Group and the Inter-District Group, in 1910 an 'autonomous group' of SRs was set up in St Petersburg, built according to known contacts and avoiding all but the most necessary correspondence with the *émigrés*. According to its prescription, there should be no central issuing of orders and no 'bureaucratic intermedi-aries', just socialist work among workers and peasants. Similar ideas had sur-faced earlier at a conference of St Petersburg organisations in spring 1909. The resolution discussed then was symptomatic of the state of affairs among SR activists. It stressed that groups within Russia were quite capable of undertak-ing work in the localities independently of the emigration. To the leadership abroad, such groups were 'liquidators', but they wanted a looser structure to the party which would lessen the danger of provocation. No St Petersburg Committee of the SR party existed in 1910–12.[62] Just as with the social democ-rats, there were intellectuals among the SRs who interpreted such ambitions as a complete renunciation of the underground. In 1909 Avksentiev started pub-lishing abroad the journal *Pochin* (*New Beginnings*), which advocated a renun-ciation of illegal underground work in favour of more modest reformist tasks.[63] The catalyst for this was the discovery at the end of 1908 that Evno Azef, the head of the party's Combat Organisation and therefore the organiser of its most spectacular assassination successes, was a police agent.

Revolutionary recovery

During 1911, the focus for the Bolshevik–Menshevik controversy again moved from the question of organisation to that of an alliance with the liberals. *Nasha zaria*, a journal founded legally within Russia by right-wing Mensheviks, sug-gested at the start of 1911 that workers should use the fifth anniversary of the provisional regulations on the trade unions, 4 March 1911, as the occasion to send petitions to the president of the Duma asking for the workings of the regulations to be reviewed. To the editors of *Zvezda*, a weekly paper launched by the Duma deputies in December 1910, this seemed to be taking the Duma far too seriously; it was handing a working-class issue to the liberals to discuss. When *Zvezda* refused to support this petition campaign, *Nasha zaria* launched a rival weekly newspaper and made much of the support for it given by Kuz'ma Gvozdev, who had become president of the Metal Workers' Union in 1910. Gvozdev committed the union to the petition campaign and threatened to boycott *Zvezda*. However, the General City Group of underground activists and the Narva District Committee both condemned the campaign, for which only 1,295 signatures were collected.[64] Some months later, at the end of 1911, the Duma deputies introduced a bill that would have made strikes legal; it was supported by 14,000 signatures on a petition sent not to the president of the Duma, with all that implied about the ability of the Duma to respond, but to the social democrat deputies.

The question of what could be expected of the Duma surfaced again as preparations began for the Fourth Duma election campaign. The arrest of the Russian Bureau in March 1911 persuaded Lenin that the time had come to act independently. He summoned a 'meeting of members of the Central Committee', which appropriated the power to dissolve the Foreign Bureau of the Central Committee and established an Organising Commission instructed to call a 'general party conference'. The result was the Sixth (Prague) Conference of the RSDLP, which took place in January 1912.[65] This was a stormy meeting with participants criticising the way delegates had been selected from Russia and ridiculing Lenin's suggestion that *émigré* politicians were helping to resolve the situation at home.[66] Nevertheless, delegates eventually agreed to Lenin's insistence that the Liquidators be expelled from the party on the pragmatic grounds that Liquidationism had only ever been an issue in St Petersburg and had long since ceased to attract workers even there. They also endorsed Lenin's requirement that in the forthcoming elections to the Fourth Duma the Liquidators should be opposed in the workers' curia.[67]

Despite being dissolved by Lenin, the RSDLP Foreign Bureau continued to meet, summoning a conference of *émigré* organisations in August 1911 which resolved to organise a 'genuine' all-party conference. The Vienna Conference was held in August 1912. Despite all the efforts of Trotsky, its main organiser, the conference was not a success. Arrests meant it was scarcely fully representational, and gave undue weight to the views of two legal activists who arrived from St Petersburg, both of whom had supported Gvozdev during the petition campaign. Although the Vienna Conference expelled no party groups, it did make radical changes to the social democrats' election programme: the demand for 'a democratic republic' became 'a sovereign popular representation'; land confiscation was replaced with 'a revision of the agrarian legislation of the Third Duma'. These changes were deemed necessary as part of the same tactic which lay behind the petition campaign. Mensheviks still detected 'a left turn in the bourgeoisie'. It therefore made sense to 'give the leftward-leaning bourgeoisie the help it needed' by adopting slogans liberals would find easier to accept.[68]

Despite the decisions taken in Prague and Vienna all underground groups in St Petersburg co-operated in the Fourth Duma election campaign. That situation changed only on the eve of the poll. In April 1912 those Duma deputies who had produced the weekly *Zvezda* started to publish the legal daily newspaper *Pravda*. It condemned factional struggle, but was loyal to the party's traditional slogans. In mid-September 1912, just prior to the elections, the Mensheviks launched their daily *Luch* as a rival to *Pravda*. As the elections in the workers' curia took place, these rival dailies published rival lists of candidates. However, this had no impact on the choice of a Bolshevik as St Petersburg deputy. Like all of the other deputies, he was mandated by the working-class curia to work for unity, and to defend the traditional slogans of the party, reflecting the mood of most worker activists.[69]

The social democrats faced no competition from the SRs in these elections. The SR Central Committee held an 'enlarged meeting' to clarify its stance in November 1911. A questionnaire was then circulated to surviving committees and the responses showed a small majority for the status quo of a boycott; however, because there were relatively few responses, it was agreed that the call for a boycott should be considered 'guidance' rather than an 'instruction'.[70] It was clear from the tenor of the report from St Petersburg that support for the status quo was the result of lethargy and apathy, rather than any serious debate;[71] this was a far cry from the official motivation which saw the boycott as a sign of political consciousness.[72] Some groups favouring a boycott did so simply because they felt the party was in too disorganised a state to put up a good showing and ensure the election of deputies with sufficient authority.[73] Since the decision to boycott the Duma elections had the status of guidance, rather than an instruction, several organisations ignored it.[74]

The elections to the Fourth Duma were followed immediately by the social insurance campaign. Like the petition campaign before it, this presented worker activists associated with the social democratic party with a clear choice between two strategies, one reflecting traditional social democratic slogans and the other reflecting the need to taylor demands with an eye to the concerns of liberal politicians. When the issue of insurance was first seriously discussed by worker representatives from eight pilot factories at the end of January 1913, it was agreed that social democrats should seek to amalgamate the factory-based insurance funds envisaged by the legislation into a general fund. However, the commission elected to negotiate with the employers made no progress in this direction. When metal workers became involved in the campaign in autumn 1913, the issue of the general fund became highly politicised.

The 'Theses on Insurance' drawn up by the St Petersburg Central Bureau of Trade Unions in 1909 had been clear that the factory-based insurance funds should be united into a general fund based on territorial area; that stance had been reaffirmed by the Metal Workers' Union as late as September 1911. However, the Mensheviks now argued that, since such an arrangement was ruled out by the legislation, it would have to be a long-term aim, one supplemented in the short term by general funds associated with individual professions, a professional fund not a territorial fund. Like the petition campaign before it, the social insurance campaign revolved around principles hidden by apparently similar political stances. To the uninitiated there might seem little difference between sending a petition to the president of the Duma or to the social democratic deputies; the initiated knew that one symbolised a liberal strategy, the other the traditional social democratic strategy. The working-class rank and file might be puzzled by the difference between a professional fund and a general fund, but worker activists knew at once that one signified kowtowing to the liberals and the other demanded militant struggle.[75]

Support for militancy was already clear in April 1913 when the Bolsheviks won control of the St Petersburg Metal Workers' Union, a victory which became even clearer in August the same year. The Bolshevik victory was essentially a rebellion against Gvozdev and his support for the petition campaign. Many of those elected to run the union in 1913 had been second-level Bolshevik activists for several years who had tired of the way Mensheviks condemned 'strikomania', a word they coined to describe *Pravda*'s indiscriminate support for striking. Gvozdev denounced the new Bolshevik leadership for supporting any and every strike and for ignoring the task of 'culturally educating' the workforce, in other words lecturing them on the need for an accommodation with the liberals. Workers now whistled down those who expressed such views. The Bolshevik victory in the Metal Workers' Union as the social insurance elections began in metal-working factories ensured that the Bolshevik call for a city-wide, territorially-based general fund won the day. It also persuaded Lenin's Central Committee in September 1913 that the time had come to split the social democratic Duma deputies into Bolshevik and Menshevik fractions.[76]

Yet if worker activists rejected Menshevik policies which smacked of collaboration with the liberals, they also opposed Bolshevik policies to tie them down organisationally. During spring 1914 workers' representatives were elected to three insurance bodies, the Insurance Council and the Insurance Boards of both St Petersburg City and St Petersburg Province. *Pravda* proposed that all those elected should report on their activities only through *Pravda*. When workers' meetings protested at this, the paper called on those elected 'to bring all their activity into agreement with organised Marxists'.

The issue did not come up at the election meeting to the Insurance Council in February 1914, but when the elections took place to the St Petersburg City Insurance Board in March 1914 the representative of the Metal Workers' Union proposed that those elected should not be responsible to 'organised Marxists' but to those who elected them in the form of a workers' insurance council; this was then amended to read that they should be responsible both to an insurance council and 'organised Marxists'. This stance was repeated at the final election to the St Petersburg Provincial Insurance Board in April. This wording suggested worker representatives should not act as mere ciphers for a Central Committee but co-ordinate policies with their electorate in the spirit of social democracy.[77]

The social insurance campaign was also the occasion for a revival of labour activity among the SRs. Their boycott of the Fourth Duma elections was linked to a call for the social insurance campaign to be boycotted as well. However, as the social insurance campaign evolved, so SRs' views changed.[78] Workers from the SR stronghold of the Nevskii District, as well as the Vyborg District, wrote to the editor of the legal SR paper *Znamia Truda* complaining that too much space was devoted to the concerns of the *émigrés* and not enough to practical issues like the social insurance campaign; the authors called for articles explaining the provisions of the law and how best to act on them.[79] Active involvement in the social insurance campaign restored the SRs to their traditional strength among workers of the capital. In 1914 it was estimated that one-third of the labour force sympathised with the SRs, the same proportion as their representation on the 1905 St Petersburg Soviet.[80]

This recovery was equally clear in the state of the underground committees. If in autumn 1912 the surviving party organisations were intellectual-led and only weakly attached to the factories, by May 1913 a conference had been held to form a St Petersburg Committee and clear guidelines issued on how to relate the work of the underground and that of the legal workers' organisations.[81] On May Day 1914 the SRs and the Bolsheviks issued a joint proclamation in St Petersburg, a sign of the SRs' support for the Bolsheviks when it came to the Menshevik policy of a liberal alliance.[82] During the years 1913–14 a new SR party was born which operated according to its own agenda and took little notice of the disagreements taking place in the *émigré* press.[83]

The war

During the war years, the *émigré* leaderships had even less influence over party activists in Russia. Of the various social democratic groups in the capital the Inter-District Group remained the most influential. Without the need for guidance from abroad, local activists condemned the war, as did all the Duma deputies, whether Bolshevik or Menshevik; the government's decision to arrest the Bolshevik deputies and put them on trial stemmed from its own agenda of perpetuating divisions among the social democrats. Throughout the war, worker activists retained their commitment to revolutionary rather than reformist politics. By September 1915 worker activists from all revolutionary parties had created a city-wide strike committee and were calling for the recreation of the Soviet.[84] Among the SRs the victory of the left among worker activists was just as clear. With the outbreak of war Kerensky helped restore some sort of party organisation in the capital and beyond, but the views these groups adopted were not those he shared; in St Petersburg the worker-oriented Organising Commission was well to the left of him. While Kerensky organised conferences of SRs, Trudoviki and Popular Socialists, worker activists met with Bolsheviks to plan joint action and came out even more clearly against the war.[85]

In July 1915 the liberal-inspired War Industry Committee resolved to invite worker representatives to join it. Elections took place in two stages in September 1915. At the second stage, the electors voted not to send representatives to the War Industries Committee since to do so would signify cross-class collaboration in favour of the war effort; the SRs joined with the Bolsheviks in voting not to participate. Having lost the vote, Gvozdev, who favoured participation, cried foul. The Bolsheviks had smuggled into the electors' meeting the underground activist S. Ia. Bagdatiev, posing as one of the electors; this was how Khrustalev-Nosar had joined the Shidlovskii Commission in 1905 and at first there was no objection. However, it provided the pretext for Gvozdev to demand a new vote, which took place in November. On this occasion the Bolsheviks and the SRs walked out in protest at the arrest of several of their electors in the intervening month. The rump electors then chose ten Mensheviks to sit on the national War Industry Committee and three Mensheviks and three SRs, loyal to the right-wing journal *Pochin*, to sit on the Petrograd district committee.[86] In such a contentious election, moral victory went to the Bolsheviks and SRs. In 1916 these two parties co-operated in plans to mark the anniversary of Bloody Sunday,[87] and by November 1916 were negotiating to form an inter-party information bureau.[88]

There was a further victory for militancy among labour activists in October 1916. Since the first elections of 1913 most of the worker representatives on the insurance councils had been arrested. After pressure from the Duma, the government agreed to new elections. Early in October 1916 elections were held to the Petrograd City Insurance Board, resulting in victory for four Bolsheviks and one SR, while a fortnight later it was the turn of the Petrograd Provincial Insurance Board, resulting in victory for three Bolsheviks and two Mensheviks. However, this assembly also saw a repeat of the situation in 1914 when the elected worker representatives sought to distance themselves from any resolution which might turn them into mere ciphers of an *émigré*-based central committee. The electors were presented with two instructions, one drawn up by the Bolsheviks and one by the Mensheviks. The victorious Bolsheviks voted for the Menshevik instructions and did so because, while on the substantive issue of insurance the instructions were identical, the Bolshevik instructions called for the new Labour Group on the Insurance Council to be 'responsible to organised Marxists', while the Mensheviks proposed that they be responsible to 'the collective of the funds', in other words, those workers, both social democrat and SR, who elected them.[89]

Those Mensheviks who supported the petition campaign, criticised strikes, favoured the revised elections slogans, proposed a professional rather than a territorial insurance fund and supported the war industries committees – all in the name of opening up avenues to the liberals – were the politicians who in 1917 favoured the perpetuation of a coalition government between liberal and socialist politicians, and did so in alliance with *Pochin* SRs. Worker activists from both the RSDLP and SRs rejected all these policy initiatives, just as they would reject a coalition with the liberals in 1917 in favour of the formation of a soviet government. The divisions of 1917 were already firmly entrenched during the Duma years.

Notes

1   A. K. Wildman, *The Making of a Workers' Revolution* (Chicago, 1967), pp. 27, 44.
2   G. D. Surh, *1905 in St Petersburg* (Stanford, CA, 1989), p. 53.
3   These issues are discussed in ch. 4 of Wildman, *Making*.
4   Wildman, *Making*, pp. 121–3.
5   M. Hildermeier, *The Russian Socialist Revolutionary Party Before the First World War* (New York, 2000), p. 77.
6   M. Perrie, 'Political and Economic Terror in the Tactics of the Russian SR Party before 1914' in W. J. Mommsen and G. Hirschfeld (eds), *Social Protest, Violence and Terror in Nineteenth and Twentieth Century Europe* (Basingstoke, 1982), p. 64.
7   Ibid., p. 70. For Chernov's early career and details on the Peasant Union, see Perrie, *The Agrarian Policy of the Russian Socialist Revolutionary Party* (Cambridge, 1976), pp. 13–83, 88.
8   Perrie, 'Political and Economic Terror', p. 65. For agrarian terrorism, see Perrie, *Agrarian Policy*, p. 95.
9   Surh, *1905*, p. 115.
10 Ibid., p. 139; U. A. Shuster *Peterburgskie rabochie v 1905–07* (Leningrad, 1977), pp. 64–82.
11 S. Harcave, *The Russian Revolution of 1905* (London, 1970), p. 93.
12 Shuster, *Peterburgskie*, pp. 101–4; Surh, *1905*, p. 206.
13 Shuster, *Peterburgskie*, pp. 151–3.
14 L. Trotsky, *1905* (London, 1971), p. 265; Surh, *1905*, p. 330.
15 M. Melancon, 'The SRs from 1902–07: Peasant and Workers' Party', *Russian History*, 12(1), 1985, pp. 15–22; C. Rice, *Russian Workers and the SR Party through the*

Revolution of 1905–07 (Basingstoke, 1988), p. 93. For the SRs and the Railway Workers, see Hildermeier, *The Russian Socialist Revolutionary Party*, p. 171.

16   M. Melancon, 'Neo-Populism in Early Twentieth Century Russia: The SR Party from 1900–17' in A Geifman (ed.), *Russia under the Last Tsar* (Oxford, 1999), p. 79.

17   Perrie, *Agrarian Policy*, pp. 101–39; the quoted passage is p. 112.

18   Ibid., p. 160.

19   J. L. H. Keep, *The Rise of Social Democracy in Russia* (Oxford, 1963), p. 167.

20   J. L. H. Keep, 'Russian Social Democracy and the First State Duma', *Slavonic and East European Review*, 34(82), 1955, p. 188.

21   Ibid., p. 186.

22   *Ocherki istorii Leningradskoi organizatsii KPSS* (Leningrad, 1980), p. 144.

23   *Volna* no. 20, 18 May 1906.

24   *Volna* no. 22, 20 May 1906.

25   *Kurier* no. 13, 31 May 1906.

26   *Ekho* no. 1, 22 June 1906.

27   'Protokoly PK RSDRP za 1905–06', *Krasnaya letopis'*, 1, 1931, p. 93.

28   *Proletarii* no. 16, 2 May 1907.

29   'Protokoly i dokumenty PK RSDRP (1907)', *Krasnaya letopis'*, 2, 1931, p. 61.

30   Perrie, *Agrarian Policy*, p. 171.

31   Perrie, 'Political and Economic Terror', pp. 72, 75; Melancon, 'The SRs', pp. 25, 29, 34.

32   Rice, *Russian Workers*, pp. 102, 109.

33   *Proletarii* no. 12, 25 January 1907.

34   *Proletarii* no. 16, 2 May 1907.

35   A. Levin, *The Second Duma* (New Haven, CT, 1940), p. 77.

36   Ibid., pp. 188, 227.

37   G. R. Swain, 'Freedom of Association and the Trade Unions, 1906–14' in O. Crisp and L. Edmondson (eds), *Civil Rights in Imperial Russia* (Oxford, 1989), pp. 172–7.

38   G. R. Swain, *Russian Social Democracy and the Legal Labour Movement* (Basingstoke, 1983), pp. 17–20.

39   Swain, 'Freedom of Association', p. 177.

40   Swain, *Russian Social Democracy*, pp. 38–40.

41   Ibid., p. 45.

42   Ibid., p. 49.

43   Ibid., pp. 52–4.

44   Ibid., pp. 62–8.

45   R. B. McKean, *St Petersburg between the Revolutions* (New Haven, CT, 1990), pp. 55, 58.

46   Swain, *Russian Social Democracy*, pp. 62–8.

47   Ibid., pp. 76–9.

48   Ibid., pp. 88, 89, 91.

49   Ibid., pp. 99, 102–3.

50   Ibid., p. 94.

51   Ibid., pp. 111–15.

52   McKean, *St Petersburg*, p.108.

53   M. Melancon, *The Socialist Revolutionaries and the Russian Anti-War Movement, 1914–17* (Columbus, OH, 1990), p.14.

54 Perrie, *Agrarian Policy*, p. 195.
55 Melancon, 'Neo-Populism', p. 82; and his '"Marching Together!": Left Bloc Activities in the Russian Revolutionary Movement, 1900 – February 1917', *Slavic Review*, 49(2), 1990, p. 246.
56 K. N. Morozov, *Partiia Sotsialistov-revoliutsionerov v 1907–14gg.* (Moscow, 1998), p. 41.
57 Ibid., p. 310.
58 Melancon, *The Socialist Revolutionaries*, p. 15.
59 Melancon, 'Stormy Petrels': The Socialist Revolutionaries in Russia's Labor Organisations, 1905–14, The Carl Beck Papers No. 703 (Pittsburgh, 1988), p. 2.
60 Melancon, 'Stormy Petrels', pp. 14–22, 31. See also McKean, *St Petersburg*, p. 69 and this author's unpublished card index.
61 Morozov, *Partiia*, p. 48.
62 Ibid., pp. 80, 84, 202.
63 Melancon, *The Socialist Revolutionaries*, p. 13.
64 Swain, *Russian Social Democracy*, pp. 120–3.
65 Ibid., pp. 134–9.
66 Swain, 'The Bolsheviks' Prague Conference Revisited', *Revolutionary Russia* 2(1), 1989, p. 138.
67 Swain, *Russian Social Democracy*, pp. 142–4.
68 Ibid., pp. 145–8.
69 Ibid., pp. 154–6.
70 Morozov, *Partiia*, p. 318.
71 Ibid., p. 543.
72 *Partiia sotsialistov-revoliutsionerov: dokumenty i materialy, iiun' 1907 g. – fevral' 1917 g.* (Moscow, 2001), p. 409.
73 Ibid., p. 420.
74 Morozov, *Partiia*, p. 91.
75 Swain, *Russian Social Democracy*, pp. 166–70.
76 Ibid., pp. 171–3.
77 Ibid., pp. 176, 179–82.
78 McKean, *St Petersburg*, p. 164; Melancon, 'Stormy Petrels', p. 40. The original government plan was to avoid separate social insurance elections and use the electors put forward in the workers' curia. This meant that boycotting the elections inevitably meant boycotting the start of the social insurance campaign.
79 Morozov, *Partiia*, p. 576.
80 Melancon, 'Stormy Petrels', p. 38.
81 McKean, *St Petersburg*, pp. 97, 109–10.
82 Melancon, 'Marching Together!', p. 249.
83 Morozov, *Partiia*, p. 89. Morozov therefore takes a very different line from Hildermeier, who suggests that at this time the SRs 'regressed' to their pre-1905 position, giving the emigration increased importance; see Hildermeier, *The Russian Socialist Revolutionary Party*, p. 299. Morozov's argument seems the more convincing.
84 McKean, *St Petersburg*, pp. 371, 376.
85 Melancon, *The Socialist Revolutionaries*, pp. 60–88.

86 McKean, *St Petersburg*, pp. 383–4, 393. For Bagdatiev's participation in the Women's Congress and the Temperance Congress, see the unpublished card index compiled by this author. This piece of theatre cannot have gone unnoticed at the time, since Bagdatiev was distributing the 'instructions' which the Bolsheviks wanted the meeting to adopt. Bagdatiev was an established Bolshevik figure. He had been staunchly opposed to Recallism and had taken part in the work of the Women's Congress and the Temperance Congress, and it was immediately after the Temperance Congress, in January 1910, that he had been arrested. Gvozdev had only arrived in St Petersburg in 1910, so personally may have known nothing of Bagdatiev's background, but it is hard to believe that other labour activists did not recognise him. For the SR role, see Melancon, *The Socialist Revolutionaries*, pp. 95–6.
87 Melancon, *The Socialist Revolutionaries*, p. 104.
88 McKean, *St Petersburg*, p. 397.
89 Ibid., p. 402, note 134; p. 558.

10

The origins, development and demise of M. N. Pokrovskii's interpretation of Russian history

James D. White

For historians of late imperial Russia, Mikhail Pokrovskii is significant in a number of respects. For one thing his biography itself is an intriguing chapter from the history of the period, revealing, as it does, the evolution towards Bolshevism of a person from a relatively privileged background by way of an involvement in liberal politics. Pokrovskii was also the only one of the leading Bolsheviks who was a trained historian, and who is credited with being the first person to present the history of Russia – including late imperial Russia – from a Marxist perspective. This interpretation of modern Russian history, which became the dominant one in the Soviet Union in the 1920s, sought to explain the political events of the time with reference to developments in economics, a method which, in Pokrovskii's estimation, embodied Marxist principles. In this endeavour Pokrovskii was innovative in that he introduced the concept of 'merchant capitalism' to account for the various directions taken in tsarist internal and foreign policies. However, Pokrovskii's version of a Marxist interpretation of Russian history was not the only one on offer, and he had to defend it against alternative schemes put forward at various times by Plekhanov, Trotsky and the followers of Bukharin.

An instructive dimension to the study of Pokrovskii is the inter-relation of scholarship and ideology in the Soviet period. At that time it became increasingly clear that Marxist interpretations of Russian history could not take place in a vacuum; they had immediate implications for the political struggles of the day. Pokrovskii tried to resist these pressures, but towards the end of his career they proved irresistible and the interpretation of Russian history became a function of the official ideology of the Stalin regime.

Perhaps the most intriguing aspect of Pokrovskii's interpretation of late imperial history is its demise. Why did it have to go? What exactly did Stalin have against it? These are interesting questions because they tell us something not only about Pokrovskii's historical thought, but about Stalin's political thinking as well.

It is only from the time Pokrovskii joined the Bolshevik party in 1905 that it is possible to follow his activities and writings in some detail. But when he joined the party he was already 37 and by that time a trained historian. Pokrovskii himself was not particularly forthcoming about his pre-1905 intellectual evolution. But since this undoubtedly influenced his later conceptions of history, it is important to try to establish what elements made up Pokrovskii's early political and ideological standpoint.

Mikhail Nikolaevich Pokrovskii was born in Moscow on 17 (29) August 1868, the son of a senior civil servant. The young Pokrovskii's highly respectable family background was to have its effect on his outlook on life, giving him a somewhat jaundiced view of the upper strata of society. Pokrovskii recalls: 'My father's attitude to the authorities . . . and to the church was very realistic, to say the least. From childhood I listened to stories about the abuses of the administration, the unedifying life of the aristocracy, the tsar's entourage and so on. Thanks to this, I was never a monarchist for a single moment of my life.'[1] Even if one makes allowances for the gloss Pokrovskii might have put on this recollection for a Soviet audience, it is nevertheless credible and accords with what we know of his early political attitudes.

At school Pokrovskii was an exemplary student and on his graduation he was awarded a gold medal, having distinguished himself in all of his subjects. In 1887 he was accepted into the Historico-Philological Faculty of Moscow University, where he studied history under two of the most distinguished scholars of the day: Vasilii Kliuchevskii and Paul Vinogradov. Kliuchevskii taught Russian history and Vinogradov taught Ancient and European history. Both deeply impressed the young Pokrovskii, especially Vinogradoff, whose seminars on historical methods attracted not only general European historians, but historians of Russia as well.[2]

In 1891 Pokrovskii graduated with a first-class diploma and eagerly accepted the offer to proceed to study for a postgraduate degree. After three years of intensive study which included both Russian history and the history of medieval Europe, he passed his master's examination in 1894. The next step ought to have been research for his master's dissertation which would have been presented as part of Pokrovskii's formal training as an academic, but this did not happen. Due to a disagreement with Kliuchevskii, Pokrovskii quit the University and went to teach history at an education college and at the Women's Institute which had been founded by Vinogradov's predecessor Guerrier (Ger'e). He nevertheless continued with his academic studies and was able to publish his first academic works in collaboration with Vinogradov. In the latter half of the 1880s Vinogradov edited a multi-volume collection of essays on European medieval history to which Pokrovskii contributed extensively. These essays provide abundant material to illustrate his approach to history at that time.[3]

A striking feature of the essays is the range of subjects they embrace; Pokrovskii wrote in considerable depth about the emergence of the Western Roman Empire, Simeon the Bulgarian tsar, the rule of the Medici in Florence, the Greeks in Italy and the renaissance of Platonic philosophy. The most extensive essay was on the economic life of Western Europe at the end of the middle ages. The first essay, that on the Western Roman Empire, contains a passage remarking that:

> The Empire was, if one may use the expression, a psychological necessity for the medieval man. Notwithstanding all the reversals and failures which beset this institution, the *idea* continued to live on until such times as together with the Renaissance and the Reformation *new concepts* made their appearance which shook the medieval world to its foundations.[4]

In retrospect the essay is something of a curiosity, because in his more mature writings Pokrovskii would never have dreamt of explaining historical developments in terms of 'psychological necessities', 'ideas' or 'concepts'. He would have sought an economic explanation for what happened in history.

The essay in which Pokrovskii took some pride in later years was the last one in the series, that on the economic life of Western Europe at the end of the middle ages. Because its theme was economic history it bore at least a superficial resemblance to the works Pokrovskii would produce in his Marxist period. Pokrovskii in fact recalled that the essay had ended by giving an account of primary capitalist accumulation according to Marx, but that when Vinogradov had read the pages in question he thought them quite out of place and demanded that they be removed.[5] Although there is no reason to doubt Pokrovskii on this matter, the general context of the article suggests that its author had no ideological affiliation with Marx, but was interested in Marx's work primarily as a source on English economic history.

At the turn of the century it was Vinogradov's brand of liberalism that determined the direction of Pokrovskii's early writings on political themes. Vinogradov's political ideas closely corresponded with his views on history. He was an Anglophile who ended his career teaching at Oxford. Vinogradov admired the British constitution and looked forward to the time when Russia too would have a parliamentary system on the Westminster model. In the Russian context this was an ambitious aim and had formidable arguments ranged against it. The most widespread of these was that in Russia the relationship between state and society was quite different from what it was in England. Whereas in England with its long tradition of local self-government, it was society which determined the actions of the state, in Russia it was the other way round: society was weak while the state was strong, so that developments in society were brought about by the initiative of the state. The salient example of this was that of the enserfment of the peasantry. This had been a measure which the state had enacted, and conversely, the liberation of the Russian serfs had also been implemented by the action of the state. Since Russia had quite different social and political structure from England, it was argued that a parliamentary system could never be successfully established there. This was the view of Russian history propounded by the great historians of Russia, S. M. Soloviev, B. N. Chicherin and Pokrovskii's contemporary Paul Miliukov.

The method Vinogradov used to counter arguments of this kind had been supplied by those nineteenth-century scholars who had specialised in the study of primitive agrarian communities, writers like Henry Maine, Georg Maurer and Emile de Laveleye. These scholars had been impressed by the great similarity which existed between agrarian communities in various parts of the world: in Germany, India, Russia and Anglo-Saxon England. It appeared that almost every nation had passed through or was passing through a historical phase in which society took the form of collectivist communities. It was the further evolution of these communities which would decide the social, political and economic structure of the given nation.

This school of thought quickly attracted adherents in Russia, because Russia was the country of the peasant community *par excellence*. These included Maxim Kovalevskii, Savin, Petrushevskii and Vinogradov. Vinogradov focused his attention on the Anglo-Saxon village community and the way it adapted itself to feudal relations. His English-language work *Villeinage in England* was the outcome of this kind of research. The English historian Maitland remarked that Vinogradov's first-hand acquaintance with Russian agrarian conditions enabled him to see many things in English medieval documents which remained obscure to people who had lost contact with the workings of communal village life.[6] These insights were of course in the very nature of Vinogradov's approach; he was concerned to demonstrate that the social evolution of England and Russia were basically the same, though Russia's development lagged considerably behind England's.

Pokrovskii wrote two articles in the cause of Russian constitutionalism directed towards showing that there was nothing in Russia's historical development that was inimical to the emergence of a parliamentary system. The first of these was in 1903 and was titled 'Local Self-Government in Ancient Russia'. In this he took issue with those historians such as Chicherin and Miliukov who considered that in Russia the state had been formed prior to society and that in Russia the historical process had taken place from the top down rather than from the bottom up as in Western Europe. Pokrovskii argued that this conception owed nothing to an empirical study of the facts but everything to the Hegelian approach adopted by the historians concerned.[7] Pokrovskii went on to show that in the sixteenth and seventeenth centuries there had been a strong network of local elected institutions in Russia which were comparable to similar bodies of local self-government in Western Europe.[8] Two years later in the article 'Zemskii Sobor and Parliament' Pokrovskii took issue with the Slavophile Aksakov and the Westerner Chicherin. Aksakov asserted that Russia was a country like no other in that it had given rise to democratic representative institutions. Chicherin, on the other hand, was of the opinion that Russian historical development offered close parallels to that of Western countries in that its representative assemblies had always been weak, and had been displaced by a strong centralised state. Pokrovskii's case was that in the middle ages in both Russia and the West there had been a division of power between the central government and the assembly representing 'the land'. A concord had existed between these two institutions. The representative assemblies had been strong because they existed prior to the formation of the centralised state with its standing army, its fiscal machinery, its powerful bureaucracy.[9] It was the opinion of Pokrovskii and the other contributors to the volume that in all civilised countries absolutist governments had been replaced by constitutional regimes, and this would be the case in Russia as well.[10]

The article 'Zemskii Sobor and Parliament' was published in 1905, by which time Pokrovskii had joined the Bolshevik party. This was a remarkably rapid progression across the political spectrum, even in a time of such political flux as the eve of the 1905 revolution. It was noted by Pokrovskii's contemporary A. A. Kizevetter, who recalled that:

> already in 1905 Pokrovskii took part in meetings connected with the foundation of the Constitutional Democratic party, and in the discussions on the party programme he took the side of the more right wing. Not long prior to this there appeared his article in the collection of the Small Zemstvo Unit published by the Beseda group headed by Prince Dolgorukov. And so, literally on the eve of becoming a Bolshevik, for whom the Kadets were guilty of the most mortal sins, Pokrovskii had rather close connections with Kadet circles.[11]

Kizevetter confuses Pokrovskii's two liberal articles, but the point he makes is sound enough: Pokrovskii's conversion to Bolshevism was remarkably rapid.

On the other hand, on the ideological plane, it was a short step from Vinogradov's brand of constitutionalism to what passed in those days for 'Marxism' or 'historical materialism'. Both doctrines rejected Russia's specificity in relation to Western Europe, and both propounded the idea that all countries pass through distinct historical stages. Both envisaged the end of the autocratic regime in Russia and its replacement by a democratic order. Both also shared the doctrine that the state, or the political realm, was not autonomous, but was conditioned by a close connection with the social and economic base.

The transition to Bolshevism was also eased for Pokrovskii because the group which he joined did not impose upon him any ideological demands. In 1903 Skvortsov-Stepanov had returned from exile and in conjunction with Alexander Bogdanov and his friends set about publishing a radical monthly journal which was called Pravda. The journal was the first collective publishing venture to be undertaken by Bogdanov's group and carried articles mainly on philosophy by Lunacharskii, Bazarov, Rozhkov and Bogdanov himself. Pokrovskii contributed a lengthy review of Rickert's book *Die Grenzen der naturwissenschaftlichen Begriffsbildung* titled 'Idealism and the Laws of History'.[12] In his discussion of Rickert's conceptions Pokrovskii did not come up with any ideas that could be described as particularly Marxist. Only in 1906 in the pamphlet *Economic Materialism* did Pokrovskii attribute any special importance to the work of Marx and Engels. But having defined 'Marxism' or 'economic materialism' as 'that conception of history which attributes chief significance to the *economic* structure of society and explains all changes in history with reference to *material* conditions, to people's *material* needs',[13] he then proceeded to translate this approach into terms he was already familiar with, and illustrate it with material he had used in his previous historical studies. The only work by Marx or Engels that Pokrovskii showed any familiarity with was the *Communist Manifesto*.

In 1907 Pokrovskii wrote a series of articles for the multi-volume *History of Russia in the Nineteenth Century* published by Granat. The topics included Alexander I, the Decembrists and Russia's foreign policy in the first decades of the nineteenth century. This series of articles represented Pokrovskii's first attempt to tackle the history of Russia in more modern times. But most Russian historians of Pokrovskii's generation would have been in the same position, for, as Daniel Field reminds us, recent history was outside the pale of historical scholarship in imperial Russia; serious Russian historians specialised in more remote eras.[14] This had been true of Pokrovskii too until he undertook the commission for Granat.

The chapters Pokrovskii wrote for the Granat *History of Russia in the Nineteenth Century* are for the most part fairly conventional works of historical narrative, couched in a lively style and with much picturesque and often amusing detail. In the chapters Pokrovskii was concerned to show that the class interest of the nobility determined the actions of the rulers. As he explained: 'The Russian tsar of the eighteenth century could rule only with the consent of the nobility. Anna Leopol'dovna and Peter III were ominous examples for those who might think of putting into effect a different sort of government. Paul I did not understand this and paid with his life for his mistake.'[15] The example of Emperor Paul I, who did not, apparently, act in the interests of the ruling class, confronted Pokrovskii with a serious methodological problem: how to account for the ability of a ruler to implement policies which ran counter to the interests of the ruling class. He had been able to rebut the contention of Chicherin and his followers that the Russian state was an autonomous entity by arguing that in the middle ages the government and the rest of society had been mutually dependent due to the feudal contract which existed between them. However, as he had indicated in his 1905 article '*Zemskii Sobor* and Parliament', this was true as long as the modern state with its standing army, its taxation system and its bureaucracy had not come into existence. But after the emergence of the modern centralised state a new situation existed, which Pokrovskii described in the article on Paul I. There in speaking of the change-over from feudal to capitalist relations he remarked:

> With the development of a money, capitalist economy the picture changes: the state acquires a reliable and constant source of income; it is now in a position to purchase personal services and not to beg for them; instead of unreliable *vassals* with whom it was necessary to negotiate and dispute, whose individuality had to be respected, there are now obedient *civil servants*. As exchange and centralisation of the economic life of the country develops, the sphere of operation of the central power widens: into the field of personal supervision come not only individual, but general interests. The fate not only of persons, but of whole social groups comes to depend on the caprice of the ruler.[16]

Having provided this explanation, Pokrovskii was then free to deal with the Emperor Paul in the way previous historians had done: in largely psychological terms. Thus, in Pokrovskii's opinion Paul 'was guided entirely by momentary caprice or an instinctive antipathy to every limitation of his personal will. To the first of these causes one may attribute the ukase on the three-day *barshchina* . . . to the second the vast majority of Paul's legislation.'[17]

In 1910 there appeared M. S. Aleksandrov's book *The State, Bureaucracy and Absolutism in Russian History*. The author, who normally wrote under the pseudonym 'Ol'minskii', had set out to investigate how Russian history might be written from a Marxist point of view. This involved showing that the Russian autocracy was motivated by definite class interests and was by no means the arbitrary tyrannical organisation depicted by conventional historians. In reading the literature on the subject Ol'minskii was rather surprised to find that there were very few historical works which attempted to trace the class roots of the Russian autocracy. It seemed to him that the only writer who had made any appreciable progress in this direction was N. A. Rozhkov. To illustrate the mistaken approach currently adopted by historians on the question of the Russian autocracy Ol'minskii cited in his book the passage from Pokrovskii's article in the *History of Russia in the Nineteenth Century* quoted above. Ol'minskii sent Pokrovskii a copy of his book, and the latter acknowledged it in a letter understandably tinged with some irritation. According to Pokrovskii:

> The theory of 'enserfment' and 'disenserfment' has not enjoyed any credit among younger Russian historians for about the last ten years. If we did not come out against it specifically, then you may easily see that we have systematically ignored it. We have not written to refute it simply because there has been no external pretext for doing so. None of us has so far undertaken such a large and comprehensive work as, for example, the *History of Russia* which is now being published. In it I

shall, of course, take this prejudice into account, and I hope that the corresponding chapters will meet fully with your approval.[18]

The *History of Russia* in question was the four-volume *Russian History from the Earliest Times* published by the 'Mir' company in Moscow which appeared between 1910 and 1913. Pokrovskii wrote most of the book, with the chapters on ecclesiastical history being supplied by N. M. Nikol'skii. As Pokrovskii and Nikol'skii explained in their introduction, the originality of their approach was not in terms of new factual material, but in re-working the material collected by *idealist* historians from a *materialist* point of view. The originality was to be in the interpretation.[19]

In fact the interpretation of Russian history embodied in the *Russian History from the Earliest Times* represented only a small variation on that found in the equivalent chapters in the *History of Russia in the Nineteenth Century*. The difference is that references to economic phenomena appear in the narrative more often. There is a more determined effort on Pokrovskii's part to show that the autocracy represents the interests of the nobility. Thus, Catherine II's proposal to liberate the serfs had to be abandoned because the rise in grain prices made *barshchina* labour more profitable for the landowners.[20] The chapter on the Emperor Paul, which Ol'minskii had found fault with, had been revised to reduce the emphasis on his personality. Now Paul's actions were explained by his anxiety to forestall peasant discontent and in this way safeguard the long-term interests of the serf-owners. Pokrovskii in evident satisfaction drew his readers' attention to the fact that he had managed to explain the general direction of Paul's policies without resorting to the method adopted by the majority of historians of his reign: to psychopathology. In this connection Pokrovskii confessed that when writing about Paul in the *History of Russia in the Nineteenth Century* he too had succumbed to using this mode of explanation.[21]

Pokrovskii must have believed that his approach to modern Russian history was sufficiently materialist to meet the objections raised by Ol'minskii to his earlier work. When the first volume of his *Russian History from the Earliest Times* appeared in the spring of 1910 Pokrovskii instructed the publisher to send a complimentary copy to Ol'minskii. Of the latter he wrote: 'This is an old Marxist author who . . . wrote the book *The State, Bureaucracy and Absolutism in Russian History*. There, without mentioning my name, he forcefully attacked my articles in *History of Russia in the Nineteenth Century*. He sent me his book, and I should like to repay him, especially since he is one of the few Marxist historians in Russia.'[22]

But Pokrovskii did not remain satisfied with the approach he had adopted for long, and when he published his *Studies in the History of Russian Culture* in 1914 his treatment of Russian history had undergone something of a transformation. In *Russian History from the Earliest Times* the economic factor is in a subsidiary position in relation to the historical events; it peeps through between them intermittently. In *Studies in the History of Russian Culture* it is the economic factor which dominates the book, the concrete historical events being treated as outcomes of the economic processes. In this way Pokrovskii had managed to elaborate a more consistent economic approach to history.

The economic interpretation of Russian history which Pokrovskii propounded in *Studies in the History of Russian Culture* utilised the concept of 'merchant capital'. In the book he showed how commerce had been a determining factor in the development of the Muscovite state from its very origins, since 'the population had worked to a large measure not only to satisfy their own needs, but to produce articles of exchange for the market'.[23] Drawing upon his wide knowledge of Russian history, he illustrated the involvement of Russian rulers in commercial ventures with extracts from chronicles and other first-hand sources. In the section of his book devoted to the state structure Pokrovskii returned to the subject of the relationship of the state to society, putting a new argument against those historians who maintained that in Russia the autocratic state was autonomous and stood above society. This was that merchant capital provided the key to the policies of the autocracy, and that these policies reflected the class interests of the mercantile community.[24] In the pamphlet *Tsarism and Revolution* published in 1918 Pokrovskii described the class-nature of the Russian autocracy epigrammatically in the phrase 'merchant capital rules in the cap of Monomakh'.[25] In the Soviet period he developed this interpretation of Russian history in *A Brief History of Russia* (1920)[26] and *Studies in the History of the Russian Revolutionary Movement* (1924).[27]

A Brief History of Russia was Pokrovskii's most celebrated work and it represents a synthesis of his two earlier books *Studies in the History of Russian Culture* and *Russian History from the Earliest Times.* It gives prominence to the economic factor, tracing the evolution of merchant capitalism, as *Studies in the History of Russian Culture* had done; but it is also to some extent an abridgement of *Russian History from the Earliest Times,* focusing on the more modern period, but ending at the beginning of the twentieth century. *Studies in the History of the Russian Revolutionary Movement* was the book in which Pokrovskii ventured into the twentieth century and took the history of Russia as far as the February revolution in 1917. This led the author into a discussion of the conflict between merchant and industrial capital in modern times and to consider to what extent Russia was an imperialist country on the eve of the 1917 revolution.

Pokrovskii's conception of merchant capitalism had been barely formulated before it encountered its first critics from within the Marxist camp. It is important to appreciate in this connection the institutional framework within which Pokrovskii worked in the early years of the Soviet regime. This was a regime whose legitimacy was based on the way it had come to power, so that from the very outset the history of the October revolution became thoroughly politicised.

In September 1920 Lenin established a special commission for the study of the October revolution and the Russian Communist Party. Initially this commission, known by the abbreviation 'Istpart', was attached to the Commissariat of Education, but in 1921 it was made into a department of the Secretariat of the Central Committee, making clear its political and ideological significance. Originally Istpart's chairman was Pokrovskii, but he almost immediately stepped down in favour of Ol'minskii, his erstwhile critic, whom he believed to be better suited to the position than himself. Pokrovskii had not approved of Istpart's creation; it was a political rather than an academic institution and the historical interpretations it promulgated were dictated by the party ideologists not historians. It is probably for this reason that Pokrovskii wrote very little on the subject of the Russian Revolution, though he was the best qualified among the Bolsheviks to do so.[28] The creation of Istpart *de facto* divided the Soviet historical study into two sections: the area of history covered by Istpart, and the rest, which was then perceived as being of no particular political significance. This was the – rather wide – historical sphere in which Pokrovskii preferred to work.

In keeping with its function of promoting the standing of members of the party leadership, Istpart published, or re-published, the writings of Lenin, Zinoviev, Kamenev and Trotsky. These writings were also intended to provide ideological guidance and to furnish the approved interpretation of the historical events with which they were concerned. It was in this spirit that in October 1921 Ol'minskii wrote to Trotsky, offering to publish his book *1905*, adding that a complete collection of his writings would be highly desirable lest the younger generation, 'not knowing as it should, the history of the party, unacquainted with the old and recent writings of the leaders, will always be getting off the track'.[29] Trotsky's book and the historical interpretations contained in it – which were completely at variance with Pokrovskii's own – had obviously the approval of the party. In face of the danger of his life's work being trampled underfoot, Pokrovskii felt compelled to make his objections known.

Trotsky's book, which had first been published in German in 1909, gave an exposition of his theory of permanent revolution. Since Trotsky expected that the victorious proletarian revolution would utilise the state for a socialist transformation of society, an essential part of his theory was that the Russian state should stand above society. According to Trotsky:

> The more centralised the state and the more independent of the ruling classes, the more it could become a self-willed organisation standing above society. The greater the military-financial strength of such an organisation, the more protracted and more successful can be its struggle for existence. The centralised state with a budget of two milliard roubles, with an eight milliard debt and with an army of over a million under arms is able to maintain itself long after it has ceased to satisfy the elementary requirements of social development – including protection from military threats for which purpose it was originally intended.[30]

This conception was singularly repugnant to Pokrovskii, who declared that it was alien to Marxism and that it should be contested no less resolutely than religious prejudices. In his judgement it was less important to prove that there was no historical Jesus Christ than to show that a supra-class state never existed in Russia.[31]

Pokrovskii's method of doing this was to argue that the autocracy had always represented class interests, those of merchant and industrial capitalists. Trotsky, on the other hand, denied completely the influence of merchant capital as the motive force behind tsarist policies on the grounds that Russia had been an economically backward country and the strength of its merchant class insignificant. He was of the opinion that: 'Russian capitalism did not develop through manufacture to the factory, because European capital, first in trade and afterwards in industrial form, poured down on us during that period when Russian handicraft had not in the mass divided itself from agriculture'.[32] The real stimulus for Russian industrial development, in Trotsky's view, came from the West in the form of foreign investment so that what existed in Russia was an enclave of highly developed imported industry superimposed on a country where economic backwardness prevailed. As for the state machine, it was precisely this economic imbalance which ensured its supra-class nature, for: 'In the last epoch of its existence, the autocracy was not only the organ of the possessing classes in Russia, but also the organisation of European stock markets for the exploitation of Russia. This double role again gave it very considerable independence.'[33] Trotsky did not deny completely the economic strength of the native Russian bourgeoisie. It was owing to its existence that Russia only became a semi- and not an outright colony of the Western powers.[34]

Pokrovskii was fortunate in his polemic that in the following year Trotsky fell foul of the party leadership and Pokrovskii's articles against Trotsky's conception of Russian historical development merged into the general anti-Trotsky campaign. Because Pokrovskii had argued in favour of Russia's having an autonomous economic development, one not dominated by foreign capital, his articles against Trotsky were held to lend weight to the case for the building of socialism in one country. This impression was reinforced in 1927, when two students of the Institute of Red Professors Alypov and Tsvetkov asked Stalin to clarify what his position was on the origins of the Russian autocracy. They had noticed that in his speech at the Tenth Party Congress Stalin had said that the centralised state in Russia had not been formed by the economic development of the country, but as a means of defence against the Mongols and other eastern peoples. Did this mean that Trotsky was right when he asserted that in its development the Russian state had overtaken economics? Stalin replied that: 'As for the theory of the "autocratic structure", I must say that basically I do not share comrade Trotsky's theory, whereas I consider comrade Pokrovskii's theory correct in the main, although it is not without its overstatements in simplifying the economic explanation of the rise of the autocracy'.[35] This passage was omitted from Stalin's *Works*, but it was referred to in a report of Pokrovskii's address to the First Congress of Marxist Historians published in the journal *Istorik-Marksist*. In his address Pokrovskii had confessed that in the explanation of historical events he tended to overstate the economic factor and that: 'This was noticed by comrade Stalin during the discussion between Pokrovskii and Trotsky. Recognising Trotsky's scheme as completely un-Marxist, comrade Stalin noted the correctness of Pokrovskii's scheme, only pointing out that it suffered from some simplification, consisting in the exaggeration of the role of the economic factor.'[36]

By the end of 1924 Pokrovskii's scheme of Russian history came under attack from a different quarter: from two of Bukharin's supporters, A. N. Slepkov and G. Maretskii. First Slepkov published a review of Pokrovskii's *Studies in the History of the Russian Revolutionary Movement*, then in the following year Maretskii reviewed Pokrovskii's collection of articles against Trotsky entitled *Marxism and the Peculiarities of Russia's Historical Development*. Both took issue with Pokrovskii's contention that the Russian autocracy represented the interests of merchant capital. In their view in the period before the 1917 revolution the Russian state represented the interests of finance capital, so that in opposing the landowners, who were allied financially with the bourgeoisie, the Russian peasants thereby were instrumental in overthrowing the power of finance capital. The peasant movement would not have this significance, however, if the Russian state was merely the political organisation of merchant capital. For this reason Slepkov and Maretskii were led to challenge Pokrovskii's scheme of Russian history.

Although Pokrovskii's polemical abilities were more than a match for those of Slepkov and Maretskii, it is likely that their arguments had raised serious doubts in his mind. He admitted that his conceptions of finance capital and imperialism were derived from Hilferding rather than Lenin, and in this respect needed revision. A further stimulus for Pokrovskii to re-think his position on Russia's economic situation on the eve of the revolution came in 1925 with the publication by N. N. Vanag, one of Pokrovskii's students, of the monograph *Finance Capital in Russia before the World War*. Vanag took as his starting-point Lenin's conception of imperialism as being the merger of finance or bank capital with industrial capital. This merger had taken place in Russia, but whereas the industry had been Russian, the finance capital had been foreign. Russian monopoly capitalism, therefore, was not an independent system, but more a link in a chain of a more powerful system: that of Anglo-French-Belgian finance capital. According to Vanag, foreign capital controlled three-quarters of the whole banking system, and of this the largest share was in the hands of the French banking consortium (53.2 per cent). The Germans controlled 36.4 per cent and the British 10.4 per cent. That is, the Entente powers controlled 63.6 per cent and the Germans 36.4 per cent of all foreign investment in Russian industry.[37]

Vanag's study was followed by that of S. Ronin, who concluded that not only the banking system in Russia but also the industrial capitalist monopolies were mainly branches of foreign capital. In his introduction to Ronin's book L. N. Kritsman declared that instead of a system of Russian finance capital there were on Russian territory elements of three systems of finance capital: the French, the German and the British.[38] Other researchers, like A. L. Sidorov and F. L. Granovskii, were reluctant to accept that Russia had been a colony of Western European imperialism, but they nevertheless found a great deal of foreign investment in the Russian economy. The only difference among the authors concerned the exact extent to which Russian industry was indebted to foreign capital. Vanag, Kritsman and Ronin represented the extreme dependence wing while Sidorov and Granovskii held more moderate positions. But, as Pokrovskii remarked:

> the debate is taking place on a very narrow front, within a matter of ten or twenty per cent, expressing the dependence of Russian industry on foreign capital. According to Vanag, the percentage is 70–75, and to Sidorov no more than 60. But that Russian capital before the war to a very great extent was a branch of Entente is not open to doubt and, in this respect, 'Russian imperialism' should appear in quotation marks.[39]

Pokrovskii accepted fully Vanag's findings, and adjusted his conception of modern Russian history accordingly. In an article written in 1926 he expressed the view that capitalism in Russia, railway construction in particular, had been stimulated by the merchant capitalist state out of military considerations. This swift economic development, originated by the autocracy and financed by foreign capital (here Pokrovskii cites Vanag's research), led to the creation of a social order which quickly made the autocracy itself an anachronism, a state machine which had no relation to actual social requirements. Yet from this situation there inescapably followed the proletarian nature of the revolution which swept away the autocratic state structure. For the Russian bourgeoisie itself, being a prisoner of foreign capital, was too feeble to carry out this task; it was: 'not in a condition to resolve this disproportion between the country's political structure and its economic development . . . and to give the country the kind of government it required'. The Russian proletariat, on the other hand, which had begun to organise itself politically long before the Russian bourgeoisie, was in such a position.[40]

This presentation of events brings Pokrovskii very close to Trotsky's viewpoint. Russian capitalism, then, is not an indigenous development, but a foreign importation – in this Pokrovskii and Trotsky are now in agreement. The revolution in Russia did not take place on the foundation created by indigenous monopoly capitalism, so that the economic argument for socialism in one country no longer exists. But since Pokrovskii will not follow Trotsky's reasoning to its logical conclusion – that socialism in one country is impossible – he was forced to argue that economic considerations are not in themselves decisive, and that the subjective factor, the human will, plays a major part in determining what is accomplished. Pokrovskii admitted that in this respect the Narodniki had been right.[41]

If Pokrovskii saw Vanag's work chiefly as a means of perfecting his own historical conceptions, others were more sensitive to its political implications. In 1928 at the First Conference of Marxist Historians, P. O. Gorin expressed what must have been in the minds of many delegates. He pointed out:

> the views of Vanag on the role of foreign capital in Russia are close to those of Trotsky. The latter in the preface of his book *1905* also ignores the role of indigenous capital in Russia. The ideas of Vanag and Trotsky are exactly alike. Of course, I am not saying that Vanag is a Trotskyist, but Trotsky's error of ignoring the role of indigenous accumulation should be taken into account by those who subscribe to the theory of 'denationalisation'.[42]

In his memoirs Sidorov also recalled the political context in which the discussion of Vanag's findings took place:

> My part in the discussion was modest. Besides my work in *Ocherki*,[43] I published an article in *Proletarskaia revoliutsiia*[44] where I outlined my own attitude to the discussion. I was closer to Granovskii's point of view, but I did not like his extravagant concessions to Vanag or his unfounded attacks on M. N. Pokrovskii. Besides this, I gave a radio talk from the lecture theatre of the Sverdlov University. In this talk the academic question of imperialism in Russia was linked with the question of Leninist theory of socialism in one country and of the 'maturity' of Russian capitalism for such construction. Although I was then politically in agreement with Granovskii and Vanag, it is true that Vanag's views found many supporters among the oppositionists. Therefore, the problem of Russian imperialism took on a great political significance in the struggle against the Trotskyists.[45]

Eventually the Trotskyist label began to be applied to Pokrovskii himself. It occurred in 1931 in a chapter written by an 'anonymous author' (actually A. L. Sidorov) in the *History of the Communist Party* edited by E. Iaroslavskii. It was asserted that: 'in denying the independent character of Russian imperialism, Pokrovskii, Vanag and Kritsman have regarded Russia as a colony of French and English imperialism'. There then followed accusations of a 'revision of Leninism', 'Trotskyist prose' and other political abuse which Pokrovskii rejected as having no justification.[46]

From 1929 onwards the academic climate in the Soviet Union deteriorated considerably and Pokrovskii and his conceptions of Russian history came under fire from several quarters in discussions about People's Will, the Asiatic mode of production and Chernyshevskii. Accusations of political heresy were bandied about on all sides. On 5 February 1931 Pokrovskii wrote to Stalin protesting against the unhealthy atmosphere which prevailed in academic circles, and against the campaign of slander which was being waged against him and his pupils. He deplored the fact that for his opponents it was not enough that he should admit his individual errors but that they wished him to prove that '*Pokrovshchina* in history was the same thing as *Rubinshchina* in economics and *Deborinshchina* in philosophy'.[47]

Pokrovskii at this time was trying to strengthen his position, for at the end of 1929 his attitude towards Vanag underwent a final modification. In a note to Stalin he described his pupil's ideas as 'semi-Trotskyist' and disclaimed them completely.[48] Vanag himself in 1932 had published a letter in *Istorik marksist* in which he said that he considered it necessary 'to condemn most decisively the point of view which presents tsarist Russia as a colony of Western European imperialist countries. This theory serves as a basis for the Trotskyist thesis that the building of socialism is impossible in our country.'[49]

Stalin made his presence felt by Soviet historians in a dramatic and forceful manner in October 1931 when *Proletarskaia revoliutsiia* published his letter to the editorial board of the journal. The letter, titled 'Some Questions Concerning the History of Bolshevism', complained that the journal had published an article by a certain Slutskii, which suggested that Lenin might have underestimated the danger of centrism in the German Social Democratic Party. There were some historical matters, Stalin asserted, which were axiomatic truths and were not subject to discussion. Any attempt to do so was, in his opinion, the smuggling of 'Trotskyist contraband' into historical literature. Stalin's letter singled out for special criticism Iaroslavskii's four-volume party history in which Pokrovskii had been criticised. Thus it was Pokrovskii's opponents who now found themselves under a cloud. This was particularly the case since in 1932 both Slepkov and Maretskii's brother were arrested for their participation in the conspiracy to oust Stalin organised by M. N. Riutin.[50]

When Pokrovskii died in April 1932 his reputation as an outstanding Marxist scholar was intact, but he left behind a historical profession in turmoil. According to Postyshev, the treatment which historians received 'either broke them completely or left them cowed'.[51] What disoriented Iaroslavskii in particular was that although he had approached Stalin personally and had written him a number of letters, he was still unable to discover precisely where he had been in error and how he might correct his mistakes. As Iaroslavskii noted in 1932: 'People are afraid to write. It is a very dangerous thing.'[52]

In retrospect it is clear what Stalin's objectives for Soviet historiography were. He wanted to be recognised by historians as the infallible guide on all questions of historical theory; and he wanted to be mentioned frequently in historical works and in a tone of extreme reverence. These objectives would be attained in 1938 with the publication of the *History of the Russian Communist Party (Bolsheviks)*, but in 1931 this was still some way off. Iaroslavskii's history of the party had made no secret of Stalin's divergences from Lenin in April 1917, and in the entire debate about Russian imperialism no one had made the slightest reference to Stalin's essay 'The Foundations of Leninism', written in 1924. This had explained the revolution in Russia as the 'chain of imperialism' breaking at its 'weakest link'.[53] Stalin himself had never based his arguments for 'socialism in one country' on the strength of Russia's indigenous economy, but on its weakness.

One major obstacle to Stalin's attaining his desired result was the status still enjoyed by Pokrovskii and his historical writings. In October 1932 the Soviet government resolved to attach Pokrovskii's name to Moscow University. In April of the following year the Presidium of the Communist Academy decided to petition that the History Institute of the Institute of Red Professors should be named in honour of Pokrovskii.[54] In 1933 a collection of Pokrovskii's articles was published under the title *Historical Science and the Class Struggle*.[55] Although the collection included the articles Pokrovskii had written against Trotsky, the ones concerned with the Vanag discussion had been omitted.

The means for Stalin to discredit Pokrovskii presented itself when the Commissariat of Education felt the need to commission new textbooks for Soviet schools. This was a matter in which Stalin intervened personally, despite the incongruity of a head of state concerning himself with the content of school history textbooks. As A. I. Gukovskii explains in his memoirs, the existing history textbooks, including one which he himself had written, had proved too dull and schematic.[56] A resolution 'On the Teaching of Civil History in the Schools of the USSR' was duly passed by the Soviet government on 16 May 1934, recommending that school textbooks should be produced which presented their factual material in a chronological order and avoided 'abstract sociological schemes'. A number of groups were established to draw up outlines for the proposed textbooks, Vanag being put in charge of the group concerned with the history of the USSR. In August of 1934 the outlines were read and commented upon by a panel consisting of Stalin, A. Zhdanov and S. Kirov. The panel found that Vanag's outline was unsatisfactory in a number of ways, including the rather surprising one that 'the dependent role both of Russian tsarism and Russian capitalism on that of Western Europe . . . remains unexplained'.[57] Vanag was to pay dearly for this oversight and was shot as an 'enemy of the people'.[58] On 26 January a governmental directive was issued setting up a commission headed by Zhdanov and including Bukharin and Karl Radek which would organise a competition for the writing of school textbooks.

The directive was published the following day, when *Pravda* and *Izvestiia* initiated the campaign against Pokrovskii and his 'school'. It was done in a rather subtle way, by juxtaposing a number of items under the general rubric 'On the Historical Front', only some of which were related. The key document was a bulletin headed 'In the Council of People's Commissars and the Central Committee of the Russian Communist Party' which reproduced the resolution of 16 May on school textbooks and recounted how the subject groups had been set up and the outlines commented upon. The comments on the groups concerned with the History of the USSR and Modern History were reproduced in full. None of this had anything to do with Pokrovskii. However, this was not the impression the newspapers conveyed, because side by side with the items on the schematic presentation of history found in school textbooks was a lengthy article denouncing the alleged errors of Pokrovskii and his 'school'. The article in *Izvestiia* was by Bukharin and the one in *Pravda* by Karl Radek. Bukharin's article was devoted to the more philosophical aspects of Pokrovskii's writings,[59] while Radek's concentrated on their political implications.[60] But what was common to both articles was that they accused Pokrovskii – quite unjustly – of being schematic and not paying due attention to concrete facts and events. In this way the content of both articles linked themselves to the resolution on school textbooks. The point was reinforced by an unsigned editorial in *Pravda*.

The finishing touch, to provide an internal connection between the denunciations of Pokrovskii and the resolution on school textbooks, was the presence of two brief references in the bulletin titled 'In the Council of People's Commissars . . . to the errors of Pokrovskii and his "school"'. The mentions only needed to be brief, because the nature of Pokrovskii's supposed errors had been elaborated on in the articles of Bukharin and Radek. According to M. V. Nechkina, who had examined the manuscript of the bulletin, the references to Pokrovskii in it were handwritten interpolations in Zhdanov's typescript by Stalin.[61] The impression created by the newspaper treatment of the item on school textbooks was that the directive of 26 January had been one condemning Pokrovskii and his 'school', and historians of the time wrote of the directive in exactly this way.[62]

The report of the jury for the history textbook competition was published in *Pravda* on 22 August 1937. The authors had in the main complied with the guidelines, and avoided abstract sociological schemes, but among the shortcomings which remained a prominent defect was that 'the Stalin thesis that Russia was beaten because of its military backwardness, because of its cultural backwardness, because of its governmental backwardness, because of its industrial backwardness, because of its agricultural backwardness, which provides one of the most important keys to Russian history in the last centuries, has not been understood by several authors of textbooks'. The report went on to say that if Russia's backwardness was not understood, the part played by Soviet power in transforming it from a poor and weak country into a rich and powerful one would not be appreciated.[63] Now, apparently, the theme of Russian backwardness, which had been associated with Trotsky until 1930, was to be attributed to Stalin.

In the same year as the jury reported, Stalin drew up an outline for the projected textbook on the history of the Russian Communist Party, the book which was to be his 'Encyclopedia of Marxism'. Symptomatically he was especially anxious that the authors of the textbook should mention the 'petty-bourgeois' nature of the country in order to explain the great variety of currents and fractions within the party and in the working class as a whole, against which it was necessary to wage an unrelenting struggle. The published version of the *History of the Russian Communist Party (Bolsheviks): A Short Course*, which appeared in 1938, duly stressed Russia's backwardness with the assertion:

> That Russia entered the imperialist war on the side of Entente . . . was not accidental. It should be borne in mind that before 1914 the most important branches of Russian industry were in the hands of foreign capitalists, chiefly those of France, Great Britain and Belgium, that is, of the Entente countries . . . All these circumstances, in addition to the thousands of millions borrowed by the tsar from France and Britain in loans, chained tsardom to British and French imperialism and converted Russia into a tributary, a semi-colony of those countries.[64]

It is ironic that Stalin should favour a scheme of Russian history hitherto associated with Trotsky. Of course it did not imply any sympathy on Stalin's part with Trotsky's point of view. It signified that Stalin was imposing his preferences *quite irrespective* of what associations they may have had previously; he was making irrelevant and consigning to oblivion the historical thinking of the early Soviet regime. He was wiping the slate clean, removing the ideological significance of the 1920s debates on Russia's economic development. Stalin had no longer any need to take into account the political implications of particular historical findings or align his pronouncements with them. Henceforth Russian and Soviet history would become what Stalin said it was. The anti-Pokrovskii campaign was to create a barren era for Soviet scholarship, dominated as it was by the *Short Course* commissioned and partly written by Stalin.

The anti-Pokrovskii campaign ended a current in historiography which had deep roots in Russian social and political thought. But the same prohibitions which Stalin had placed on the study of Russian capitalism and the Russian bourgeoisie also extended to the investigation of the liberal ideas from which Pokrovskii's interpretation of Russian history had emerged. The considerable element of continuity between the pre-revolutionary era and the Soviet period was thus obscured. In this way it became possible for Western historians to form the mistaken impression that Soviet historiography came into being as a result of 'a concerted effort to recast Russia's history in a Marxian ideological mold'.[65] That is very far from the way things actually happened. There was no concerted effort to re-interpret Russian history in this way after the Bolsheviks came to power, because the process of re-interpretation had begun well before the 1917 revolution, much of it in the service of Russian liberalism. The mistaken impression does, however, illustrate nicely the need to study the development of early Soviet historiography, and also the importance of Pokrovskii's

political and intellectual biography in reconstructing some key aspects of late
imperial Russia's history.

Notes

1 O. D. Sokolov, *M. N. Pokrovskii i sovetskaia istoricheskaia nauka* (Moscow, 1970),
   p. 46.
2 M. N. Pokrovskii, 'P. G. Vinogradov (1854–1925)', *Izvestiia*, 29 April 1926.
3 M. N. Pokrovskii, *Izbrannye proizvedeniia, 4, Russkaia istoriia v samom szhatom
   ocherke*, ed. M. N. Tikhomirov, V. M. Khvostov, L. G Beskrovnyi and O. D Sokolov
   (Moscow, 1967), p. 266.
4 M. N. Pokrovskii, 'Vosstanovlenie Zapadnoi Rimskoi imperii' in P. G. Vinogradov
   (ed.), *Kniga dlia chteniia po istorii srednikh vekov sostavlennaia krugom prepoda-
   vatelei*, vol. 1 (Moscow, 1896), p. 424.
5 M. N. Pokrovskii, *Istorizm i sovremennost' v programmakh shkol II stupeni* (Moscow,
   1927), p. 9.
6 H. A. L. Fisher, *Paul Vinogradoff: A Memoir* (Oxford, 1927), p. 21.
7 M. N. Pokrovskii, 'Mestnoe samoupravlenie v drevnei Rusi' in K. K. Arsenev (ed.),
   Melkaia zemskaia edinitsa (St Petersburg, 1903), p. 187.
8 Ibid., p. 190.
9 M. N. Pokrovskii, 'Zemskii sobor i parlament', in E. Avalov, V. V. Vodovozov and
   M. B. Gorenberg (eds), *Konstitutsionnoe gosudarstvo* (St Petersburg, 1905), p. 456.
10 Ibid., p. v.
11 A. A. Kizevetter, *Na rubezhe dvukh stoletii (vospominaniia 1881–1914)* (Prague,
   1929), p. 285.
12 M. N. Pokrovskii, '"Idealizm" i "zakony istorii"', *Pravda*, February–March 1904.
13 M. N. Pokrovskii, *Ekonomicheskii materializm* (St Petersburg, 1920), p. 3.
14 D. Field, 'The Reforms of the 1860s' in S. H. Baron and N. W. Heer (eds), *Windows
   on the Russian Past* (Columbus, OH, 1977), p. 94.
15 M. N. Pokrovskii, 'Rossiia v kontse XVIII veka. Khoziaistvo. Obshchestvo. Gosudarstvennaia vlast'' in *Istoriia Rossiia v XIX veke* (Moscow, 1907), p. 62.
16 M. N. Pokrovskii, 'Pavel Petrovich' in *Istoriia Rossiia v XIX veke* (Moscow, 1907),
   pp. 21–2.
17 Ibid., p. 27.
18 M. S. Aleksandrov, *Gosudarstvo, biurokratiia i absoliutizm v istorii Rossii*, 2nd edn
   (Moscow and Petrograd, 1919), p. 70.
19 M. N. Pokrovskii, pri uchastii M. N. Nikol'skogo i V. N. Storozheva, *Russkaia
   istoriia s drevneishikh vermen*, vol. 1 (Moscow, 1913), p. 1.
20 M. N. Pokrovskii, *Izbrannye proizvedeniia, 2, Russkaia istoriia s drevneishikh vermen*,
   ed. M. N. Tikhomirov, V. M. Khvostov, L. G Beskrovnyi and O. D Sokolov (Moscow,
   1965), p. 113.
21 Pokrovskii, *Russkaia istoriia s drevneishikh vermen*, p. 168.
22 A. I. Gukovskii, 'Kak sozdavalas' "Russkaia istoriia s drevneishikh vremen"',
   Voprosy istorii, 9, 1968, p. 132.
23 M. N. Pokrovskii, *Ocherk istorii russkoi kul'tury*, part 1 (Moscow, 1915), p. 88.

24   Ibid., pp. 270–1.
25   M. N. Pokrovskii, *Tsarizm i revoliutsiia* (Moscow, 1918), p. 13.
26   M. N. Pokrovskii, *Izbrannye proizvedeniia, 3, Russkaia istoriia v samom szhatom ocherke*, ed. M. N. Tikhomirov, V. M. Khvostov, L. G Beskrovnyi, and O. D. Sokolov (Moscow, 1967).
27   M. N. Pokrovskii, *Ocherki russkogo revoliutsionnogo dvizheniia XIX–XX vv.* (Moscow, 1924).
28   M. N. Pokrovskii, 'O vozniknovenii Istparta', *Proletarskaia revoliutsiia*, 7–8, 1930, pp. 138–9; O. Lezhava and N. Nelidov, *M. S. Ol'minskii: Zhizn' i deiatel'nost'* (Moscow, 1973), p. 208.
29   L. D. Trotsky, *The Stalin School of Falsification*, introduction and explanatory notes by M. Schachtman, translated by J. G. Wright (New York, 1962), pp. 23–4.
30   L. D. Trotskii, *1905* (Moscow, 1922), p. 21.
31   M. N. Pokrovskii, 'Pravda li, chto v Rossii absoliutizm "sushchestvoval naperekor obshchestvennomu razvitiiu"?' in *Marksizm i osobennosti istoricheskogo razvitiia Rossii. Sbornik statei 1922–1925 gg.* (Leningrad, 1925), p. 23.
32   Trotskii, *1905*, p. 300.
33   Ibid., p. 307.
34   L. D. Trotskii, 'Parakhod – ne parakhod, a barzha', *Pravda*, 7 July 1922.
35   M. V. Nechkina, 'Vopros o M. N. Pokrovskom v postanovleniiakh partii i pravitel'stva 1934–1938 gg. o prepodavanii istorii i istoricheskoi nauke', *Istoricheskie zapiski*, 118 (1990), pp. 232–46, at pp. 242–3.
36   M. N. Pokrovskii, 'Leninizm i russkaia istoriia', *Istorik marksist*, 11 (1929), pp. 234–5.
37   N. Vanag, *Finansovyi kapital v Rossii nakanune mirovoi voiny* (Moscow, 1925), pp. 24–7.
38   S. Ronin, *Inostrannyi kapital i russkie banki (K voprosu o finansovom kapitale v Rossii)* (Moscow, 1926), p. v.
39   M. N. Pokrovskii, *Imperialistskaia voina* (Moscow, 1928), p. 267.
40   M. N. Pokrovskii, 'K deviatoi godovshchine', *Nauchnyi rabotnik*, 11, 1926, p. 12.
41   Ibid., pp. 9–12.
42   P. O. Gorin, 'Discussion on Vanag's Paper', *Istorik marksist*, 11, 1929, p. 234.
43   A. L. Sidorov, 'Vliianie imperialisticheskoi voiny na ekonomiku Rossii' in M. N. Pokrovskii (ed.), *Ocherki po istorii Oktiabr'skoi revoliutsii*, (Moscow and Leningrad, 1927).
44   A. L. Sidorov, 'O finansovom kapitale v Rossii', *Proletarskaia revoliutsiia*, 5, 1929.
45   A. L. Sidorov, 'Nekotorie razmyshleniia o trude i opyte istorika', *Istoriia SSSR*, 3, 1964, p. 129.
46   M. N. Pokrovskii, 'Po povodu nekotoroi putanitsy', *Istorik marksist*, 1–2 (1932), p. 18.
47   L. V. Ivanova, *U istokov sovetskoi istoricheskoi nauki. Podgotovka kadrov istorikov-marksistov 1917–1929* (Moscow, 1968), p. 180.
48   K. N. Tarnovskii, *Sovetskaia istoriografiia rossiiskogo imperializma* (Moscow, 1964), p. 51.
49   N. Vanag, 'Letter to the Editors', *Istorik marksist*, 4–5 (1932), p. 357.
50   R. Medvedev, *Let History Judge: The Origins and Consequences of Stalinism* (Oxford, 1989), p. 296.
51   P. Postyshev, 'Misinterpretations of Stalin's Letter to the Proletarskaya Revolyutsia'

in *Questions Concerning the History of Bolshevism: A Symposium* (Moscow, 1932), p. 36.

52   E. N. Gorodetskii, 'Vystuplenie' in *Vsesoiuznoe soveshchanie o merakh podgotovki nauchno-padagogicheskikh kadrov po istoricheskim naukam* (Moscow, 1962), p. 363.

53   J. Stalin, *Problems of Leninism* (Moscow, 1953), p. 37.

54   A. I. Alatortseva and G. D. Alekseeva (eds), *50 let sovetskoi istoricheskoi nauki 1917–1967* (Moscow, 1971), pp. 170, 178.

55   M. N. Pokrovskii, *Istoricheskaia nauka i bor'ba klassov*, 2 vols (Moscow and Leningrad, 1933).

56   A. I. Gukovskii, 'Kak ia stal istorikom', *Istoriia SSSR*, 6 (1965), pp. 95–8.

57   I . Stalin, A. Zhdanov and S. Kirov, 'Zamechaniia po povodu konspekta uchebnika po istorii SSSR' in *K izucheniiu istorii* (Moscow, 1937), p. 23.

58   Tarnovskii, *Sovetskaia istoriografiia rossiiskogo imperializma*, p. 69.

59   N. I. Bukharin, 'Nuzhna li nam marksistskaia istoricheskaia nauka? (O nekotorykh sushchestvenno vazhnykh, no nesostoiatel'nykh vzgliadakh M. N. Pokrovskogo)', *Izvestiia*, 27 January 1936.

60   K. Radek, 'Znachenie istorii dlia revoliutsionnogo proletariata', *Pravda*, 27 January 1936.

61   The passage from the document in question is reproduced in D. Brandenberger, 'Who Killed Pokrovskii (The Second Time): The Prelude to the Denunciation of the Father of Soviet Marxist Historiography, January 1936', *Revolutionary Russia* 11(1), 1998, p. 70.

62   Nechkina, 'Vopros o M. N. Pokrovskom v postanovleniiakh partii i pravitel'stva 1934–1938 gg. o prepodavanii istorii i istoricheskoi nauke', pp. 236–40.

63   'Postanovlenie zhuri pravitel'stvennoi komissii po konkursu na luchshii uchebnik dlia 3 i 4-go klassov srednei shkoly po istorii SSSR' in *K izucheniiu istorii* (Moscow, 1937), p. 33.

64   *Istoriia vsesoiuznoi kommunisticheskoi partii (bol'shevikov): Kratkii kurs* (Moscow, 1938), p. 156.

65   S. H. Baron and N. W. Heer, 'Introduction' in Baron and Heer (eds), *Windows on the Russian Past*, p. iii.

11

Late imperial Russia in the imperial world

Paul Dukes

Dominic Lieven has appropriately argued: 'The demands of international power politics and of membership of the European and then global system of great powers were of overwhelming importance in Russian history. More probably than any other single factor they determined the history of modern Russia.'[1] In this chapter, my aim will be to show my agreement with this observation and to present supporting evidence for it while concentrating on late imperial Russia in the imperial world. However, I will widen the 'system of great powers' to add economic and cultural considerations to the political.

Before 1914, neither 'empire' nor 'imperialism' was a bad word in Europe, except for a few critics. From Portugal to Russia, patriots celebrated the participation of their own country in a movement that had very nearly taken over the whole world. Among the first negative views was that of J. A. Hobson in 1902:

> The scramble for Africa and Asia has virtually recast the policy of all European nations, has evoked alliances which cross all natural lines of sympathy and historical association, has driven every continental nation to consume an ever-growing share of its material and human resources upon military and naval equipment, has drawn the great new power of the United States from its isolation into the full tide of competition; and by the multitude, the magnitude, and the suddenness of the issues it throws on to the stage of politics, has become a constant agent of menace and of perturbation to the peace and progress of mankind.[2]

A dozen years later, as the crisis leading to war loomed, imperial rivalries meant even more passionate assertion of one's own cause accompanied by denunciation of the cause of one's own rivals.

These rivalries were by no means the same as they had previously been. For example, from the British point of view, the German Empire had seemed relatively benign before the naval arms race began at the end of the nineteenth century, and talk of an Anglo-Saxon alliance including Britain and Germany along with the USA lasted into the early twentieth century. As W. H. Roobol commented in 1991: 'The democratic institutions of Great Britain and the

United States were supposed to have originated in the German forests and to have been brought to England in a remote past'.[3] Back in 1905, Robert Seton-Watson wrote: 'The three great Teutonic nations – Britain, America and Germany – are the natural allies of the future; and such an alliance, once realized (not on paper, but in fact), would be almost as great a gain to the peace of the world as a European Federation'. In 1906, he expressed the view that the Habsburg monarchy of Austria-Hungary would remain the pivot of the balance of power, and its disappearance would be 'a European calamity'. The ailing Ottoman Empire should be partitioned between Germany and Russia, which he had recently denounced as 'not a civilized state'. Although Seton-Watson's estimate of Russia had not changed, he was prepared to satisfy its age-old ambition for the acquisition of Constantinople and the Straits as part of the appeasement of Germany in the Middle East. If Germany were not pacified, 'with Britain and Germany ranged on opposite sides, general war is sooner or later inevitable'.[4] When general war broke out in 1914, the Anglo-Saxon alliance was quickly forgotten in Britain, replaced by denunciation of the beastly Huns, transfixing Belgian babies on their bayonets.

Conversely, Russia, which had been a deadly rival through the years of the Great Game, had by then become Britain's ally along with France – itself no British favourite in spite of the so-called Entente Cordiale. In 1860, defences against Napoleon III had been built as far north as Aberdeen. In 1898, Britain and France were on the brink of war over Fashoda on the Nile. But then, differences over Egypt and Morocco were resolved in the *entente* of 1904. As for Russia, throughout the nineteenth century it had been feared as a menace to freedom-loving Europe. An anonymous *Description of Sevastopol* published in 1855 caught the mood of many other books before, during and after the Crimean War in its observation that:

> Russia, by fraud or force, has succeeded in extending the limits of her empire from the Polar Regions of America to the centre of Europe, from the Arctic Circle to the sunny regions of Persia. Whatever territories her armies may have conquered, her treacherous and cruel diplomacy has acquired positions more dominant, and places of attack and defence still more important.[5]

After the Crimean War, the determination that the Russians should not seize Constantinople nor defeat Great Britain in the Great Game of empire played out in Central Asia was resolute indeed, and Russophobia often reached fever pitch. Small wonder, then, that German ministers in the early twentieth century 'practically staked their reputation on the prophecy that no British Government sufficiently bullied and frightened would stand by France, who had for centuries been England's ubiquitous opponent, and was still the ally of Russia, England's "hereditary foe"'.[6] Nevertheless, neither Francophobia nor Russophobia persisted without some attempts at rapprochement. To take an example from A. J. P. Taylor's masterpiece, in 1871 Salisbury invited the French fleet to visit Portsmouth in order to demonstrate, as he wrote to Queen Victoria, that 'England has no antipathy to France, or any particular partisanship against her'. In his autobiography, Taylor asserted: 'I held with the great Lord Salisbury that cooperation with Russia was a wiser course than hostility and that Russia, whether Tsarist or Soviet, sought security, not world conquest'.[7]

The struggle for imperial expansion that had been largely the affair of Europe was joined at the turn of the century by two powers from the wider world – the USA and Japan. Both of these clashed with Russia in the Far East, Japan most seriously in the Russo-Japanese War of 1904–5, after which the USA acted as peacemaker. Arguably, the USA constitutes the most appropriate comparator for Russia, partly because of their situation as outliers of Europe, even more because of their imperial rivalry reaching new heights in 1917 with the clash of the world-views of Lenin and Wilson.

In broad context, modern empire was dominated at first by Portugal and Spain, then by the Netherlands, followed by an Anglo-French condominium. Towards the end of the nineteenth century, well-established Britain was joined by a dynamic USA in a new leadership of the imperial race.

While there was a succession of victors in the struggle for mastery of the seas, Russia was consolidating its landward empire, in rough parallel with its neighbours, Austria and Germany. The gathering together of the lands around Moscow was followed in the sixteenth century by probes into Siberia and, less successfully, towards the Baltic. Much of the Ukraine was assimilated in the middle of the seventeenth century and the Baltic region – more certainly – at the beginning of the eighteenth. These acquisitions were important not only politically, but economically and culturally too. So were the partitions of Poland (with Austria and Prussia) towards the end of the eighteenth century, accompanied by further expansion towards the Black Sea and the Caucasus. The major development in the nineteenth century was into Central Asia and the Far East, hence the clashes with Britain, the USA and Japan. But the major crisis leading to the First World War was centred on Europe.

There, Austria had emerged from the ruins of the Holy Roman Empire to dominate the Balkans and contiguous Central Europe in the Austro-Hungarian Empire of 1867. Meanwhile, spreading from its consolidated base in Prussia, Germany completed its continental expansion in Europe by 1871. Along with Austria and Germany, Russia demonstrated apartness from Western peers in the early modern period. While most of the empires of the rest of Europe developed in a freer manner stemming from their access to the sea, the three at the centre and east of the continent moved towards a more landlocked consolidation based on variants of the institution of serfdom. Their collaboration from the partitions of Poland through to the formation of the Three Emperors' League in 1873 was based on shared autocratic values. From the beginning, there was rivalry, too, leading to the realignment of the pre-1914 period.

Within the framework of Europe alone, many similarities could be made between Germany, Austria and Russia. However, on the global scale appropriate for the twentieth century, especially from 1917 onwards, I have suggested that another appropriate comparator for Russia is the USA.

By the middle of the nineteenth century, radiating from the thirteen former original colonies, the USA had rounded out its boundaries. Having eliminated most of the Native Americans, fought with Mexico and agreed with Canada, Americans rushed for gold in '49 to consolidate their presence on the Pacific coast. There, Russian settlements had already played a part in the formation of US policies, especially the Monroe Doctrine first enunciated in 1823 and declaring that 'the American continents, by the free and independent condition which they have assumed and maintain, are henceforth not to be considered as subjects for future colonization by any European powers'. Moreover, Russian involvement in the Greek war for independence helped to prompt a second principle of the Doctrine: 'In the wars of the European powers in matters relating to themselves we have never taken any part, nor does it comport with our policy so to do'.[8]

Thus, the USA played no active part in the Crimean War of 1854–56, although immediately afterwards, in the estimate of historian Frank Golder, 'the United States was the only nation in the world that was neither ashamed nor afraid to acknowledge boldly her friendship for Russia'.[9] Then, during the American Civil War, 1861–65, Russia appeared to be pursuing a policy of benevolent neutrality, and mutual good feelings were fostered by the announcement of two emancipations, of the Russian serfs in 1861 and of the American slaves in 1863. *Harper's Weekly* could go so far as to compare Alexander II's repression of the Polish Insurrection in 1863 with the attempt of Abraham Lincoln to prevent the South from seceding from the Union, predicting that:

> Russia, like the United States, is a nation of the future . . . Like the United States, Russia is in the agonies of a terrible transition: the Russian serfs, like the American negro, are receiving their liberty; and the Russian *boiars*, like the Southern slave-owners, are mutinous at the loss of their property . . . To two such peoples, firmly bound together by an alliance as well as by traditional sympathy and good feeling, what would be impossible? . . . An alliance between Russia and the United States at the present time would relieve both of us from all apprehensions of foreign interference.[10]

A year later, in 1864, the Russian Chancellor Prince Alexander Gorchakov issued a defence of expansionism: 'The United States in America, France in Algeria, Holland in her Colonies, England in India – all have been irresistibly forced, less by ambition than by imperious necessity, into this onward march, where the greatest difficulty is to know where to stop'.[11] Russia conformed to this pattern: in 1860, the Russian imperial flag was hoisted on the Pacific coast over a small collection of huts named Vladivostok, 'Lord of the East'. But in 1867 Russia took a step back as the USA took one forwards with the sale of Alaska. Historian Norman E. Saul comments:

> While many Americans felt they were paying for a worthless burden and assuming an untimely obligation out of appreciation for past favors, Russians sensed a wound to their grand empire that had become infected with American ingratitude. Russia did in fact lose the American part of its national psyche, an important but incalculable feature of its imperial outreach.[12]

Possibly for this reason, at least in part, Russians pushed deeper into Central Asia. The perceptive analyst David Mackenzie has pointed out that the advances of the 1860s, although begun by the government's decisions, went much further than its plans and intentions. Ministers wanted to promote commerce and security. Mackenzie comments: 'Their public opposition to unchecked imperialism was sincere, but they proved impotent against the generals and their supporters . . . . What eventually set limits to Russian expansion in Central Asia were not ministerial resolutions but mountain barriers and British power.'[13]

While the Great Game of empire was played mainly against Britain in and around Afghanistan, there were many rivals to be found in the Far East by the end of the nineteenth century, especially in China. Among them was the USA, which had spent the 1870s and 1880s completing its victory over Native Americans before a final massacre at Wounded Knee, South Dakota, in 1890.

Already, in the 1870s and 1880s, the USA had asserted its position in the wider world, in particular in Latin America and across the Pacific to Asia.[14] The most positive response to infiltration from the USA and Europe came from Japan. A popular voice arguing that if his country could not defeat the imperialist powers it should join them was Fukuzawa Yukichi, who pointed to the fate of the American Indians as an object lesson. 'Among the countries touched by the Westerners', he asked, 'was any able to maintain real independence?' To show the way forward, Fukuzawa translated the American Declaration of Independence and Constitution, pointing out that 'Heaven did not create a man above or below another man'. Nevertheless, he argued, if Japan were to be a full member of the imperialist club, it too should seek its local spheres of influence in Korea and elsewhere.[15]

The models for Japanese modernisation were by no means exclusively American. Indeed, Dominic Lieven asserts, 'Imperial Germany was its preferred role-model'.[16] Russia cut a much smaller figure in this respect, although the sweeping reforms from 1868 including the reorganisation of the army, the creation of a navy and the adoption of Western dress certainly recalled those of Peter the Great at the beginning of the eighteenth century.

By the 1890s, as the race for empire accelerated throughout the world, the scene was being set in the Far East for the first major global clash involving the European powers, the USA and Japan. It was the last of these, only recently emerged from centuries of isolation and attempting to enter a wider world already carved up by the old imperial powers, that triggered the crisis. In disagreement with China about influence in Korea and elsewhere, Japan engaged in a short, sharp and successful war in 1894, concluded by the Treaty of Shimonoseki in 1895. Japan obliged China to recognise the independence of Korea, also taking the island of Formosa and the mainland peninsula of Liaotung with its ice-free harbour, Port Arthur. Russia was outraged by this infiltration into what it liked to think of as its own sphere of influence. Germany and France joined in an international rebuke to Japan, which was obliged to hand back the Liaotung peninsula to China. In 1896, Russia received the right to construct the Chinese Eastern Railway (CER) through northern Manchuria to Vladivostok, and entertained the aim of extending its sphere of influence into China and Korea. After Germany seized Kiaochow on the Shantung peninsula in 1897, Russia seized Port Arthur, while Great Britain and France also took new bases. The USA increased its influence enormously in 1898 by taking Cuba and the Philippines from Spain and annexing Hawaii, previously of interest to Britain and Russia. But Murav'ev, the Russian Foreign Minister from 1897, wrote to his appointee as ambassador to the USA Cassini, who had previously served in China, that Far Eastern developments needed special attention: in particular, American control of Hawaii, the 'Malta of the Pacific', was a far preferable alternative to that of Japan, which had to be contained.[17]

While the Japanese smouldered, some Chinese took action against foreign intervention in the shape of the nationalist Boxer rising of 1900. Russia's subsequent move in force into Manchuria alarmed the other European powers and the USA, especially keen to maintain the policy of the Open Door. In 1899 and 1900 US Secretary of State John Hay put forward his proposal that the powers should respect the administrative and territorial integrity of China. Zhang Zhidong, one of the leading figures in the pro-Western elite wrote: 'It will be better to open up, without any reservations, the Three Eastern Provinces [that is, Manchuria] to all the powers of the world for commerce than yield to Russia only'.[18] While China grudgingly accepted the Open Door, the combined threat of the USA, Great Britain and Japan was enough for Russia to promise in 1902 to withdraw its troops from Manchuria and to abandon other plans of expansion.

At the beginning of 1902, Japan signed a treaty with Great Britain committing each side to come to the assistance of the other if it were attacked by two further powers. Neither power was to enter into further arrangements to the prejudice of the alliance, while the special interest of Japan in Korea was recognised. On the Korean and other questions, the tension between Japan and Russia intensified as Russia delayed its departure from Manchuria. Meanwhile, as Walter LaFeber points out, the USA was 'an informal member' of Japan's alliance with Great Britain, and American loans to Japan 'marked the birth of Wall Street as a force in international diplomacy.' He quotes a Japanese war song to the effect that Great Britain, 'Lion, Lion, the king to the Beasts', was in approval and the USA sympathised with Japan's 'war for civilization'.[19] Russia's ally, France, attempted to avert war, but on the night of 8–9 February 1904 Japanese destroyers took the Russian fleet in Port Arthur by surprise. While only one Russian battleship was seriously damaged, the whole Pacific fleet was rendered powerless in subsequent engagements. A worse fate awaited the Baltic fleet, which, having mistaken British fishing vessels in the North Sea for Japanese warships and sunk some of them, itself met with almost total destruction in the Tsushima Straits on 27 May 1905. On land, the biggest battle of the war at Mukden in Manchuria had ended in March with heavy losses on both sides and certain defeat if short of disgrace for Russia.

The rising tide of revolution in Russia and the near exhaustion of Japan persuaded both sides to accept the offer of President Theodore Roosevelt of the USA to come to the negotiating table in Portsmouth, New Hampshire, in August 1905. Sergei Witte played a weak Russian hand as best he could, giving up the Liaotung peninsula to the Japanese and conceding the supremacy of their interests in Korea, but maintaining dominance in northern Manchuria and the northern half of the island of Sakhalin. In the estimate of Hugh Seton-Watson:

> The impact of the first victory of an Asian over a European power in modern times was felt beyond the theatre of war. Defeat put an end to the designs of the extreme expansionists in Russia, but with the Maritime Provinces [the hinterland of Vladivostok] and the Chinese Eastern Railway still in its possession, the Russian empire remained a Great Power of the Pacific.[20]

In 1910 Japan formally annexed Korea. Then in 1912 a Russo-Mongolian Treaty extended Russian interests in the Far East.

Nevertheless, after the Russo-Japanese War of 1904–5 and the first Russian Revolution of 1905, the primary focus of imperial attention was Europe. Already, by the beginning of 1904, a Franco-Russian Alliance was concluded, promising mutual military aid should either side be attacked by a member of the Triple Alliance of 1882 comprising Germany, Austria and Italy. Germany, the main cause for concern, now suggested an alignment with both Russia and France in the person of Kaiser William II in a meeting with Nicholas II on the tsar's yacht in the Gulf of Finland in the bay of Björkö in July 1905. France flatly refused the offer, and reinforced the Alliance with Russia in the spring of 1906 with a huge loan of 2.25 billion francs.

Russia now entered into negotiations with its rival during the years of the Great Game, Britain, culminating in the Anglo-Russian Convention of August 1907. Agreement was reached on spheres of influence in Persia, while Russia accepted that Afghanistan was beyond its sphere of interest and that Britain had particular concerns over Tibet. In April 1908 a treaty was signed by Russia, Germany, Denmark and Sweden regarding the Åland Islands in the Baltic Sea, and in November 1910 a bilateral convention with Germany recognised Russian interests in Persia and German interests in Turkey.

Agreement on the Balkans was elusive, however, especially as far as the Slav peoples were concerned. As the Turkish empire disintegrated, big brother Russia sought to protect its smaller siblings, while still harbouring ambitions to annex the Straits and other strategic areas. Already worried about its waning influence in the face of Balkan nationalism, both Slav and non-Slav, Austria sought to consolidate its position in Bosnia and Hercegovina. Neighbouring Serbia and its protector Russia gave way to pressure from Germany as well as Austria, but with a smouldering resentment that was soon to lead to the outbreak of hostilities.

In October 1912 an alliance of Balkan states attacked Turkey, and achieved considerable success. Alarmed especially at Serbia's pretensions to an outlet on the Adriatic Sea, Austria managed to restrain them as part of a general Treaty of London in May 1913. However, war broke out again in June, as Bulgaria attacked Serbia and Greece over the question of influence in Macedonia. Romania took advantage of the situation to invade Bulgaria, which had to concede defeat.

Meanwhile, great power tensions grew as Russia, France and Britain became alarmed about growing German influence in Turkey. However, the Russian government in particular was not unanimous, the Minister of the Interior P. N. Durnovo speaking for many in a memorandum arguing that the future of Germany was via the sea while Russia was the most continental of the powers. Therefore, Durnovo argued, there was no fundamental conflict between Germany and Russia, whose probable defeat in a European war would lead to hopeless anarchy.

War came when the assassination of the Archduke Franz Ferdinand on 28 June 1914 led to renewed and greater Austrian determination to reduce the power of Serbia. Russian mobilisation in support of Serbia was the next significant step on the road to a wider conflict.

As elsewhere, the war began for Russia with widespread popular enthusiasm. By 1917, however, its unpopularity had sunk lower than elsewhere. In August 1914, in order to take German pressure off Paris, a Russian army invaded East Prussia. At the end of the month, the Russians suffered a massive defeat at the battle of Tannenberg, and their commander committed suicide. By the middle of September, they were driven from German territory. To the southwest, there was more success as another Russian army took nearly half of Austrian Galicia. A counter-attack into East Prussia was a failure, however. Turkey's declaration of war on the allies on 31 October 1914 cut the sea route to the Mediterranean while the Baltic was closed by a German blockade.

If 1914 had brought some success for Russia, 1915 was unmitigated disaster. In March, France and Britain agreed that their ally should have what they had previously fought to deny her, Constantinople and the Straits. But the refusal of the Russians to allow their Greek Orthodox rivals to participate in the action was followed by the failure of the British and Anzac expeditionary force in the Dardanelles campaign. Bulgaria was encouraged to join the Central Powers in October. By then, the Russian armies had been driven from Galicia, Warsaw and the rest of Poland. In May, there had been a wild bout of xenophobia in Moscow, with German and Jewish houses and shops as prime targets. In September, Tsar Nicholas II made a distinctive personal contribution to his own downfall by moving to the front early in September to take control of his forces against the advice of many of his own leading supporters.

Elsewhere in 1915, there was stalemate on the western front. Events of longer-term significance for the world war and its aftermath occurred on the high seas and in the Far East. On 7 May 1915, as part of a submarine campaign in retaliation for the British naval blockade of Germany, the British liner *Lusitania* was torpedoed off the Irish coast, and 128 Americans were among the victims. In the authoritative view of Walter LaFeber, 'the episode marked a turning point' as President Wilson 'had now decided to separate, both openly and formally, British and German sea warfare'.[21] The USA's path to entry into the war was beginning to take on a clear direction. On 18 January, Japan pressed China to accept Twenty-One Demands regarding acquisition of German rights in the Shantung peninsula among other concessions. On 7 November, a Japanese force with British detachments in support entered Tsing-tao, the Hamburg of the Orient, and soon occupied the whole of the province. In the long run, Wang-Li observes, 'Japan and its wartime policy towards China not only sowed the seeds of deep mistrust between the two countries and a strong anti-Japanese sentiment in China but also impaired Japan's relations with other powers'.[22]

1916 produced some successes for the Russian armies from the Caucasus to Lithuania. In June and July, to give the most significant example, General A. A. Brusilov led his forces deep into Galicia, helping to persuade Romania to enter the war on the Allied side in August. However, the human costs were high: 1.3 million killed, 4.2 million wounded and more than 2.4 million taken prisoner.[23] This heavy toll contributed to the resentment against the tsarist regime building up behind the lines. At sea, the failure of the British fleet to defeat its German enemy in the battle of Jutland at the end of May 'ruined all hope of opening the Baltic to Russia' in the estimate of C. R. M. F. Cruttwell, who suggested: 'Thus Jutland may be reckoned among the many converging causes which brought the March Revolution of 1917'.[24]

While Wilsonism and Leninism were in most respects poles apart, they shared at least one tenet: rejection of traditional imperialism. During the First World War, Lenin wrote *Imperialism: The Highest Stage of Capitalism*, drawing on the publications of several of his contemporaries, and helping to give imperialism a bad name among a fairly broad circle.

Bearing in mind the appraisals made of imperialism by Lenin and Wilson, let us now turn to further analysis of the phenomenon, especially as it affected Russia, the USA, and the other great powers. In 1890, the US Census indicated that the continental frontier had disappeared and inspired the historian Frederick Jackson Turner to produce famous essays on the subject three years later. In 1890, Captain Alfred Thayer Mahan of the US Navy published an equally famous book, *The Influence of Sea Power upon History, 1660–1783*, drawing the conclusion that America must now look outward. In 1897, Mahan produced *The Interest of America in Sea Power*, arguing that the sea powers of Britain, Japan and the USA faced the land powers of France, Germany and Russia.[25] By the end of the nineteenth century, in the view of Lenin amplifying the observations of the geographer A. Supan, 'the characteristic feature of the period under review is the final partitioning of the globe'.[26]

In 1904, influenced no doubt by this kind of consideration, Halford John Mackinder, who had enjoyed a varied career in travel, politics and education after graduating in history from Oxford, gave a significant lecture to the Royal Geographical Society entitled 'The Geographical Pivot of History', giving emphasis to the concept of the 'Heartland' of central Russia.

Undoubtedly, emphases on land and sea tended to separate the principal imperial powers at the beginning of the twentieth century, although there can be debate about where these emphases and other characteristics lay.

Apologists for Britain would assert the superiority of the freer path to empire pursued by Britain along lines recommended by Adam Smith: for example, J. Shield Nicholson, Professor of Political Economy in the University of Edinburgh, in his book *A Project of Empire: A Critical Study of the Economics of Imperialism, with Special Reference to the Ideas of Adam Smith*, published in London in 1909. At the very beginning, Nicholson seeks to disabuse his readers of a fundamental misunderstanding of Adam Smith (still all too much with us today) as 'a kind of parrot who could only say "cheap food", "competition", "let alone", "devil take the hindmost", and other simple cries'. In Smith's own words, he had planned 'a connected history of the liberal sciences and elegant arts', and for this purpose had collected much material and written many papers, including an essay on the formation of languages, another on the history of astronomy and a fragment on the affinity between music, dancing and poetry. Nicholson himself went on to make use of the ideas of Adam Smith to present arguments concerning imperial defence and a system of representation as well as the benefits of a vast market, customs union and common policy in commercial relations with other countries – 'a policy adverse to every kind of monopoly, and favourable to everything that increases the revenue and the prosperity of the great body of the people throughout the empire'. Moreover, 'The greater the extension of the commerce of the British empire so much the greater would be its moral and political influence in promoting the general advance of civilisation'.[27]

In his *The National System of Political Economy*, first published in 1841, the German/Prussian Friedrich List wrote of Britain and its system of free trade that: 'It is a rule of elementary prudence, when you have reached the top, to kick away the ladder you have used, in order to deprive the others of the means of climbing up after you'.[28] Those on lower rungs would have to resort to tariffs and to other legislative and administrative steps in order to catch up. Britain's move at the end of the century from free trade towards imperial preference indicated that the position at the top of the ladder was under threat at a time when other powers also believed that they were exerting moral and political influence in promoting the general advance of civilisation.

In Russia, a disciple of Friedrich List was Sergei Witte, Minister of Finance from 1892 to 1903, who published a pamphlet on List in 1889. From Witte's point of view, the lessons drawn by List from a sojourn in the USA applied also to Russia, deeply in debt to Germany and France, heavily dependent on grain exports in an increasingly competitive market with plummeting prices, and with a credit rating lowered not only by uncertain exports but also by debts already incurred and the use of paper money. List's cure for all these ills, national industry, was taken up with enthusiasm by Witte. With specific regard to Russia, List had written in 1841:

> The want of civilization and proper political institutions may prove a great obstacle to the advance of Russia in industry and commerce, unless the Imperial government should succeed in advancing general civilization in accordance with the claims of industry by establishing good municipal and provincial organizations, by first regulating and then completely abolishing all servitude, by improving the methods of interior communication, and finally by facilitating the means of transportation to Asia. Such are the measures which Russia has to accomplish within this century, such is the condition of her further progress in agriculture, manufacturing, industry, as well as in commerce, mercantile navigation, and naval power. But that such reforms may be possible, that they may be accomplished, it is necessary that the Russian nobility comprehend that their material government interests are closely connected with them.[29]

By 1889, serfdom had gone, and new systems of municipal and provincial government had arrived. Methods of interior communication were being improved.

As Minister of Finance from 1892, Witte strove to take the process of modernisation further, realising from the beginning that there could be no clear separation of domestic and foreign policy. In particular, in 1896, in order to avert a unilateral Russian seizure of control of the Straits from the Ottoman Empire, he leaked the plan to the British. At about the same time, he played an important part in Far Eastern affairs, negotiating a Franco-Russian loan to China to enable it to pay indemnities to Japan agreed in the Treaty of Shimonoseki of 1895. He persuaded his government along with the French and the German to force Japan to leave the Liaotung peninsula, while scheming for Russian infiltration into China, especially via the agency of a Russo-Chinese Bank to pay for the construction of a Chinese Eastern Railway to link up with the Trans-Siberian. Witte made Manchuria the virtual preserve of his Ministry of Finance, while extending communications from railway into shipping in the Yellow Sea and Pacific Ocean, and organising a Russo-Korean Bank.

Russia's long-term prosperity would depend on a satisfactory solution to its peasant problem and the preservation of peace. P. A. Stolypin, Prime Minister from 1906 to 1911, believed that, given twenty years of peace, his wager on the strong, that is the creation of a sturdy independent farmers, would prove to be a winner. However, he could not ignore foreign policy. Indeed, he made use of such patriotic appeals as 'no second Tsushima' to build up the navy while not neglecting the army. For Geoffrey Hosking, Stolypin's overall programme is most aptly described as a 'constitutional nationalism' similar to that which 'Joseph Chamberlain had been preaching in Britain a few years earlier: an Empire for the common man'. However, 'Germany was the model to which the centre and the right in Russian politics tended to look as an example of the successful integration of an authoritarian monarchy, an imperial patriotism and parliamentary institutions'.[30]

Ironically, tsarist Russia's economic progress was one of the major reasons why it became embroiled in war since it provoked the apprehension of Germany in particular. As A. J. P. Taylor observed: 'Where most of Europe felt overshadowed by Germany, she saw the more distant Russian shadow; and many Germans thought of anticipating the Russian danger almost as genuinely as others thought of combining against the weight of Germany'.[31]

In our examination of the Russian Empire in its global context, we must not neglect Nicholson's insistence that there was much more to Adam Smith than recommendation of the free market. While, as Dominic Lieven observes, some of Smith's arguments 'could be described as the official ideology of liberal capitalism, of the IMF [International Monetary Fund] and today's other multilaterals and indeed of the contemporary world economic order',[32] that official ideology does not take into consideration Smith's other concerns, taken up wittingly or unwittingly by later analysts of empire. For example, let us recall along with Simon Schama the Netherlands in the seventeenth century, a leading seapower with a flourishing economy and an ebullient culture.

We can certainly agree with Dominic Lieven that 'the most interesting and important empires have been those linked to some great religion and high culture, thereby leaving a major impact on the history of world civilisation'.[33] This was, so to speak, the Russian Empire's strongest suit, outstripping the political and economic cards that history had dealt her. Unfortunately, however, it was not trumps, since brute force was the ultimate arbiter. At least, in the period leading up to the First World War, Eyre Crowe from the British

Foreign Office talked of alternatives before Germany: either it was aiming at 'a general political hegemony and maritime ascendancy' or it was seeking to follow a more peaceful path, including the spread of 'the benefits of German culture'.[34]

Orthodoxy could be deemed a great religion, but could hardly be said to have made a global impact. Moreover, like the nineteenth-century Church of England, which was said to be the Tory party at prayer, the Orthodox Church was even more the official support of the Russian Empire in its last years and rendered unto the tsar more than his due. It lost much of its influence with the tsar's fall. Russia's high culture in general could not be said to have rendered much assistance in high councils of diplomacy and war, even if such individuals as Tolstoy and Tchaikovsky were celebrated throughout the Western world.

If we take as a succinct indicator of Russian ideology, Orthodoxy, autocracy, nationality, we can see that it was of little use to tsarism internationally. Even fellow Orthodox Slavs were averse to autocracy, while further afield the image of Bloody Nicholas and his cruel regime, however accurate or inaccurate, was clearly stamped on the public consciousness throughout Europe and beyond. The USA was especially averse to anti-Semitism and the convict system.

Nationality is the customary translation of *narodnost*, but the term means more, something like the special character of the Russian people. In this connection, we should note the fact that the Russian Empire was not as diverse as some of its fellows. According to the census of 1897, nearly half of the 125 million people in the empire were Russian and nearly three-quarters were Slavic. (In more detail, 44.31 per cent were Russians, 17.81 per cent were Ukrainian, 6.31 per cent were Poles and 4.68 per cent were Belorussians.) Asiatics constituted little more than a tenth of the whole, a far smaller minority than their equivalents in many other empires.[35] In the greatest of the pre-1914 empires, for example, the British constituted a minority overall, especially in India – the so-called jewel in the crown. Siberia, which Dominic Lieven calls 'the jewel in Russia's imperial crown',[36] was almost empty. To put the point another way, Russia's metropolis was much more populous than its periphery, and while its many non-Slavic peoples deserve more attention than is customarily given, say, in histories of the USA to Native Americans, their influence on the destinies of tsarism can be exaggerated.

To sum up, in the years leading to its collapse, the Russian Empire was about number five in the imperial league, below Britain, Germany, the USA and France. Although beaten by Japan in the war of 1904–5, it was still ahead of Japan according to some indices. For example, its army was one of the world's largest. However, as far as the indispensable economic support was concerned, in 1913 Russia was fifth overall in world industrial production, in some branches even fourth, but its share was little more than 4 per cent of the total. While on the eve of the war it was advancing to an extent that alarmed potential enemies, its progress was uneven and precarious. The abandonment of the gold standard and the introduction of prohibition were grievous wounds to the economy even before the strains of the actual conflict began to show.

Whatever the case that can be made for it as a going concern, however great the intrinsic worth of Orthodoxy, the romanticisation of autocracy (or at least of the autocrat and his family) and the enduring fascination of the Russian or Slavic 'soul' and other aspects of nationality, imperial Russia failed the ultimate test for great powers constituted by the First World War. The question has often been asked: would tsarist Russia have avoided revolution if it had not been caught up in the war? However, as we have seen in our discussion of Witte and Stolypin, the two statesmen who made the greatest contributions to pre-revolutionary modernisation before 1914, they were both intimately connected with foreign policies taking their country towards a showdown with its peers.[37]

Notes

1   D. Lieven, *Empire: The Russian Empire and its Rivals from the Sixteenth Century to the Present* (London, 2003), p. ix. For once, I agree with reviewers: in particular with John Lloyd in the *Financial Times* that the book is 'a very great intellectual achievement' and with Anne Applebaum in the *Sunday Telegraph* that '*Empire* is a quirky hybrid: part straight history, part comparative politics, part international relations . . . . a joy to read'. However, my own exposition differs significantly from that of Lieven. I disagree with him most strongly in his interpretation of the part played by the USA.

2   J. A. Hobson, *Imperialism: A Study* (London, 1902), p. 11.

3   W. H. Robool, 'In Search of an Atlantic Identity' in J. Th. Leerssen and M. Spiering (eds), 'National Identity – Symbol and Representation', *Yearbook of European Studies*, 4, 1991, p. 4.

4   H. and C. Seton-Watson, *The Making of a New Europe: R. W. Seton-Watson and the Last Years of Austria-Hungary* (London, 1982), pp. 16, 19, 30.

5   Cited in P. Dukes, *The Last Great Game: USA versus USSR: Events, Conjunctures, Structures* (London, 1989), pp. 148–9.

6   'Memorandum on the Present State of British Relations with France and Germany', 1 January 1907, by Mr. Eyre Crowe, Senior Clerk, British Foreign Office, 1906–1912, later Permanent Under-Secretary, 1920–5, as in G. P. Gooch and Harold Temperley, *British Documents on the Origins of the War, 1898–1914. Vol. 3: The Testing of the Entente, 1904–6* (London, 1928), p. 402.

7   A. J. P. Taylor, *The Struggle for Mastery in Europe, 1848–1918* (Oxford, 1980), p. 335; A. J. P. Taylor, *A Personal History* (London, 1983), p. 181.

8   R. W. Leopold and A. S. Link (eds), *Problems in American History* (Englewood Cliffs, NJ, 1957), pp. 178–9.

9   F. A. Golder, 'Russian–American Relations during the Crimean War', *American Historical Review*, 31, 1926, p. 474.

10   L. A. Rand, 'America Views Russian Serf Emancipation', *Mid-America*, 50, 1968, pp. 47–8.

11   Cited in *Correspondence Respecting Central Asia* c. 704 (London, 1873), pp. 72–5.

12   N. E. Saul, *Concord and Conflict: The United States and Russia, 1867–1914* (Lawrence, KS, 1996), p. 13.

13   D. Mackenzie, 'Expansion in Central Asia', *Canadian–American Slavic Studies*, 3, 1969, p. 310.

14   W. LaFeber, in the chapter 'Laying the Foundations for "Superpowerdom"' in *The American Age: United States Foreign Policy at Home and Abroad since 1750* (New York, 1989), pp. 160, 175–6.

15   W. LaFeber, *The Clash: U.S.–Japanese Relations Throughout History* (New York, 1997) pp. 36–7.

16   Lieven, *Empire*, p. 8.

17   Saul, *Concord*, p. 438.

18   Wang Li, 'Sovereignty, *Status Quo* and Diplomacy: A Case Study of China's Interaction with the Great Powers, 1912–22', unpublished PhD thesis, University of Aberdeen, 2003, p. 45.

19   LaFeber, *The Clash*, pp. 76, 77, 81.

20   H. Seton-Watson, *The Russian Empire, 1801–1917* (Oxford, 1967), p. 597.

21   LaFeber, *The American Age*, p. 271.

22   Wang Li, 'Sovereignty', p. 119.

23   N. N. Golovin, *The Russian Army in the World War* (New Haven, CT, 1931), pp. 82–92.

24   C. R. M. F. Cruttwell, *A History of the Great War, 1914–1918* (Oxford, 1934), p. 337.

25   LaFeber, *The Clash*, pp. 56, 61.

26   V. I. Lenin, *Imperialism: The Highest Stage of Capitalism*, written in 1916 and republished in V. I. Lenin, *Selected Works* (London, 1971) p. 223.

27   J. S. Nicholson, *A Project of Empire: A Critical Study of the Economics of Imperialism, with Special Reference to the Ideas of Adam Smith* (London, 1909), pp. 1–2, 268, 271.

28   J. Droz, *Europe Between Revolutions, 1815–1848* (Glasgow, 1967), p. 55.

29   T. H. Von Laue, *Sergei Witte and the Industrialization of Russia* (New York, 1974), pp. 59–61. Von Laue makes use of an American translation by G. A. Matile of Friedrich List's work, *The National System of Political Economy* (Philadelphia, 1856).

30   G. A. Hosking, *The Russian Constitutional Experiment: Government and Duma, 1907–1914* (Cambridge, 1973), pp. 106, 113.

31   A. J. P. Taylor, *The Struggle*, p. xxvi. See also, for example, R. Ropponen, *Die Kraft Russlands: Wie beurteilte die politische und militärische Führung der europaischen Grossmächte in der Zeit von 1905 bis 1914 die Kraft Russlands* (Helsinki, 1968).

32   Lieven, *Empire*, p. 18.

33   Ibid., p. xiv.

34   'Memorandum' by Crowe, p. 417.

35   A. Kappeler, *The Russian Empire: A Multiethnic History* (London, 2001), pp. 397–9.

36   Lieven, *Empire*, p. 224.

37   For an attempt to place the events of 1917 in a broad perspective, see P. Dukes, *October and the World: Perspectives on the Russian Revolution* (London, 1979).

Index